Understanding
Les Fleurs du Mal

Understanding
Les Fleurs du Mal
Critical Readings

EDITED BY
William J. Thompson

FOREWORD BY
Claude Pichois

Vanderbilt University Press
Nashville and London

First printing 1997
97 98 99 00 4 3 2 1

This publication is made from recycled paper and meets the minimum
requirements of American National Standard for Information Sciences—
Permanence of Paper for Printed Library Materials ⊚

Library of Congress Cataloging-in-Publication Data

Understanding Les fleurs du mal : critical readings / edited by
    William J. Thompson.
      p. cm.
    Includes bibliographical references and index.
    ISBN 0-8265-1290-9 (alk. paper). — ISBN 0-8265-1297-6 (pbk. :
    alk. paper)
    1. Baudelaire, Charles, 1821-1867. Fleurs du mal. I. Thompson,
    William J., 1961– .
    PQ2191.F63U54 1997
    841'.8—dc21   97-4698
                                                                          CIP

Manufactured in the United States of America

CONTENTS

FOREWORD

After nearly half a century of involvement in Baudelaire studies, I take great satisfaction in noting the prominence of Baudelaire and *Les Fleurs du Mal* throughout the international world of poetry.

Understanding Les Fleurs du Mal: Critical Readings, edited by William Thompson, provides a spectacular example of how *Les Fleurs du Mal* and its author are at the center of a vast audience. As Thompson himself says, the gathering of interpretations in this volume is addressed to several audiences: undergraduate and graduate students alike, teachers, and all those Baudelaire-lovers in the general public who feel drawn to a deeper appreciation of his work.

The works of some poets—I am thinking of Rimbaud, Mallarmé, Ezra Pound—are screened from the reader by an accumulation of burdened interpretations, which must be cleared away if the serious reader is to gain access to the work, come to grips with it, and subject it to questioning. The situation is quite different with Baudelaire, perhaps because his work, though opening onto the future, is firmly anchored in literary tradition. Unless the modern reader maintains an intimate contact with that tradition and with Baudelaire's use of it, full understanding will be elusive. This book will take its place among the amazingly diverse critical efforts that usefully serve this purpose.

The numerous interpretations of *Les Fleurs du Mal* have already been the subject of two bibliographical inventories.* The astute essays of this collection, referring as they do to many other readings of the poems, suggest the need for a new listing. They also suggest the need for still another collection, one devoted to *Le Spleen de Paris,* now that Baudelaire's poems in prose have finally been acknowledged as a major work whose eminence prolongs that of *Les Fleurs du Mal.*

We are all greatly indebted to William Thompson and to all of the contributors of this volume for adding to the texture of our understanding of Baudelaire's work, for challenging old assumptions, and for stimulating new ideas.

Claude Pichois

---

* Henk Nuiten, William T. Bandy, Freeman G. Henry, *Les Fleurs expliquées. Bibliographie des exégèses des "Fleurs du Mal" et des "Epaves" de Charles Baudelaire* (Amsterdam, Rodopi, 1983)—"Les Fleurs expliquées. Supplément," *Bulletin Baudelairien* 21:2 (1986).

INTRODUCTION

Perhaps no poet's life and œuvre are more capable of fascinating the reader, student, and scholar of French literature than those of Charles Baudelaire. His timeless poetic vision, his evocation of a rapidly changing society, and his ability to capture his personal anguish in verse have guaranteed Baudelaire immortality and have made *Les Fleurs du Mal* one of the most frequently read and studied poetic works in the French literary canon.

At the university level in the United States, Baudelaire is frequently included in both introductory courses on French literature and in upper-division and graduate-level seminars on poetry and the nineteenth century. The entirety of Baudelaire's œuvre is also the focus of a tremendous amount of impressive and diverse scholarly analysis throughout the world. Yet one need only consider the tumultuous events of Baudelaire's life, including his numerous and well-chronicled struggles with family, creditors, women, drugs, illness, and the law (*Les Fleurs du Mal* was condemned for obscenity upon its publication in 1857) to realize that the reasons for this interest transcend his remarkable poetic achievements. All of these aspects of Baudelaire's biography continue to fascinate a wide range of people, from professional scholars to casual readers of French literature.

In spite of the great amount of critical work on Baudelaire, few of the available book-length studies approach the poems in *Les Fleurs du Mal* individually and in depth, providing scholarly "explications" of the poems. Even fewer take into account the broad appeal of Baudelaire's poetry, especially to undergraduate students reading French literature for the first time and looking for critical perspectives on specific poems or to graduate students seeking comprehensive, scholarly readings.

One of the goals of this collection is to give students a clear, scholarly introduction to the widely studied poems of *Les Fleurs du Mal* through analyses that each focus on one particular poem, that offer a broad range of critical perspectives, and that display a genuine interest in theoretical concerns in combination with a close textual analysis. Presentation of the many critical paths available can only benefit the student unfamiliar with the methods of poetry analysis or with literary criticism. At the same time, the intellectual quality of the analyses included in this collection means that they are not only accessible to students but also of interest to scholars: they make a valuable contribution to the body of criticism devoted to Baudelaire's poetry.

Each of the contributors to this volume takes a different critical approach to *Les Fleurs du Mal*. All of the contributors are scholars of French literature; most are primarily nineteenth-century specialists; and all of them, of course, share a common interest in, and a genuine affection for, Baudelaire's poetic œuvre. All contributors chose the specific poems that they analyze, so that even the formulation of the table of contents was not the decision of any one individual.

The broad range of critical approaches evident in these essays enables the collection to demonstrate that the reading of poetry does not lead to one "definitive" interpretation and that there is no single "correct" manner in which to evaluate the work of a particular author. Baudelaire's poetry is the perfect model for such a demonstration. The complexity of his subject matter, combined with the varied interests and approaches of the contributors to this collection, results in the elucidation of an amazing range of themes and topics.

Some of the readings evaluate the impact of Baudelaire's personal life on his poetic inspiration. Several chapters, for example, consider Baudelaire's portrayal of the female figure, one of the most prominent subjects in *Les Fleurs du Mal* and a popular one for analysis. Chapters by DalMolin, Schultz, Olmsted, Giacchetti, Harrington, Thompson, and Burton either document Baudelaire's relationships with specific women (such as Jeanne Duval) or explore his ambivalent attitude toward women in general. Other details about Baudelaire's life and times that receive attention include his often difficult relationship with his mother (Mahuzier) and the impact on his poetry of the sociopolitical atmosphere in France during his life (Chambers).

Other chapters focus on the various themes that recur throughout *Les Fleurs du Mal*, many of which are also inextricably linked to Baudelaire's personal experiences: death (Olmsted and particularly Putnam), exoticism and travel (Whitaker, Harrington, Putnam, and Burton), idealism and antiidealism (Whitaker and Olmsted), drugs (Tucci) and wine (Chambers), the poetic imagination (Giacchetti and Miner), and poetic alienation (Blood, Gasarian, and Chambers). Since Baudelaire is often considered one of the first poets of the modern urban scene, it is hardly surprising that several chapters also treat the notion of the flaneur, the wandering poet who captures in his verse the phenomena of the modern city landscape (Gasarian, Maclean, Thompson, and Chambers).

In several chapters, the analysis focuses on intertextual elements, as the poem in question is compared to other poems (Schultz and Thompson), compared to earlier versions of the same poem (Blood and Mahuzier), considered in terms of its position in *Les Fleurs du Mal* (Mahuzier and Putnam), and compared to other art forms, such as painting and sculpture (Harrington, Thompson, and Burton). References to various poets and writers also abound, including Hugo (Blood, Gasarian, and Maclean), Gautier and Musset (Miner), Flaubert (Blood), and Proust (Mahuzier).

Some chapters exhibit a particular theoretical methodology: the Jungian approach adopted by Nina Tucci in her analysis of "La vie antérieure"; Ross Chamber's sociohistorical perspective on "Le vin des chiffonniers"; and Marie Maclean's rigorous structuralist analysis of "Les sept vieillards." These examples clearly demonstrate that an unlimited number of perspectives can illuminate one poet's work. While the analysis in some of the chapters proceeds line by line or stanza by stanza, even devoting considerable space to the study of one word (in the case of Eliane DalMolin's lengthy analysis of the title of "Tout entière"), other chapters trace individual themes or use a particular methodology to evaluate the poem as whole. Some stress poetic structures (form), while others focus exclusively on content.

This collection does not aim to provide the reader with an all-encompassing view of *Les Fleurs du Mal* and of all the critical perspectives relevant to this work. To facilitate and encourage further study, the bibliography includes works not cited in the chapter that deal with the poems in question.

The definitive edition of *Les Fleurs du Mal* can be found in the two-volume "Bibliothèque de la Pléiade" edition of Baudelaire's complete works, edited by Claude Pichois, which is the edition used in all of the chapters. By far the most thorough biographical study of Baudelaire is the volume by Pichois and Ziegler, available both in the original French edition and in an excellent English translation. The wealth of resources available to the reader attests to Baudelaire's enduring place in France's literary heritage as well as to the constant appeal of his poetic vision.

Understanding
Les Fleurs du Mal

Chapter 1

Mimesis and the Grotesque in "L'Albatros"

SUSAN BLOOD

Souvent, pour s'amuser, les hommes d'équipage
Prennent des albatros, vastes oiseaux des mers,
Qui suivent, indolents compagnons de voyage,
Le navire glissant sur les gouffres amers.   (4)

A peine les ont-ils déposés sur les planches,
Que ces rois de l'azur, maladroits et honteux,
Laissent piteusement leurs grandes ailes blanches
Comme des avirons traîner à côté d'eux.   (8)

Ce voyageur ailé, comme il est gauche et veule!
Lui, naguère si beau, qu'il est comique et laid!
L'un agace son bec avec un brûle-gueule,
L'autre mime, en boitant, l'infirme qui volait!   (12)

Le Poète est semblable au prince des nuées
Qui hante la tempête et se rit de l'archer;
Exilé sur le sol au milieu des huées,
Ses ailes de géant l'empêchent de marcher.   (16)

Baudelaire's poem "L'Albatros" has elicited little critical commentary. The reason may be that the poem is structured somewhat like a fable, and fables often provide their own commentary, in the form of the moral. The first three stanzas contain the brief story of an albatross that has been caught by a group of bored sailors looking for amusement. They drag the stunned bird aboard ship and then marvel at its clumsiness. There is little more to the story than this. Baudelaire gives a few background details—one sailor imitates the bird's limp, another pokes at it with a pipe—and emphasizes how curious it is that the same creature could be so graceful in flight and so awkward on foot. But the narrative remains minimal. As is often the case with fables, the narrated events can be understood as having a kind of logical necessity only after the moral has been given. In this instance, the moral (which is what I am calling the final stanza) transforms an aimless little story into a rigorously organized allegory of the Poet. The identification of poet and albatross is so explicit, and the interpretation of the preceding narrative provided by these four lines is so convincing, that one tends to feel relieved of any further interpretive burden.

If there is any mystery surrounding "L'Albatros" at all, it involves not the question of the poem's meaning but the date of its composition. "L'Albatros" was first published, along with "Le Voyage," in February 1859. Baudelaire arranged for the two poems to be printed side by side on fine paper and then sent them as gifts to five or six of his acquaintances. There is no doubt that "Le Voyage" was composed shortly before this original publication. But as for "L'Albatros," friends from Baudelaire's youth claimed to have heard the poem recited in 1842, soon after the poet's return from the Indian Ocean. "Il est certain que 'L'Albatros' lui fut suggéré par un incident de sa traversée. Il nous le récita dès son retour" (Pichois, *Baudelaire,* 15). This was Ernest Prarond's statement to Eugène Crépet in 1866. It would indicate an extremely early date of composition. If Prarond's memory can be trusted, one might justifiably wonder why Baudelaire would keep his poem hidden for seventeen years. Some critics have found such a silence so inconceivable that they have dismissed Prarond's testimony and have argued for a late date of composition. Jean Pommier, in "A propos de 'L'Albatros,'" summarized this alternative position with a wealth of detail that is highly intriguing but that does not really concern us here.

Only one thing is certain in this textual mystery: the third stanza of "L'Albatros" was written in 1859, after the first printing of the poem. When Charles Asselineau received his early copy, he immediately wrote to Baudelaire, thanking him and offering a suggestion: "La pièce de 'L'Albatros' est un diamant!—Seulement je voudrais une strophe entre la deuxième et la dernière pour insister sur la gaucherie, du moins sur la gêne de l'albatros, pour faire tableau de son embarras. Et il me semble que la dernière strophe rejaillirait plus puissante comme effet" (Pichois and Pichois 18). Baudelaire took Asselineau's advice and composed the third stanza, which was added manually to the copy of the poem that he sent to Flaubert. Thus the composition of the third stanza can be traced with great precision to the period between late February and early March 1859.

In a careful article from 1950, Margaret Gilman decided to go beyond circumstantial evidence and to see what a stylistic analysis might reveal about the poem's genesis. She discovered noticeable differences between the three original stanzas (I, II, and IV) and the added one. In general, the third stanza resembles poems that belong to Baudelaire's maturity: its exclamations, prosaic vocabulary, and use of the "discours indirect libre" (which Gilman calls "direct speech") all characterize a later period of poetic production. By contrast, the rest of the poem seems to fit solidly within the romantic tradition, which influenced Baudelaire in his early writings. The theme of the isolated poet, the narrative structure, and the schematic use of simile ("Le Poète est semblable . . .") attest to this influence. Gilman concludes, not surprisingly, that what we have in "L'Albatros" is neither an early poem nor a late poem but a hybrid piece, part youthful, part not. Implicit in her analysis is the idea that Baudelaire became Baudelaire in the course of writing this poem, that the poet discovered his own idiom by breaking with romanticism and romantic topoi.

With such a reasonable resolution to the puzzle of the poem's genesis, it might seem that little remains to be said about "L'Albatros." As I mentioned at the outset, the poem's critical interpretation appears never to have troubled anyone. At the risk of mystery-mongering, however, I propose to examine the following hypothesis: that the gradual clarification of the poem's origins, while it has satisfied most textual scholars, has actually made the interpretation of "L'Albatros" more difficult.

The difficulty comes once we admit, in the spirit of Gilman's analysis, that questions of style can have hermeneutic implications. If style can be used in the study of textual genesis, it may also be pertinent to the investigation of textual meaning. In this particular instance, the division of "L'Albatros" into two distinct styles may introduce some nuance into what has been perceived as the poem's blinding simplicity. The fablelike structure, which describes a forward-moving narrative and its summation in the moral, is disturbed by a very different temporal sequence. In stylistic terms the poem "matures" in the third stanza and relapses, at the end, into juvenilia. What we have are two conflicting senses of poetic development, or poetic finality, that pit the third and fourth stanzas of "L'Albatros" against one another as alternative endings for the poem. The critical challenge is to determine what, if anything, this alternative might mean.

Before attempting to address the question of the poem's complexity, it would be useful to explicate the moral in all its apparent simplicity. We might say that by comparing the plight of the poet with that of a bird, Baudelaire is giving us an example of his famed theory of correspondances: nature contains symbols that permit communication between the physical realm and another dimension that Baudelaire variously calls "le spirituel" or "le moral." The albatross works as a natural symbol for solid, anatomical reasons. Its massive wings, which both enable it to fly through tempests and prevent it from walking, depict with admirable economy the coincidence of power and powerlessness, capacity and incapacity. As Pommier remarks, this same anatomical peculiarity is noted by Michelet in *L'Oiseau* and by Buffon in his *Histoire naturelle* (with respect not to the albatross, however, but to the martlet and the frigate bird). By linking Baudelaire's "L'Albatros" with the French naturalist tradition, Pommier is not just indulging in a bit of aimless pedantry. The analogy between poet and bird derives much of its simple power from our sense that it is grounded in nature and anatomical fact. (We might contrast Baudelaire's "naturalist" treatment of the albatross with Coleridge's "supernatural" treatment in *The Rime of the Ancient Mariner*. Coleridge's bird is a mythic figure from the first. Its complex function—as good omen and curse—has nothing to do with its anatomy.)

The moral that "corresponds" to this natural portrait of the albatross may be summarized as follows: poets are alienated from the rest of humanity by being both more and less capable. Their great gifts, which enable them to fly in a spiritual sense, hamper them in the realm of everyday activities. They are, for this reason, objects of ridicule, misunderstood by prosaic individuals who are impressed only with pedestrian abilities. This moral is, as Gilman suggests, thoroughly compatible with a romantic tradition that in France can be traced back at least to Rousseau. By the time Baudelaire enters the tradition, it has become a cliché. Again, the self-evident character of "L'Albatros" is partly linked to the familiarity of its moral. We recognize here the concise formulation of an idea we already knew.

This simple explication of "L'Albatros" and its moral can be problematized in several ways. We might call attention, for example, to an apparent contradiction between the poem's form and its content. Why should an allegory of incomprehension be itself so comprehensible? "Ce sont des vers anthologiques par excellence, qu'un écolier aborde sans peine" (376). This was Paul Rémy's evaluation of "L'Albatros," and it enables us to pose a kind of riddle: why should any schoolchild enter effortlessly into the pathos of the poet/bird if the latter is in fact so strange? The very simplicity of the poem becomes a problem when we view it in this light.

Flaubert must have sensed this difficulty when he included "L'Albatros" among the materials he was collecting for the "sottisier" of *Bouvard et Pécuchet*. The sottisier contains, not surprisingly, samples of what Flaubert considered stupidity on the part of great writers and savants. Among other things, Flaubertian stupidity involves the disclosure of banality at the heart of aesthetic or intellectual pretension. If "L'Albatros" is a stupid poem, then, its thematics of poetic alienation are more than accessible to an average audience; the average schoolchild, as Rémy affirms, has no difficulty donning a pair of imaginary wings and feeling at odds with "le commun des mortels." Such flights of fancy prove, not that one is a poet, but that one is average (or they prove, alternatively, that poetry itself is not so very rare). In the absence of more extended critical commentary, we might read Flaubert's inclusion of "L'Albatros" in the sottisier as a kind of minimal critique, ironizing the poem's pathos and revealing that the sense of alienation is "la chose du monde la mieux partagée."

From the standpoint of literary history, Flaubert's critique of "L'Albatros" can also be considered a critique of romanticism. By indicating the banality of the romantic subject, Flaubert is displaying his own postromantic sensibility. His position is one that Harold Bloom would call belated. It is defined by a distance that is both historical and critical: "la situation de l'écrivain qui vient après tout le monde, de l'écrivain retardataire, comporte des avantages que n'avait pas l'écrivain prophète, celui qui annonce le succès, qui le commande, pour ainsi dire, avec l'autorité de l'audace et du dévouement" (*OC II*, 76). This thought introduces Baudelaire's essay on *Madame Bovary*. It is intriguing that Baudelaire applies the description of the belated writer not to Flaubert but to himself as critic of Flaubert's work. Given the incessant transitivity of Baudelaire's critical writings (with Poe, Wagner, Delacroix, and so forth, the artist and critic constantly exchange qualities), I would take this as proof of Flaubert's belatedness in Baudelaire's eyes. Flaubert would therefore be contrasted with "l'écrivain prophète," an epithet that, whatever else Baudelaire may have intended by it, applies overwhelmingly to Hugo. Something like the critical history of romanticism can thus be located between Hugo and Flaubert.

If we sketch out the critical history in this manner, "L'Albatros" becomes unexpectedly interesting. The poem seems to repeat the movement of literary history from Hugo to Flaubert. While the portrait of the poet and the use of natural analogy may be characteristically Hugolian, the "discours indirect libre" and the ironic objectivity of the third stanza are distinct Flaubertian trademarks. These comments are, of course, consistent with Gilman's observations about the stylistic differences between the third and fourth stanzas of the poem, but the stylistic observations take on added implications by being placed within a critical history of romanticism. The story of Baudelaire's personal development as a poet becomes a larger problem of aesthetic history; stylistic difference becomes the symptom of a critical difference that sets the poem against itself in an intelligible and threatening fashion.

Since I have evoked the shade of Hugo somewhat schematically, it would be appropriate to specify how Hugo might be linked to the critical problem of "L'Albatros." More is at stake than the practice of natural analogy, which other romantic poets (Gilman cites Vigny, Musset, and Gautier) used as abundantly as did Hugo. Natural analogy in "L'Albatros," however, has an added feature that deserves our attention: the comparison of poet and bird is based upon a kind of difformity. The albatross can serve as the natural analogon for a moral condition only because it itself is misshapen. To those familiar with Hugo's aesthetic terminology, the albatross is grotesque. In the argument that follows, I hope to demonstrate that the critical complexity of "L'Albatros," at which the poem's stylistic difference hints, is rooted in a Hugolian aesthetics of the grotesque. This notion will have consequences, both for our understanding of the critical history of romanticism and for the interpretation of the poem.

Hugo's theory of the grotesque was elaborated early in his creative life, in the preface to his monumental play *Cromwell*. The *Cromwell* preface has come to be accepted as the manifesto of literary romanticism in France. In it Hugo argues for a historicized understanding of aesthetic production: just as the social history of humanity can be divided into distinct epochs, so can the history of art. Hugo's exposition of the different aesthetic ages is quite detailed and really does not concern us here. His definition of the modern age is of interest, however: modernity begins, he says, with the advent of Christianity and involves an intuition of what Pascal would call "la disproportion de l'homme," the division of the human into "un animal et une intelligence" (66). To this disproportionate human reality corresponds a complex notion of art that is at antipodes from the classical or antique ideals of regularity and harmony: "Le christianisme amène la poésie à la vérité. Comme lui, la muse moderne verra les choses d'un coup d'œil plus haut et plus large. Elle sentira que tout dans la création n'est pas humainement *beau,* que le laid y existe à côté du beau, le difforme près du gracieux, le grotesque au revers du sublime, le mal avec le bien, l'ombre avec la lumière" (69).

Thus far Hugo's argument seems simple enough to follow. A dual aesthetic, grotesque and sublime, is appropriate for a dual conception of the human. Romantic art, by embracing such duality, is doubly privileged; it both brings poetry to the truth, as Hugo claims, and invests it with a historical urgency and specificity. From this perspective French classicism is doubly condemned to falsehood. Its aesthetic ideals are anachronistic (they are pre-Christian ideals in a Christian age) and its truth is unmasked as a half-truth. Here, however, the straightforward analogic structure of Hugo's argument breaks down. Romanticism becomes more than a mere alternative to classicism, the next stage in a perpetual unfolding of aesthetic history. Romanticism both contains and critiques the classical moment. The whole of truth must contain the half of truth; that is basic mathematical logic. But the whole, in this instance, holds the half at a distance, marking it as false. The relationship between part and whole thus ceases to be continuous and ceases to underwrite the conceptual unity of art, history, and society. In its theoretical articulation, the Hugolian grotesque brings a critical element to aesthetic expression: the grotesque is the part that communicates the whole of truth, not by containing that truth but by exposing the partial nature of all other values. Hugo explains this critical function as follows: "Le beau n'a qu'un type; le laid en a mille. C'est que le beau, à parler humainement, n'est que la forme considérée dans son rapport le plus simple, dans sa symétrie la plus absolue, dans son harmonie la plus intime avec notre organisation. Aussi nous offre-t-il toujours un ensemble complet, mais restreint comme nous. Ce que nous appelons le laid, au contraire, est un détail d'un grand ensemble qui nous échappe, et qui s'harmonise, non pas avec l'homme, mais avec la création tout entière. Voilà pourquoi il nous présente sans cesse des aspects nouveaux, mais incomplets" (73–74).

With this passage the systematic exposition of Hugo's thought attains its greatest complexity. When Hugo writes that in nature "le laid . . . existe à côté du beau," we might be inclined to think that the truth claims of romanticism involve a simple affirmation of natural variety. But more is at stake in Hugo's aesthetic program than the exhortation to represent both Beauty and the Beast in the name of diversity. The grotesque figure does not merely complete the aesthetic spectacle, filling in the canvas of perceivable nature. It also provides the intuition of "un grand ensemble qui nous échappe," of a realm that lies beyond human powers of perception and representation. If the grotesque figure is manifold, presenting a "thousand types," the reason is not that it represents the variety in nature. Its variety and multiplicity are due instead to its harmony with what cannot be represented. Thus the grotesque both completes the canvas of nature and critiques it, revealing that any appearance of completion is the effect of an incomplete, human perspective. The paradox of the grotesque can be seen as a radical treatment of classicism's mimetic principle: by generalizing the classical imperative to imitate nature, by insisting that *all* of nature become an object of imitation, Hugo induces the collapse of mimetic art. For this reason the valorization of "le laid" does not lead to a sober, realist conception of the aesthetic. Hugo's grotesque figures are either fabulous or comic. In their frank lack of realism, or their parodic relationship to reality, they call into question their own status as representations.

Now it remains to determine how this brief summary of Hugolian aesthetics might influence the interpretation of "L'Albatros." Clearly Baudelaire's bird presents a problem of perspective, similar to the one that Hugo outlined: the albatross may seem ugly to the sailors aboard ship but only because the bird is not in its element. Its ugliness is not an innate characteristic but a function of the perspective from which it is viewed. In and of itself the albatross has no determinate aesthetic quality. This aspect is consistent with Hugo's critical understanding of the grotesque, more consistent than Hugo himself often proved to be in his poetic practice. In poems like "La Chouette" or "J'aime l'araignée et j'aime l'ortie," Hugo pleads the cause of ugly plants and animals but does not provide the shift of focus that would enable them to be seen as anything but ugly. In theory we might intuit their potential beauty; in practice we are merely asked to love them as they are. With "L'Albatros," however, there is no longer a divergence between the theory and the practice of the grotesque. The full critical potential of the figure is realized within the poem itself.

Where "L'Albatros" seems to differ from Hugo's aesthetics is in its apparent preservation of a mimetic mode. As Jean Pommier noted, Baudelaire's bird is an anatomically sound representation. There is nothing supernatural about its difformity, nothing in its description that strays beyond the limits of naturalist discourse. Even though the albatross is viewed in two incommensurate contexts, each of these contexts is natural. Only when Baudelaire subjects his naturalist description to metaphorical interpretation does another, transcendent dimension of meaning enter the poem. The "moral" of the story marks this passage of meaning from a natural to a spiritual dimension. And yet I would argue that in "L'Albatros" Baudelaire stretches the mimetic principle to its limit. No matter what perspective we as readers take on the poem, whether we read from the vantage point of the third stanza or of the fourth, "L'Albatros" enacts a kind of mimetic crisis.

To understand better how this crisis works, we would do well to pinpoint just what is at stake in the alternative perspectives that the poem offers to its readers. Since the question of perspective is crucial to the theory of the grotesque, the position of the reader cannot be ignored in the interpretation of "L'Albatros." Like the bird itself, the poem does not present a determinate aesthetic character but allows itself to be read from two different angles. We could even say that "L'Albatros" is aimed at two different audiences, or two types of reader. The ingenuous reader, Rémy's schoolboy perhaps, will follow the poem's fablelike logic and survey its message from the standpoint of the moral. The schoolboy will understand the poem by identifying with the metaphorical poet-bird, thereby adopting the loftiest perspective, one that will enable the bird's dual character to be perceived. In contrast, a more suspicious reader (Flaubert, for example) might resist the seductions of the moral, noting a conflict between the poem's message of alienation and its invitation to share in the poet's isolation. Furthermore, the suspicious reader might prefer not to identify with a ridiculous, limping figure and might doubt that such a figure could be rendered beautiful from any angle of vision. This reader's cynicism is consonant with the attitude of the sailors in the third stanza of the poem; it acknowledges that, in the allegory of the misunderstood poet, the sailors must represent the unappreciative readership. In a sense the cynic gives the poet what he wants by laughing at him, thereby fulfilling the poet/reader relationship as it is allegorized in the poem. The cynical perspective is not comprehensive in any respect; it is a down-to-earth, limited perspective that refuses sympathetic understanding.

What is striking in these alternative perspectives is that neither can be said to be superior. The cynic may be the more careful reader, but as I have suggested, the fastidiousness of the reading is bought at the price of understanding. What the schoolboy understands by failing in some sense to read the poem is the full complexity of the central figure. The cynic reads and does not understand, which is what the poem tells us readers do. In either case something is missing, something that will undermine any position taken by the reader. We could say that the poem poses a constant critical challenge to its own interpretation. How, though, does such critical instability affect the mimetic character of "L'Albatros"?

As I have already mentioned, the moral of Baudelaire's poem rests upon the metaphorical transposition of a mimetically sound representation. The realistic plight of the bird comes to figure the spiritual condition of the poet in an apparently stable process of identification. In other words, metaphorical transposition seems to preserve rather than undermine the mimetic integrity of the representation. This harmony between metaphor and mimesis is consistent with the theory of natural correspondances; it also marks a crucial point of divergence between this theory and the Hugolian theory of the grotesque, which, in its affirmation of the noncorrespondency of nature and spirit, seems to be at odds with the very possibility of metaphor. Yet I have argued, and will continue to argue, that "L'Albatros" is firmly rooted in a Hugolian aesthetics. By internalizing the notion of noncorrespondency, and by presenting nature as incommensurate to itself (the air and the land in this poem are radically noncorresponding), Baudelaire has simply displaced the mimetic crisis that we found in the theory of the grotesque. The moral of "L'Albatros" teaches the reader that all mimetic representation is partial, that the portrait of a bird in flight of necessity excludes the portrait of a bird on foot. In order to get a complete picture, we are compelled to an activity of metaphorical totalization that is essentially nonmimetic, nonrepresentational, because it brings together two perspectives that cannot be perceived simultaneously. The mimetic crisis of "L'Albatros," far from conflicting with the possibility of metaphor, actually cries out for metaphorical interpretation. We might even say that the possibility of metaphor is a consequence of the mimetic crisis: the inability of the natural world to find completion within itself leaves a door open, so to speak, to metaphor. This crisis gives a significant twist to the theory of natural correspondances. While nature in "L'Albatros" invites its own metaphorical transposition, it does so only insofar as nature is in crisis, unable to stabilize its self-presentation.

Clarification is necessary at this point. By reading Baudelaire's poem in terms of the grotesque, I have affiliated it with an aesthetics of crisis or critique. I have also noted that Baudelaire displaces the mimetic crisis that occurs in Hugo as the frank proliferation of imaginary figures. With this displacement it becomes possible to speak, not only of a mimetic crisis, but also of a crisis in nature. More is at stake here than an accidental shift of terms. The classical aesthetics of natural imitation conceals a critical moment within its apparent simplicity. The imitation that would seem to affirm the claims of nature to adequacy, to self-sufficiency, actually critiques them: if nature were truly self-sufficient, there would be no aesthetic impulse to reduplicate it, in whole or in part. The prestige of aesthetic imitation points indirectly to some deficiency in nature. So mimesis, by definition, is predicated upon a kind of natural crisis. What we learn from "L'Albatros" is that crisis is infectious, that the mimetic impulse itself comes to be in crisis, and that this crisis in turn impels mimesis toward metaphor. At each stage, the critical instance both preserves and negates: mimesis preserves and negates the natural world while being preserved and negated by metaphorical transposition.

Let us return to my characterization of two different readers for "L'Albatros." Only the naive reader is capable of grasping the mimetic crisis for what it is. Only the naive reader identifies with the albatross and in so doing affirms the existence of an identity that can reflect upon its own disproportion. The cynical reader refuses such identification and thus resists the critical character of the poem. This resistance is quite surprising, since we tend to affiliate pathetic identification with an acritical attitude in readers. What, however, is the status of the cynical response to "L'Albatros"? Can the cynic, by refusing to understand the mimetic crisis, remain free from its contagion?

The answer to this question may come from a closer look at the poem's third stanza. There the sailors' cynicism, which stands for the attitude of the unsympathetic reader, takes the form of laughter. Instead of identifying with the pathos of the bird's condition, the sailors think it is funny: "Lui, naguère si beau, qu'il est comique et laid." Such laughter marks an affirmation of difference: the sailors do not see themselves in the bird's position, and so they find it comical. It is striking that the sailors should use the adjectives "comique" and "laid" to describe the humiliated albatross. The coupling of the two terms has a peculiarly technical ring to it, as does the entire series of exclamations attributed to the bird's persecutors. For all the apparent realism of the poem, and particularly of the third stanza, these sailors speak suspiciously like aestheticians. The language recalls both Hugo's *Cromwell* preface and Baudelaire's own *De l'essence du rire,* which develops the theory of the grotesque in the direction of comedy. Baudelaire's critical work on laughter was produced between the early and the late versions of "L'Albatros"—in other words before the composition of the poem's third stanza—so it is not unreasonable to think that his theoretical speculations on comedy might inform his poetic depiction of laughter.

In *De l'essence du rire,* Baudelaire associates laughter with an attitude very similar to the one displayed by the sailors in "L'Albatros": "[Le rire] est dans l'homme la conséquence de l'idée de sa propre supériorité," he writes (*OC* II, 532). Where this sense of superiority is lacking, in children or in infant civilizations, there can be no real comedy. From this perspective laughter appears to be at odds with expressions of pity or compassion, which involve "fellow feeling," that is, the affirmation of similarity, not difference. And yet laughter is fraught with a diabolic complication. The sense of superiority, which is crucial to laughter, is in fact a consequence of human imperfection: "Comme le rire est essentiellement humain, il est essentiellement contradictoire, c'est-à-dire qu'il est à la fois signe d'une grandeur infinie et d'une misère infinie" (*OC* II, 532). The one who laughs is of necessity caught in the ironic drama of "la disproportion de l'homme." Here Baudelaire's argument is induced by its Pascalian underpinnings to take an eccentric turn; human laughter, Baudelaire claims, measures simultaneously the inferiority of man with respect to the divinity and the superiority of man over the animals. The essential structure of laughter, or "l'essence du rire," thus comes to involve the oddly particular phenomenon of laughing at animals: "Les animaux les plus comiques sont les plus sérieux; ainsi les singes et les perroquets" (*OC* II, 532). The fundamental difference that underwrites "l'idée de sa propre supériorité" is the difference between man and animal.

The laughter of the sailors in "L'Albatros" follows this theoretical sketch in several respects. There is the clear confrontation between man and animal, which contributes to the poem's simple, almost archaic quality. And the unstable dynamic of laughter derives from this simple, apparently stable confrontation. The fundamental difference between man and animal, which is affirmed by the sailors' laughter, is also undermined by it. Through a kind of diabolic logic, the laugh of superiority takes the form of *mimesis*: "L'un agace son bec avec un brûle-gueule, / L'autre mime, en boitant, l'infirme qui volait!" The sailors come to imitate the grotesque figure of the fallen bird in what could also be called a mimetic crisis, since it too obscures the structures of identity and difference. Like it or not, the sailors are engaged in the drama of human disproportion: they seek difference through imitation and are degraded by their very efforts at self-elevation. Unlike the poet, they do not embrace such disproportion as their own and do not seem aware of the irony that makes them resemble the albatross in spite of themselves. But their very lack of self-awareness testifies to the power of the poem's mimetic machinery. All figures, whether cynical or sympathetic, imitate the strange bird in the end. This may be Baudelaire's somewhat comical version of the mythic curse of the albatross.

How do these comments on the mimetic crisis in "L'Albatros" affect the thematic and historical interpretation of the poem? To begin with, the theme of the poet's alienation takes on a slightly different shading. Poetic alienation, since it involves the experience of human disproportion, is not such an isolated phenomenon. It appears, instead, as an integral part of the human condition. The poet may realize this condition more fully than other humans, but the distinction is a matter more of degree than of kind. In other words, poetic distinction does not make one a radically strange bird, detached from the human species. If anything, the poet is the least alienated of humans, since he sees and understands his alienation for what it is. This interpretation of "L'Albatros" forces us to reconsider some of the stylistic and historical premises that Gilman used in her analysis of the poem. In particular, Baudelaire's engagement with romanticism appears deeper and less schematic, and the critique of romanticism that takes place in the third stanza appears less definitive than we might have thought. Once the alienated romantic subject is understood as the figure of subjectivity per se, then we can see that figure at work, not only in the persecuted poet, but in the persecuting sailors as well. Baudelaire does not simply discover his own, postromantic subjectivity in the poem's third stanza, with a stylistic "coming of age." The Baudelairean subject is produced instead by a peculiar friction between the third and fourth stanzas that opposes and unites persecutor and persecuted, cynicism and pathos, self and other. We have in "L'Albatros" a fascinating example of the same subjectivity that is expressed programmatically in "L'Héautontimorouménos":

> Je suis la plaie et le couteau!
> Je suis le soufflet et la joue!
> Je suis les membres et la roue,
> Et la victime et le bourreau.

Thus the romantic subject is capable of playing not only the victim but also the executioner. Part of the mimetic game of "L'Albatros" involves the poet's speaking in the voice of his persecutors, fulfilling their role as well as his own. This is accomplished so successfully that one might fail to notice how poeticized the sailors' diction really is. The impossibility of speaking in one's own voice (speech in the poem is in fact "imitation speech"; we have the poet imitating a sailor or a sailor who talks like a poet) does not belie but underscores the condition of romantic alienation, which touches all the figures of the poem. In terms of a literary historical analysis, Gilman argued that "L'Albatros" contained a romantic moment and a moment that critiques or goes beyond romanticism. I would argue that "L'Albatros" is thoroughly romantic, if we understand romanticism to be an aesthetics of critique: the poem's two moments remain, but their interplay involves more than a linear, historical development. In the friction between the third and fourth stanzas, a single, if complex aesthetic problem is at work, one that we can account for within a romantic framework. Asselineau's sense that the final stanza of the poem could be rendered more "powerful" by the addition of a tableau painting the bird's predicament is consistent with these observations. The tableau and the moral of the poem, as divergent as they may seem in historical or stylistic terms, work together to produce a single aesthetic effect that is more than the sum of its parts.

Much of my argument can be taken as an extended elaboration, in Hugolian terms, of Flaubert's response to "L'Albatros." What Flaubert must have seen as the banalization of the romantic subject I am seeing as its generalization. The fact that Flaubert did not voice his critique but kept it implicit (by placing "L'Albatros" without comment in his sottisier), indicates that the critical voice is internal to the poem. Where my position differs from the one implied by Gilman's reading is that I do not believe that the critical voice can be localized. Both the third and the fourth stanzas of "L'Albatros" have marked critical potential. By the same token, I would argue that the Hugolian and Flaubertian voices in the poem cannot be restricted to the fourth and third stanzas, respectively. The profound identification between human and beast that occurs in the fourth stanza is perfectly compatible with Flaubert's idiom and with his peculiar brand of sentimentality. On the other hand, the enumerative technique used in the third stanza—"*L'un* agace son bec. . . . *L'autre* mime en boitant"—is something that we know Baudelaire borrowed from Hugo in a later period of poetic production (this would tend to discredit the thesis that Baudelaire "matured" by overcoming Hugo's influence). The dissemination of literary voices in "L'Albatros" is another indication that the critical moment of the poem cannot be isolated: if Flaubert's voice cannot be separated from Hugo's, then the critical impact of the former cannot be felt as a simple "going beyond." On the contrary, each voice might be said to criticize the other. Hugolian romanticism is not purged from "L'Albatros" but remains as part of the poem's critical character.

When "L'Albatros" is read in this manner, the poem becomes something more than a literary chestnut, lacking in critical interest. By introducing literary-historical categories to the interpretation of the poem, Gilman initiated a hermeneutic process that exceeds the limits of her analysis. This process takes the term "romanticism," which Gilman used in a limited, descriptive sense, and transforms it into a critical category with a wide-ranging field of application. "L'Albatros" may thus be seen as a privileged text, one that enables us to challenge and rethink the categories of literary-historical interpretation. In particular, the poem suggests a way in which the Hugolian theory of the grotesque might persist as a subversive principle behind Baudelaire's theory of correspondances, as a self-parodic moment in the otherwise straightforward production of beauty. This self-parody, which I have read as the tension between the two last stanzas of "L'Albatros," is neither naive nor cynical but critical. As such, it resists the simple historicization that is implicit in Gilman's interpretation that "L'Albatros" moves from a naive romantic to a sophisticated postromantic perspective. By its intimate linkage of the grotesque with a poetics of correspondances (for there to be analogy in this poem, there must be difformity; for there to be identity, there must be difference), "L'Albatros" displays in exemplary fashion the *necessity* of a critical moment in Baudelaire's aesthetic enterprise. This simple poem, whose critical commentary seems to have been obvious, offers a key to understanding the complex character of *Les Fleurs du Mal.*

Chapter 2

Baudelaire's "La Vie antérieure"

NINA TUCCI

J'ai longtemps habité sous de vastes portiques
Que les soleils marins teignaient de mille feux,
Et que leurs grands piliers, droits et majestueux,
Rendaient pareils, le soir, aux grottes basaltiques. (4)

Les houles, en roulant les images des cieux,
Mêlaient d'une façon solennelle et mystique
Les tout-puissants accords de leur riche musique
Aux couleurs du couchant reflété par mes yeux. (8)

C'est là que j'ai vécu dans les voluptés calmes,
Au milieu de l'azur, des vagues, des splendeurs
Et des esclaves nus, tout imprégnés d'odeurs, (11)

Qui me rafraîchissaient le front avec des palmes,
Et dont l'unique soin était d'approfondir
Le secret douloureux qui me faisait languir. (14)

In general, critics agree that Baudelaire's "La Vie antérieure" is a drug-induced experience, a psychedelic vision, to use a more modern term (see, for example, Claude Pichois's commentary in the Pléiade edition of Baudelaire's complete works as well as other works listed in the bibliography). Indeed, a reassessment of the poem from this point of view is a timely task, for it creates a link to the modern drug culture, but more important, it continues to underscore the universal longing of the human psyche to transcend itself.

In the modern classic *The Doors of Perception*, the noted religious scholar Aldous Huxley states: "That humanity at large will ever be able to dispense with Artificial Paradises seems very unlikely. . . . [The] urge to escape, the longing to transcend . . . if only for a few minutes is, and always has been, one of the principal appetites of the soul" (62). Huxley's statement is a commentary on his own chemically

16

induced experience with the transcendent. He ingested mescaline to alter his ordinary state of consciousness in order to understand "from the inside" the vision of the seer, the medium, the mystic, the poet, and the artist (14). The drug temporarily suppressed the localized or subjective aspect of the self to allow what Huxley calls (and indeed what contemplatives, philosophers, mystics, and artists both Eastern and Western since time immemorial have called) the "Not-Self," the objective or nontransitory aspect of the human psyche, to emerge. The drug, he explains, rendered him indifferent to ordinary time and space, and his heightened sense of perception permitted him as Not-Self to participate in the Not-Self of all that surrounds him—in a word, the pure existence or eternal Being of all things ("this timely bliss of seeing"). Subject and object became one (35, 40). Speaking from beyond the boundary of ego, Huxley finds himself agreeing with Bergson's idea that each individual is potentially a "Mind-at-Large" (Not-Self). In other words, each person is "at each moment capable of remembering all that has ever happened to him and of perceiving everything that is happening everywhere in the universe" (22–23). "Mind-at-Large," continues Huxley, is necessarily filtered through the "reducing valve of the brain and the nervous system" to protect the ordinary mortal from being overwhelmed by an utter invasion of information (23). Yet a nostalgic intuition of this inherent potential for expanded awareness is ever present in the human psyche.

In recent history, the drug culture has claimed numerous adherents; however, only the artistic elite, contends Huxley, brings back reports from the transcendent country of the mind (see, for example, the winter 1993 issue of *Gnosis*, which examines psychedelics as harbingers of an awakening of human consciousness). The distinction between the poet (artist and so forth) and the untalented visionary resides not in the quality of the vision but rather in the inability of the latter to express and give form to the inner experience. Huxley concludes:

> From the records of religion and surviving monuments of poetry and the plastic arts, it is very plain that, in most places, men have attached more importance to the inscape than to objective existents, have felt that what they saw with their eyes shut possessed a spiritually higher significance than what they saw with their eyes open. . . . The outer world is what we wake up to every morning of our lives, is the place where . . . we must try to make our living. In the inner world there is neither work nor monotony. We visit it only in dreams and musings. . . . What wonder, then, if human

beings in their search for the divine have generally preferred to look within! (46–47)

The accounts of poets, mystics, and artists attest to the universality of the spiritual experience and have created an ahistorical fraternity that transcends the barriers of time and space. Thus we can link, for example, Huxley's classic to Baudelaire's *Les Paradis artificiels*.

The poet's chronicle of his psychedelic experience is quasi-identical to that of Huxley. Baudelaire's unquenchable thirst for the infinite ("le goût de l'infini")—his desire to escape the human condition, if only for a few moments—drives him to create his own paradise through artificial means: "créer . . . l'Idéal Artificiel . . . par la pharamacie: [L'homme] . . . a . . . cherché . . . sous tous les climats et dans tous les temps, les moyens de fuir, ne fût-ce que pour quelques heures son habitacle de fange" (*OC* I, 402–3). Though drugs temporarily obliterate the ego ("vous avez jeté votre personnalité aux quatre vents"), the experience will take on the hue of the temperament of the user: "[L'expérience] gardera toujours la tonalité particulière de l'individu" (*OC* I, 409). (This was only one of Huxley's unexpected insights during his experiment with mescaline: "But I had not reckoned . . . with the idiosyncrasies of my mental make-up, the facts of my temperament, training and habits" [*Perception* 15]).

Baudelaire describes the process as a progression from an incipient state of hyper well-being to one of inexorable ecstasy ("une extase implacable") to a state of absolute happiness ("C'est ce que les Orientaux appellent le kief; c'est le bonheur absolu"). The eyes have pierced the veil of profane reality, have opened onto infinity ("Les yeux visent l'infini") and there is a heightened acuity of all the senses: "C'est . . . à cette période de l'ivresse que se manifeste une finesse nouvelle, une acuité supérieure dans tous les sens. L'odorat, la vue, l'ouïe, le toucher participent également à ce propos" (*OC* I, 419). (Though not encompassing all the senses, Huxley reports an "enormous heightening . . . of the perception of color . . . under mescaline" [*Perception* 26]). In this radically altered state of consciousness, the Not-Self perceives and participates in the infinity of all things: "Les objets . . . se révèlent à nous sous des formes inconnues jusque-là. Puis ils se déforment, se transforment, et enfin ils entrent dans votre être, ou bien vous entrez en eux" (*OC* I, 392).

This cursory comparison of two strikingly similar accounts of chemically induced Artificial Paradises is an infinitesimal sampling of a substantial and controversial literature on the subject. It is important to mention that, although the alteration of consciousness remains constant, the experience varies from individual to individual (for additional bibliography, see the above-mentioned issue of *Gnosis*). For the modern individual whose horizons have been expanded experientially by drugs or meditation or psychologically by the study of the collective unconscious or objective psyche (Not-Self, Not-I, Mind-at-Large) as posited by the Swiss psychologist C. G. Jung, the parcel of infinity encapsulated in "La Vie antérieure" can become a moment of shared participation. Enriched by an already substantial body of critical studies on the poem, we enter Baudelaire's visionary experience with the hope of gaining further insights into the infinite complexity of the poem. To this end, in addition to Huxley, I have also consulted the work of Gaston Bachelard and have drawn extensively on the psychological premises of C. G. Jung.

From the outset of "La Vie antérieure," we are aware that a transformation has already occurred. The ego has receded to the wings and has assumed the role of witness. The drug has liberated the psychic forces, and we are immediately plunged into an "other" space that Huxley defined as the Not-Self, C. G. Jung as the collective or objective psyche, the matrix of all creativity (*Collected Works*, vol. 15, 97), and Gaston Bachelard as "l'immensité intime de la rêverie" (*La Poétique*, 168). The poet is already completely enveloped in the vision, and the reader as participant struggles to "see" and understand his personalized corner of infinity and at the same time to attach it to the primordial or archetypal image or images that have erupted from the depths of the unconscious.

A reading of the first quatrain tells us that the poet's unconscious is lodged in a familiar, serene, and well-structured space. Gaston Bachelard has noted that the inner house is our first piece of the universe, our private bit of the Cosmos: "Tout espace vraiment habité porte l'essence de la notion de maison" (24). The vast portals and the grand, majestic columns suggest that the imagination has sculpted a psychic structure that resembles a temple, an indication to our mind of the spiritual tenor of the vision. The affective tone of this first quatrain is one of leisure and passive well-being. But it is also a solemn participation in the autonomous unfolding of the idyllic scene and its subsequent transformation. Contemplating a splendid sunset from the protective grandeur of the portals (suggested by "sous"), the poet revels in the dance of sunlight on the surface of the sea that breaks into a prismatic orgy of color against the surface of the columns. In the evening, they are transmuted into columnar basaltic caves.

The use of the first person narration would seem to indicate that the essentially visual reverie of the first quatrain is anchored in a personal memory. Yet images such as the sea, the temple, the columns, and the caves, which have been individualized by the poet, belong to the immense repository of symbols of the collective psyche. The great images of mankind are both historical and prehistorical—that is, they belong to memory and to legend. Each image is rooted in an unfathomable oneiric source. On this oneiric source, the poet places the seal of his own personal past: "C'est sur ce fond onirique," says Bachelard, "que le passé personnel met des couleurs particulières" (*La Poétique,* 47). The accomplished state of extended perception is immediately rendered in the first line by the term "vastes." Bachelard, who has examined at length the use of the word in Baudelaire's poetry, helps us to understand its various shades of meaning (174–90). Drawing upon Baudelaire's essays on the use of drugs, he notes that the prerequisite for the visionary experience is an unbounded capacity for leisure: "Le mangeur d'opium, pour profiter de la rêverie calmante, doit avoir de 'vastes loisirs'" (114). Bachelard further postulates that the vowel "a" of the word ("l'immensité intérieure du mot") has the value of a mantra, or cosmic sound, that dissolves ego barriers and penetrates into the vastness of the human soul. The vibrating, ever-expanding vowel unites the double universe of the depths of the psyche and the Cosmos (181). In "La Vie antérieure," the vast inner dwelling of the human psyche, symbolized by the temple with its grand, majestic columns and the basaltic caves, mirrors the immensity of the Cosmos, symbolized by the sea. From this inner abode, the poet, in a blissful state, contemplates his reflection in an intensely illuminated sea. As previously mentioned, it is a familiar, happy locus ("l'espace heureux"). It is also a locus that the poet possesses ("l'espace de possession") because of repeated periods of introversion ("J'ai longtemps habité"). Bachelard explains that "les lieux où l'on a *vécu la rêverie* se restituent d'eux-mêmes" (26). In addition, the image of the temple suggests that the poet has moved into a sacred space that will be further substantiated in the second quatrain by the phrase "solennelle et mystique."

Since time immemorial, man has constructed temples whose architecture images his concept of the sacred. When the image of the temple was interiorized, it became, psychologically speaking, one of the archetypes of man's spiritual inscape and the sacralization of the macrocosm. The temple is, however, also an image of the microcosm. In "La Vie antérieure," the poet inhabits a temple that reflects his Occidental heritage, a symmetrical Hellenic structure, divided into upper and lower regions. Its classical proportions are reflected in the form and content of the first quatrain and, in terms of the division of light and dark, the entire poem. In the first two lines, the temple is bathed in light. The second half of the quatrain stands in direct opposition to the first yet is connected to it by the powerful columns extending from the light to be transmuted into basaltic caves in the obscure depths of its foundation.

This allusion to "grottes basaltiques" demands further attention. Basalt is a dark gray to black fine-grained volcanic rock and tends to assume a columnar structure (*Encyclopedia Americana*, III, 301). On the psychological level, this definition is significant, for the cave is also a prime symbol of the unconscious and as such is known to guard the secrets of humanity. From the eruption of the treasure house of primordial images that is the human psyche, the poet has sculpted an edifice. He maintains a delicate balance between those secrets that have surfaced and become a part of his conscious substance and those that remain unknown. This balance will become increasingly clear as the poem unfolds, particularly in the relationship between the slaves and "Le secret douloureux." "La cave," says Bachelard, "est d'abord *l'être obscur* de la maison, l'être qui participe aux puissances souterrains" (35).

A complementary image of the cave is that of the womb. The return to the womb is the return to the origin of all things, to the innocence and purity of primal beginnings. It is an amniotic space of warmth and protection, but it is also a dark space of unrevealed phenomena. Therefore, the surface expanse of the sea, irradiated by the sun, symbol of consciousness and the masculine principle, masks its dark maternal aspect, which coincides with the unconscious or the cave (Jung, vol. 5, 219). The word "vaste" comes to mind once more, for it synthesizes the experience and unites the opposing forces of light and dark, or as Jung would say, the tension of the opposites. This juxtaposition of light and dark, it seems, would invalidate Michel Quesnel's assessment that "la grotte inaugure 'La Vie antérieure'" (265). He has evidently overlooked the fact that the cave is the subterranean foundation of the temple. In addition, the dual symbols of the temple and the cave, upheld by the columns, illustrate the verticality of the inner house and represent the two poles of the psychic blueprint (Bachelard, *La Poétique*, 35). The contours of the poet's vision in this magnificently proportioned quatrain embrace the two "vast" categories of archetypal imagery, which are, to use Gilbert Durand's phraseology, "le régime diurne et le régime nocturne de l'image" (540, 543). The poet, however, has sensitized the objective immensity of these two values by creating, as we have seen, a temple to house and contain the vision. It is also significant that, despite the poet's awareness of the parallel forces of light and dark in this first quatrain, the dominant and overriding sensation is one of profound well-being. In the context of a drug-induced vision, it corresponds to the phase when the interior eye of the poet begins to apprehend the underlying aesthetic continuum in himself and in nature.

In the second quatrain, the static visual scene of the first four lines takes on an autonomous life of its own. The rounded ridges of the surf mirror the prismatic colors of the setting sun ("Les houles en roulant les images des cieux"). The collective, cadenced sound emanating from the slow, rhythmic swell and fall of the unbroken waves creates a solemn and mystical chant ("Mêlaient d'une façon solennelle et mystique / Les tout-puissants accords de leur riche musique"). The eyes of the poet become like magnets that synthesize and absorb this mighty union of heaven and earth unto himself, creating a triangle or, more pertinently, a sacred trinity ("Aux couleurs du couchant reflété par mes yeux"). It is far from the narcissistic experience of which Sartre accuses Baudelaire: "Il se regarde voir; il regarde pour se voir regarder" (25). The universe has entered the poet and has transported him beyond the boundaries of the individual self and the contradictions of relative existence. To our perceptions we may add Louis Morice's splendid appreciation of the poet's vision: "Et que fait Baudelaire dans ces deux quatrains sinon regarder et entendre le monde, comme le premier homme au matin de la création?" (45). For a precious, inestimable moment, Poet and Cosmos are one in a state of primordial innocence and purity. The form also renders the vision that has risen to consciousness and the poet's assimilation of it into his being. The rhyme scheme of the first quatrain, *abba*, is inverted in the second quatrain and becomes *baab*, suggesting that the poet has become the vessel for this sacred union. In *Les Paradis artificiels*, Baudelaire summarizes for us this final stage, which he compares to oriental "bliss consciousness": "Toute contradiction est devenue unité. L'homme est *passé* dieu" (*OC* I, 394).

It would not be an exaggeration to say that "vaste" also has a metaphysical value. Bachelard concurs: "Le mot vaste est, chez Baudelaire, un véritable argument métaphysique par lequel sont unis le vaste monde et les vastes pensées" (175). The sense of the immensity of the universe, which the poet cognizes in himself as a spiritual, aesthetic experience, converges and is recast in the second quatrain in the word "mystique." The mystical participation in which subject and object have become one is a mysterious poetic event that cannot be conveyed by rational language. "Mystique," which embraces the notion of "vaste," is an inexhaustible theme of our poem (and of poetry in general). The poem can be deciphered, and then only partially, through associative imagery. The poet, in an effort to express the inexpressible, couches the vision in symbolic language. In turn, the vision, when filtered through the individual psyche, takes on a humanized personal expression. As we saw, both Huxley and Baudelaire agreed that, despite the expansion of consciousness due to the influence of drugs, the core personality retained its identity. In this sense we can speak of the predilection of certain recurrent themes or images in an artist's work.

For the Baudelaire reader, "La Vie antérieure" is a prism that refracts a recognizable system of thought and impressions, for example: an insatiable thirst for the Absolute, the desire to escape the mundane, the ever-present tension between the forces of light and darkness, the fear of the void or the unknown (a theme that I will broach in our discussion of form at the end of our analysis), the theme of the inner voyage and the spiritual and sensual appreciation of this "other" space, the prevalence of sun and sea imagery, and above all, the concept of synesthesia, a hallmark of Baudelaire's poetry that he defined in the celebrated poem "Correspondances" and enacted in the second quatrain of our poem. The convergence of the senses transports the poet beyond the individual frame and links him with his notion of ultimate Reality. An even more detailed description of the elements of the beatific scene of "La Vie antérieure" is found in "Le Poème du hachisch":

> Le hachisch s'étend alors sur toute la vie comme *un vernis magique*: il la colore en *solennité* et en *éclaire* toute la profondeur. Paysages dentelés, horizons fuyants . . . ou illuminés par les ardeurs concentrés des *soleils couchants*,—profondeur de l'espace, allégorie de la profondeur du temps. . . . *La musique,* autre langue chère aux esprits profonds, vous parle de vous-même et vous raconte le poème de votre vie; elle s'incorpore à vous, et vous vous fondez en elle. . . . Chaque note se transform[e] en mot, et le poème entier entr[e] dans votre cerveau comme un dictionnaire doué de

vie. . . . *L'immensité bleue de la mer* s'étale comme une véritable enchanter-
esse. (*OC* I, 430–31; emphasis added)

The poet comes full circle and caps part of the event in the first two
lines of the first tercet: "C'est là que j'ai vécu dans les voluptés calmes
/ Au milieu de l'azur, des vagues, des splendeurs." Syntax effects this
partial, intertextual completion. The present perfect, "J'ai vécu"
recalls its synonym "J'ai habité" in the first line and intensifies it with
the introductory phrase "C'est là." It is as if the poet wishes to con-
vince the reader of the veracity of this vast inner dimension for which
he is the spokesman. In his prose writing, Baudelaire defines the poet
as "une âme collective." Elsewhere, he asks: "qu'est-ce un poète (je
prends le mot dans son acception la plus large), si ce n'est qu'un tra-
ducteur, un déchiffreur?" (*OC* II, 133, 139). Bachelard fleshes out
Baudelaire's definition in terminology more reflective of our analysis:
"Pour Baudelaire, le destin poétique de l'homme est d'être le miroir
de l'immensité, ou plus exactement encore, l'immensité vient prendre
conscience d'elle-même en l'homme. Pour Baudelaire, l'homme est un
être vaste" (178–79).

"C'est là" also raises the specific question: Where is "là"? This
"other" space is related to the title of the poem and has been the sub-
ject of some critical speculation. Paul Arnold sees in the title a clear
allusion to the Pythagorean tenet of palingenesis. He equates the situ-
ation of "La Vie antérieure" with that in "Le Mauvais moine," in
which the poet, he feels, despite one or several previous existences,
has failed to attain a state of purity: "Mon âme est un tombeau que,
mauvais cénobite, / Depuis l'éternité je parcours et j'habite; / Rien
n'embellit les murs de ce cloître odieux" (*OC* I, 16).

For him, the vision is a compensatory mental extravaganza that
stands in direct opposition to "le secret douloureux" of the last line.
Indeed, the painful secret invalidates the vision, says Arnold, because
the poet has not succeeded in shedding karmic accretions accumulat-
ed over many lifetimes (126–28). The vision remains a haunting intu-
ition of what was and the object of the poet's deepest longing. Louis
Morice, on the other hand, rejects the notion of palingenesis. He pro-
poses the Platonic theory of the Idea as a possible solution, admitting,
nevertheless, that Plato also adhered to the doctrine of palingenesis.
The Platonic Idea represents ultimate Reality. It is the archetype of
absolute Being imperfectly expressed by man imprisoned in the
human frame but in whom there remains the vague memory of the

Idea of perfection. In the end, Morice decides that, despite misleading allusions to oriental and Hellenic notions of palingenesis and profound Platonic resonances, the title of the poem simply represents a privileged moment of "béatitude poétique." I would like to elaborate on these conclusions.

One of the metaphors that Baudelaire himself used to describe the unconscious was the palimpsest on which is transcribed the incommensurate collective memory of man. Images, ideas, and sentiments may drop below the level of consciousness, but they are never lost: "Rien ne se perd" (*OC* I, 507). The poems hidden in the artist's soul are not dead. They sleep: "L'oubli n'est donc que momentané . . . et généralement dans les excitations créées par *l'opium,* tout l'immense et compliqué palimpseste de la mémoire se déroule d'un seul coup, avec toutes ses couches superposées de sentiments défunts, mystérieusement embaumés dans ce que nous appelons l'oubli" (*OC* I, 506).

Baudelaire's discussion of the unconscious is strikingly akin to that of Jung, who defines it as an entity that tells the "story of mankind." When the brain "becomes creative, it creates out of this history" (Jung, vol. 10, 10). The point I wish to make is that the visionary mode of artistic creativity is irrational. Therefore, the Platonic theory of the Idea, the oriental and Pythagorean concepts of palingenesis, to which we might add the influence of Swedenborg, prevalent ideas in the nineteenth century, need not be dismissed. Rather, they should be regarded as tools of expression. Through the alchemy of the creative process, the imagination of the poet has dissolved them as philosophical systems and transformed aspects of them into a network of suggestions or usable metaphors, because, by their very nature, they speak of the immensity of the soul and its potential for perfectibility.

We must also consider the concept of time in the title. Time is a matter of perception. In ordinary reality, time is linear. Therefore, it would be appropriate to interpret "ante" of "antérieure"—which means "before" or "prior to"—as an allusion to a chronological past event. Barry Ulanov, in his work *Jung and the Outside World,* helps us frame the thought: "Here in the collective unconscious is where our roots go down into a shared history of soul to reach an inheritance that both *precedes* individual consciousness and is, at the same time, its nutriment" (x; emphasis added). "Anterior," however, also means "situated towards the front: before in place, as opposed to posterior" (*Webster's Third New International Dictionary,* s.v. "anterior"). We may remember Baudelaire's concept of the palimpsest, in which the psyche, in an altered state of consciousness, is capable of participating in the simultaneity of the human experience. In this state of extended awareness, the perception of time has changed. The ego, with its notions of sequence and logically connected events, has receded to the background, and Mind-at-Large (Not-Self), with its ability to perceive "All," has moved to center stage. Time is abolished, and the purview of the inner eye is all-encompassing. With one sweeping glance, the poet sees and experiences the sublime and the grotesque aspects of the human condition concurrently. In timelessness, both states cohabit and are eternally present. A more complete interpretation, then, must include both the chronological and nonchronological aspects of the title. In our poem, drugs yielded a panoramic view of a piece of man's psychic *history*—his eternal striving to create more light in the darkness. And the echoes of reincarnation discussed above can be reinterpreted to indicate not so much the problem of *a* previous existence or existences as *the collective unconscious life* that the poet shares with all mankind—"la vie antérieure"—and of which he, by virtue of his poetic gift, is a mediator. Indeed, the unconscious *reincarnates* each time the poet wrests from and expresses a part of this fertile Ground. The poem itself is the reincarnation, because it gives birth, or more accurately, rebirth to that which lives in the darkness of the womb, that matrix of all creativity. From this most profound level of human awareness, the poet says, "Quelque incohérente que soit une existence, l'unité humaine n'en est pas troublée. Tous les échos de la mémoire, si on pouvait les réveiller simultanément, formeraient un concert, *agréable* ou *douloureux,* mais logique et sans dissonances" (*OC* I, 506; emphasis added). This significant statement helps us create a harmonious transition from our discussion of the vision to the consideration of the slaves and the secret, for "La Vie antérieure" is both an agreeable and a painful concert.

In retrospect, we may note that the vision that comprises ten lines has disrupted the mechanics of the fixed form of the sonnet and has impinged upon two lines of the first tercet for its conclusion. The last line of the first tercet, when added to the last three lines, forms an equally divided quatrain. Just as the third line of the first quatrain connected the archetypal registers of light and dark, so also can lines 11 and 12 be considered pivotal. The exotically scented, nude slaves are affiliated with the world of light and the commingling of the senses of the second quatrain *and* the dark world of the secret.

In Baudelaire's poetic universe, the bouquet of a strong perfume has frequently served as a catalyst for transcending the finite ("Parfum exotique," "La Chevelure," "Le Parfum"). In "La Vie antérieure," we can say that the poet is led by the scent of his own creative instincts, which seek expression and are symbolized by the slaves. There is more. The poet's choice of the word "front" is particularly auspicious, for it is linked to our interpretation of the term "antérieure" in the title. The notion of the poet as clairvoyant was widespread in the nineteenth century. The influx of oriental thought popularized the concept of the all-seeing third eye, located in the middle of the forehead (in oriental parlance, this corresponds to the sixth chakra). In "La Fonction du poète," Victor Hugo maintained that only the poet had the gift of vision: "Lui seul a le front éclairé" (*Œuvres poétiques* I, 1031). In "Le Poème du hachisch," Baudelaire makes the comment that "L'œil intérieur transforme tout" (*OC* I, 431).

I therefore disagree totally with Paul Arnold, who feels that "Le secret douloureux" of the final line annuls the vision. On the contrary, impending darkness, though muted by the splendor of the scene, permeates the poem. From the outset, we saw that darkness forms a part of the very structure of the poet's house ("grottes basaltiques"). That the event should occur at sunset is also psychologically telling, and critics have noted Baudelaire's predilection for sunsets. Marc Eigeldinger's interpretation is eminently appropriate for our poem: "Le soleil, à l'heure du couchant, ressuscite le passé, non seulement celui des souvenirs personnels, mais le passé immémorial et mythique de l'homme éternellement en quête de la lumière de l'âge d'or" ("La symbolique," 369). Eigeldinger adds that the setting sun in Baudelaire's poetry is often engulfed by the sea and is alchemically purified in its dark regenerative waters (368). Jung echoes the idea and completes it: "The sea devours the sun" in its maternal waters but brings it forth again. He who thirsts for the heights, adds the noted psychologist, must "descend into the dark depths," and this descent is an "indispensable precondition for climbing . . . higher" (Jung, vol. 5, 218; vol. 9i, 19). The tension between the upper and lower worlds is at the very core of Baudelaire's poetry and is an undeniable theme of our poem. Implicit in this habitually cultivated vision (note the use of the imperfect) is the cyclic movement of light to dark. These recurring encounters, which are meant to repel the darkness, are regulated by the slaves, the denizens of the inner abode.

The slaves acquire an even deeper meaning when viewed with a Jungian apperception. Jung maintains that the unconscious personifies itself to inform the individual ego (Jung, vol. 15, 81). In the structure of the poem, the slaves' function is complex. They officiate as custodians of the threshold that separates the light from the dark. If we accept them as vital inherent impulses of the psyche, as I suggested above, we can also say that they represent a deep intuition that points to things that are unknown and hidden and, by their nature, secret (Jung, vol. 15, 94). To ease the confrontation with the darkness, these incarnate elemental forces from the sea of the poet's unconscious draw refreshment for him from the corresponding sea of the Cosmos through the metrical strokes of palm leaves ("Qui me rafraîchissaient le front avec des palmes"). At the same time, this to-and-fro rhythm, which emulates the undulating movement of the waves, mesmerizes the poet and keeps the interior eye focused on the inner event. The slaves blur the boundaries of these contradictory worlds and turn the poet's attention from his experience of a spiritual union with the Cosmos to a consideration of the darkness, its psychic twin. This swing of the pendulum is necessary to authenticate the vision. "Every single virtue in this world," says the Jungian analyst Robert Johnson, "is made valid by its opposite. Light would mean nothing without dark. . . . one cannot exist without the other" (*Shadow*, 17, 82). The slaves' task, it seems, is to help the poet fold the dark into the light. These unclothed figures ("esclaves nus") lay bare the poet's inner truth, heretofore unknown, and allow it to filter up to ego consciousness gradually. Through this dialogue with the unconscious, or more precisely, through the mutual relationship between the poet and these inner "gods or daemons," as Jung sometimes calls them, the poet's Being becomes more conscious of itself and continues to expand its horizons. Jung gives a psychological explanation of the poetic experience: "However dark and unconscious this night world may be, it is not wholly unfamiliar. . . . The poet now and then catches sight of the figures that people the night world. . . . he feels the secret quickening of human fate . . . and has a presentiment of incomprehensible happenings in the pleroma" (Jung, vol. 15, 94–96). In "La Vie antérieure," the concept of the psyche in a constant state of becoming is explained by the poet's ongoing quest to deepen his knowledge of "Le secret douloureux." And the process is contained in the well-chosen verb "approfondir."

The cryptic last line of the poem yielded an assortment of views. For René Galand, the secret pain is due to the fact that "Toutes les voluptés que peut offrir un lieu terrestre, si paradisiaque qu'il paraisse, ne peuvent satisfaire l'aspiration mystique à l'Absolu. Au lieu de l'apaiser, elles ne font que l'exacerber, que l'approfondir" (269). Carlo François seeks clues in the poet's account of his experience with hachisch: "Le rêveur du 'Poème du hachisch' confesse que l'euphorie des premiers moments du rêve est vouée à l'échec en vertu de l'existence préalable de son malheur" (199). Hubert's evaluation is indecisive. He imputes the painful secret to existent causes in the actual life of the poet. The secret may be a permanent part of human nature, or it may even be linked to poetic creativity: "Ce secret douloureux marque un retour au présent, au secret qui fait souffrir le poète *maintenant* ou qui existe depuis toujours dans la nature humaine. . . . Il se pourrait que ce secret, existant semble-t-il, en dehors du temps, correspondît à la création poétique" (157).

In my opinion, we must probe the secret of "La Vie antérieure" from a double point of view: the objective, or impersonal, and the subjective, or personal. Objectively, the riddle of the secret is quite simple: the drug is the clue. Through its use, the vast, ever-present world of the human psyche that lies hidden behind the facade of ego emerges. It is secret because it cannot be perceived with ordinary vision. This secret world, which represents the psychic heritage of all mankind, is intuited and seen by the elite minority of which Huxley spoke in the statement that I quoted at the outset of this chapter. Within the context of the poem, the presence of this secret world was already implicit, as we saw, in my discussion of the word "antérieure" in the title and in the use of the word "front." Outside the framework of the poem, Baudelaire's own definition of the brain as a palimpsest whose many layers were simultaneously revealed to him under the influence of drugs further substantiates our premise. Yet the dissolution of profane vision does not make the poet immediately omniscient, for the inner world has its own inborn structure of secrets that remain dormant until ferreted out by the seer (Jung, vol. 15, 97).

Several of Baudelaire's poems reveal the various aspects of his anguish such as time, inimical to the poet ("L'Horloge," "L'Ennemi"); the isolation of the poet ("L'Albatros"); the chasm between the ideal and man's human estate ("L'Élévation"), and so on. Poetic creativity seems to be another central problem. To a degree, his pain is anchored in the conflict between simple human endurance and the imperatives of an ineluctable poetic calling. He expresses his concern in "Le Guignon," which directly precedes "La Vie antérieure":

> Pour soulever un poids si lourd,
> Sisyphe, il faudrait ton courage!
> Bien qu'on ait du cœur à l'ouvrage,
> L'Art est long et le Temps est court. (*OC* I, 17)

Though the unconscious is the cathedra of creativity, the poet access-es its treasures with much difficulty. Again in "Le Guignon," he laments:

> Maint joyau dort enseveli
> Dans les ténèbres et l'oubli,
> Bien loin des pioches et des sondes;
>
> Mainte fleur épanche à regret
> Son parfum doux comme un *secret*
> Dans les solitudes profondes. (*OC* I, 17; emphasis added)

In a general comparison between man and the sea, the poet judges that neither will ever yield its secrets entirely:

> La mer est ton miroir; tu contemples ton âme
>
> Vous êtes tous les deux ténébreux et discrets:
> Homme, nul n'a sondé le fond de tes abîmes,
> O mer, nul ne connaît tes richesses intimes
> Tant vous êtes jaloux de garder vos *secrets*!
> ("L'homme et la me," *OC* I, 19; emphasis added)

In "La Vie antérieure," the poet has prevailed on the unconscious and has wrenched one of its jewels from its clutches. Still, not only is the Source of the vision shrouded in a darkness that he can never fully penetrate, but its sparkle does not cast light on the myriad unborn secrets that remain unrevealed. As a collective man, says Jung, "the poet is everywhere hemmed round . . . by the Unconscious, the mysterious god within him; so that ideas flow to him—he knows not whence; he is driven to work and to create—he knows not to what end; and is mastered by an impulse for constant growth and development—he knows not whither" (Jung, vol. 15, 102). We may remember Jung's statement that to create more light, one must descend into the depths. Therefore, the continued deepening of the unfathomable secret of the depths of his own being, which coincides with the vision of light, both inherent facets of the psyche, is, to quote the poet once again, "logique et sans dissonances."

Reference to the mention of the "secret" in other poems in the proximity of "La Vie antérieure" emphasizes the poet's personal pre-occupation with the unknown and also facilitates further speculation on "Le secret douloureux" as part of the paradox of the creative process. I will use the medieval concept of the mandorla to illustrate my point (I am indebted to Robert Johnson for this insight). The mandorla is the almond-shaped section that is created by two partly over-lapping circles. It is, says Johnson, the home of all great poetry, the place where the poet has created a mystical synthesis of the opposites, the place where he has united the "beauty and the terror of exis-tence," "l'horreur de la vie et l'extase de la vie," as Baudelaire himself put it (Johnson, *Shadow*, 98, 103; *OC* I, 703). Within the framework of the sonnet, the poet has created such a mandorla in which light and dark unite, for the vision that was once hidden has now surfaced to consciousness. On the affective level, the tension of the opposites is expressed by the bliss that is offset by the pain caused by that part of his psyche that he has not yet reclaimed ("Le secret douloureux").

The poet also demonstrates that the process by which the opposites are sustained must be constantly renewed. The inner secret world nourishes his creativity but only at the price of a continual sounding of the depths, and as we noted above, the process is rendered by the verb "approfondir." Another important verb to be taken into consid-eration is "languir." *Le Petit Robert* gives a definition that is germane to our analysis: "souffrir de quelque peine dont la continuité épuise" (972). From the outset, the poet informed us that he had been a long-time citizen of the inner world. As we saw, his inner temple was a protective fortress that permitted him to confront and to participate in the unfolding of the inner drama. Bachelard puts this idea into per-spective: "Il faut participer au drame cosmique soutenu par la maison qui lutte. . . . Une telle maison . . . est un instrument à affronter le cos-mos" (57–58). From this inner sanctuary, he allows the slaves to track the scent of his hidden resources. The creative struggle between the poet and his secret inner world has always been a painful one. In their wisdom, acquired through repeated encounters with the poet, the slaves cautiously gauge his journey, thus preventing the prodigious richness of the imaginative material from overtaxing and outstripping the poet's power to give expression and form to the event (Jung, vol. 15, 88). And herein lies the meaning of "languir." It is this gradual unveiling that saps his creative energy. He languishes after an ulti-mate ideal whose entirety he may never grasp, for the vast and complex secrets of the unconscious may never be reflected in the mirror of a single human consciousness. Nevertheless, the sonnet is a mandorla that absorbs unto itself a part of the two vast circles of light and dark that stretch beyond its boundaries into infinity. Light and dark are two aspects of the same coin. Paradoxically, the secret is a part of the light that has yet to be revealed. And the poem is a personalized miniature version of this most profound truth of the human condition, translated into language and form.

The enclosure of the vision into the specific form of the sonnet is significant. Given our hypothesis that the edenic scene of the poem is rooted in the undifferentiated formlessness of the unconscious, we could say that form is necessary to mold and give focus to the poet's discovery. The unconscious is the poet's cornucopia. As we saw in our discussion of the title, this silent, primordial domain, incapable of expressing itself, would remain forever hidden were it not glimpsed, formulated, and made concrete by the poet. He does not create the substance of his poetic vision but recreates it through form and gives it meaning (Jouve, *Baudelaire,* 78). Baudelaire is quite specific on the point, for in the *Salon de 1859* he states: Un poème ne se copie jamais: il veut être composé" (*OC* II, 661). Through *willed* composition of the reverie, the poet rediscovers and redeems the authentic state of primordial perfection. Form, then, regenerates and projects the spiritual longing of the human spirit onto the outside world (Jouve, *Baudelaire,* 78). This idea also links form to aesthetics, as Nicole Jouve spells it out: "Beauty [is] brought about by the 'Spirit' of man. . . . [It] only begins to *exist* once a landscape bears the sign of 'spiritual interference'" (76). In our poem, the drug-mandated reverie has displaced the intellect and has put the poet in contact with his absolute subjectivity. In this state, the poet as "seer" apprehends nature in its original, untainted, eternal beauty and gives it expression. Poetic reverie, it would seem, is the state of mind that reconciles absolute subjectivity with the absolute objectivity of nature. Baudelaire himself contended that Beauty exists not in and of itself "mais par moi, par ma grâce propre, par l'idée ou le sentiment que j'y attache" (*Curiosités esthétiques,* quoted by Jouve, *Baudelaire,* 78). In connection with this idea, Nicole Jouve appropriately comments, "The mind or the sensibility become for Baudelaire the repository of the beautiful because 'perception,' as well as a sense of values in man, remains relatively untouched by the fall" (78). In aesthetic contemplation, the poet transcends his local personality and, from this vantage point, externalizes his aesthetic intuition.

Form also assures the integrity of the vision and prevents the fragmentation of the psyche that gives it expression. The terse sonnet form is a particularly apt vehicle of expression for the poet's glimpse into the inexhaustible "superhuman world of contrasting light and darkness" (Jung, vol. 15, 90). Crystallizing the vision of light as well as the unfolding secret in artistic form serves to assuage the fears of the poet in his confrontation with the unknown. He confesses in "Une Mort héroïque" that "l'ivresse de l'Art est plus apte que toute autre à voiler les terreurs du gouffre" (*OC* I, 321).

Form is also inherently paradoxical. The poet has cognized and framed this "other" space, but he has not contained it. Peering into the gaping abyss reveals to him his own image and, by extension, man's human estate, "la tyrannie de la face humaine" (*OC* I, 483). He has not been able to sustain the moment of spiritual unity that is everywhere threatened by darkness. There is a dichotomy, then, between the power of art to recover primal innocence and to conceal the void and its inability to save him from the shadows of the human condition (Jouve, *Baudelaire*, 264). And of this Baudelaire was eminently aware: "La dualité de l'art est une conséquence fatale de la dualité de l'homme" (*OC* II, 685–86). In this sense, form is also inextricably linked to the secret. It is conceptualized in the fourteenth line of the poem, and it remains thus within the parameters of the traditional sonnet form. As a psychic reality, it wends its way past the grasp of poet and critic alike. The sonnet form has become a window that opens into a zone where only the elite few tread.

In succumbing to the temptation of trying to decode the personal topography of the poet's secret by alluding to poems that surround "La Vie antérieure," we were just able to touch upon the great mystery that enshrouds the creative act. The fact remains that even this is not verbalized in the poem itself. The secret becomes a sort of vacuum, as Pizzorusso put it, that the reader must fill. To understand its transpersonal meaning, readers must allow it to mold them as it did the poet. They must descend into the depths of their own unconscious where all humans are united and from which space the poet has communicated his feelings and aspirations to humankind. Though the poet's lines seemingly express an aspect of his own personal myth— "un petit élément de mythologie spontané," as Bachelard phrases it—

in essence, this is one of the myths of mankind. For "La Vie antérieure," within the limited space of the sonnet, represents the archetypal quest for spiritual union. This "re-immersion in the state of *participation mystique*," says Jung, "is the secret of artistic creation and of the effect that art has upon us, for at that level of experience it is no longer the weal or woe of the individual that counts, but the life of the collective. . . . Great poetry derives its strength from the life of mankind" (Jung, vol. 15, 98, 105). A work of art can orient mankind toward the unfathomable depths of the secret but can never name it (Bachelard, *La Poétique*, 31).

Chapter 3

"La Géante": Feminine Proportions and Lyric Subjectivity

GRETCHEN SCHULTZ

Du temps que la Nature en sa verve puissante
Concevait chaque jour des enfants monstrueux,
J'eusse aimé vivre auprès d'une jeune géante,
Comme aux pieds d'une reine un chat voluptueux.   (4)

J'eusse aimé voir son corps fleurir avec son âme
Et grandir librement dans ses terribles jeux;
Deviner si son cœur couve une sombre flamme
Aux humides brouillards qui nagent dans ses yeux;   (8)

Parcourir à loisir ses magnifiques formes;
Ramper sur le versant de ses genoux énormes,
Et parfois en été, quand les soleils malsains,   (11)

Lasse, la font s'étendre à travers la campagne,
Dormir nonchalamment à l'ombre de ses seins,
Comme un hameau paisible au pied d'une montagne.   (14)

Big Is Better

"La Géante" offers one of the most eccentric of the variegated femi-
nine figures represented in *Les Fleurs du Mal*. She shares company
with the beautiful but cruel and sterile woman appearing in a
whole range of poems (including "La Beauté," "Je t'adore à l'égal de la
voûte nocturne . . . ," "Avec ses vêtements ondoyants et nacrés . . .");
her antithesis, the sensuous and fecund woman of the evasion poems;
the disappointing muses of "La Muse malade" and "La Muse
vénale"; the terrifying and reviled but desired vampires; the lesbians
all but banished from the collection after the 1857 trial and expurga-

tion—I will not take the time to exhaust this list of sometimes contradictory, often dangerous, and frequently problematic feminine creatures. Such a diversified representation of femininity calls into question the emphatically simple message of so many of the provocative statements sprinkled throughout Baudelaire's *Journaux intimes*. "La femme est *naturelle*, c'est-à-dire abominable": this is perhaps the most notorious, but by no means the sole, example of Baudelaire's misogynist invective that relies on the opposition of woman/body/nature/spontaneity versus man/soul/artifice/reasoned intelligence. He has also written that: "Nous aimons les femmes à proportion qu'elles nous sont plus étrangères. Aimer les femmes intelligentes est un plaisir de pédéraste. Ainsi la bestialité exclut la pédérastie" (*Fusées, OC* I, 653); "J'ai toujours été étonné qu'on laissât les femmes entrer dans les églises. Quelle conversation peuvent-elles tenir avec Dieu?" (*Mon cœur mis à nu, OC* I, 693). Indeed, his relation to femininity in his poetry is clearly more complicated than such quips would suggest. Baudelaire's ambivalent representation of femininity is a vast and fascinating problem whose study has much to teach us about his approach to the lyric.

Let me risk a sweeping statement. Despite their differences, the feminine figures represented in *Les Fleurs du Mal* (whether coded positively or negatively) share similar functions. They allow Baudelaire to address two problems central to his work and to the work of the lyric in general: the constitution of the lyric subject and the elaboration of formal issues. While seeming to talk of nothing but femininity, *Les Fleurs du Mal* actually strays far from this question just when it appears to focus on it most intently. By studying the particularity of "La Géante," I aim to illustrate these functions at work in Baudelaire's poetry.

The subjectivity in question in this sonnet, as elsewhere in the collection, is not feminine subjectivity but rather that of the lyric "I." The speaking subject is perhaps as pluralistic as the feminine figures in the collection. The lyric "I" in Baudelaire's work is largely identified explicitly as masculine, is often called "le poète" (particularly in the collection's liminal pieces), and is only rarely allowed a feminine voice (such as the personified female subject who objectifies the poet in "La Beauté," a sonnet upon which I will touch again). The genderless speaking subject of "La Géante" offers a curious exception that points to the importance of imaginary (prelinguistic) configurations in the genesis of Baudelaire's aesthetic categories.

Several French theorists have linked poetic language to the unconscious structures that are remnants of an imaginary stage. Julia Kristeva, in *Révolutions du langage poétique,* studies the relationship between poetic rhythm and the semiotic function, which she defines in this way: "Il s'agit donc de fonctions sémiotiques pré-œdipiennes, de décharges d'énergie qui lient et orientent le corps par rapport à la mère" (26). Hélène Cixous identifies the repressed feminine, rather than the mother's body, as poetic source: "La poésie n'est que de prendre force dans l'inconscient et . . . l'inconscient, l'autre contrée sans limites est le lieu où survivent les refoulés: les femmes, ou comme dirait Hoffmann, les fées" (*La jeune née,* 182).

The speaking subject in "La Géante" is one of few in Baudelaire's work that are unmarked by gender. Most critics, however, base their readings on the unfounded assumption that the "I" of "La Géante" is masculine. I am thinking specifically of Ruwet in his "Limites de l'analyse linguistique en poétique," which offers an otherwise impressive reading of the poem's linguistic structures, nonetheless concluding that linguistics must remain an auxiliary field in relation to poetics, since it fails to resolve aesthetic dilemmas such as the question of what makes a line of poetry beautiful, and I am also thinking of Spånberg, who offers Baudelaire's "La Géante" as a source for the unusually large character of Josie in O'Neill's *Moon for the Misbegotten.* Although Grimaud correctly notes the ambiguity of the speaking subject's gender (273), he nonetheless slips into referring to the relational roles of the "je" in masculine terms, as "fils" and "frère," thus implicitly suggesting that the poetic subject could not be simply ungendered or female (femaleness would in fact allow for a certain matrilinear harmony, with mother nature begetting a female giant who in turn mothers a feminine speaking subject).

Such presuppositions skew these critics' analyses of the poem by too neatly allowing them to posit binary oppositions that the poem does not uphold, such as that masculine is to feminine as child is to mother. In fact, there is a constant undoing of oppositions and slippage of positions attributable in large part to the presence of a personified third term (Nature) that is mother of the giant girl-child and, most significantly, to the instability of the speaking subject, who appears in a supervisory role to the giant (watching her play) before adopting the position of infant at her breast in the final image of the poem ("Dormir nonchalamment à l'ombre de ses seins"). That the ambiguity remains is important, since it suggests that one point of reference for the poem is an imaginary time before gender distinctions mattered or before the subject was even a subject. Where gender is most clearly delineated here is in the figure of the giant who, in her maternal incarnation, guides us to the location of this pregendered subject.

Indeed, an image proposed by Freud echoes that with which "La Géante" ends: "An infant at the breast does not as yet distinguish his ego from the external world as the source of the sensations flowing in upon him" (*Civilization and Its Discontents*, in *Complete Works*, vol. 17, 66–67). By naming this sense of unboundedness the "oceanic" feeling ("a sensation of 'eternity,' a feeling as of something limitless, unbounded" [64]), Freud seems to suggest to us that the representation of largeness and limitlessness (whether of the ocean or of Baudelaire's maternal giant) recalls a long buried, presymbolic experience.

Turning now to the interrelation of aesthetic issues and femininity, a brief comparison of "La Beauté" and "La Géante" will serve to illustrate the divergent approaches not only to sexuality and subjectivity but also to form in *Les Fleurs du Mal*. "La Beauté" exemplifies the aspect of Baudelaire's work that adheres to the neoclassical Parnassian aesthetic of objectivity, impassivity, and formal perfection celebrating the constraints of form by privileging the sonnet and a tight, symmetrical alexandrine. The personified beauty of this poem carrying her name is typical of the Parnassian incarnation (or incarceration) of woman, figured as a hard, immobile, stone-like creature in verses whose chiseled but often rigid perfection mirrors her own statuesque, unyielding beauty ("Je suis belle, ô mortels! comme un rêve de pierre"). As such, this and other Baudelairean poems that align femininity with artifice appear to contradict the poet's assimilation of things feminine with an abhorrent nature. And yet if these representations of femininity seem incompatible (does woman belong to nature or to artifice?), the value placed on the two poles of nature and art is thoroughly consistent: feminine fecundity is abhorred ("Du vice maternel traînant l'hérédité / Et toutes les hideurs de la fécondité" ["J'aime le souvenir de ces époques nues"]), while feminine sterility and artifice is praised ("La froide majesté de la femme stérile" ["Avec ses vêtements ondoyants et nacrés"]). Baudelaire's art criticism, such as "Eloge du maquillage," confirms this association between femininity and artifice: "[le] *maquillage* . . . a pour but et pour résultat de faire disparaître du teint toutes les taches que la nature y a outrageusement semées, et de créer une unité abstraite dans le grain et la couleur de la peau [qui] . . . rapproche immédiatement l'être humain de la statue, c'est-à-dire d'un être divin et supérieur" (*OC* II, 717). Moreover, several poems come to mind where the feminine costume is aestheticized and can be read as a representation of a sinuous poetic line: "Avec ses vêtements ondoyants et nacrés, / Même quand elle marche on croirait qu'elle danse" (XXVII) (*OC* I, 29); "Une femme passa, d'une main fastueuse / Soulevant, balançant le feston et l'ourlet" ("A une passante") (*OC* I, 92).

But what of the giant, figured as both feminine and natural? A product of Nature, she is characterized by movement instead of stasis ("Grand[it] librement"), merging with the natural landscape by the poem's end, and yet is at the same time majestic (compared with "une reine") rather than an abomination. Her sexuality provokes not the fear but the curiosity of the speaking subject ("Deviner si son cœur couve une sombre flamme / Aux humides brouillards qui nagent dans ses yeux"). The answer to this uncharacteristic coupling lies, I believe, in the way nature and artifice are conflated in this sonnet: nature and femininity are permitted to coexist in a representation coded positive only because the natural feminine ends up being an aesthetic figuration. The clearly maternal giant escapes "les hideurs de la fécondité" because the enormity of her body produces the love of immensity that motivates an aspect of the Baudelairean aesthetic. Consequently, "La Géante" calls into question not simply his allegiance to Parnassian doctrine but also his repudiation of feminine sexuality as abhorrent.

In order to explore the meaning(s) of femininity for this sonnet and for the collection, then, I will examine "La Géante" on the two necessarily related levels of aesthetics and psychology for what the female giant has to teach us about form and subjectivity in Baudelaire's work. The giant seems to stand apart, not only by virtue of her stature, but also because the conception of her body and its relation to the speaking subject suggest a valuation of femininity and of maternity different from the one often ascribed to Baudelaire.

In his *Salon de 1859* Baudelaire states most explicitly his love for the large: "Dans la nature et dans l'art, je préfère, en supposant l'égalité de mérite, les choses *grandes* à toutes les autres, les grands animaux, les grands paysages, les grands navires, les grands hommes, les grandes femmes, les grandes églises, et, transformant, comme tant d'autres, mes goûts en principes, je crois que la dimension n'est pas une considération sans importance aux yeux de la Muse" (*OC* II, 646). As in "La Géante," here nature and art are not placed in opposition but rather are coterminous. Indeed, in this eclectic list of large things, nature ("animaux," "paysages") appears alongside culture ("navires," "églises"). Further confused in this jumble of "choses grandes" is the distinction between the animate ("animaux," "hommes," "femmes") and the inanimate ("navires," "églises," "paysages"). What is interesting to note is that the nonhuman and/or inanimate elements contributing to this list are personified elsewhere in Baudelaire's work, as if to point to an animate, moving, human source for Baudelaire's love of physical greatness. In "L'Albatros," for example, these "vastes oiseaux des mers" (*OC* I, 9) are compared with the poet. And ships, more than simple means of transportation, appear as personified liberators: "Enlève-moi, frégate!" ("Moesta et errabunda") (*OC* I, 63).

But rather than being translated into a Balzacian or Hugolian drive to create an englobing and monumental oeuvre, Baudelaire's relation to size (and his own version of desiring recognition for his genius: "si mon nom / Aborde heureusement aux époques lointaines, / et fait rêver un soir les cervelles humaines" ("Je te donne ces vers . . . ," *OC* I, 40) is distilled in one small collection of poems where the sonnet, the lyric's miniature, predominates. He does not favor big poems: how then is size of importance to the muse?

Baudelaire's small poems are filled up with vast spaces ("les grands paysages"): the wide open sea, expanses of sky, the yawning abyss. This three-dimensional landscape, stretching from hell to the heavens, is the arena within which the speaking subject seeks definition: soars jubilantly among the clouds ("Par delà les confins des sphères étoilées, / Mon esprit, tu te meus avec agilité" ["Elévation," *OC* I, 10]), is oppressed by the heaviness of the sky ("le ciel bas et lourd pèse comme un couvercle" ["Spleen" (LXXVIII), *OC* I, 74]) perches on the edge of the void ("J'ai peur du sommeil comme on a peur d'un grand trou" ["Le gouffre," *OC* I, 143]). These spaces trace limitlessness and infinity. At the same time, as large ships glide on still waters, they make patterns suggestive of rhythm: dimension implies movement, displacement, interaction.

We find the poetic import of largeness for Baudelaire in the formal relations implied by such movement. Writing in his intimate journal *Fusées* of the "charme infini et mystérieux qui gît dans la contemplation d'un navire . . . en mouvement," he links this fascinating spectacle both to an essential appreciation ("un des besoins primordiaux") of regularity and symmetry and to "la génération de toutes les courbes et figures imaginaires opérées dans l'espace par les éléments réels de l'objet") (*OC* I, 663). Baudelaire concludes that "L'idée poétique qui se dégage de cette opération du *mouvement dans les lignes* est l'hypothèse d'un être vaste, immense, compliqué, mais eurythmique, d'un animal plein de génie, souffrant et soupirant tous les soupirs et toutes les ambitions humaines" (*OC* I, 663–64; emphasis added). The shapes and their graceful movement designed by vast interacting fields (here imaged as a ship on the sea), then, would be figures for the minute but infinitely variable poetic unit: the poetic line. If the personified speaking subject in "La Beauté" contends, "Je hais le mouvement qui déplace les lignes" (*OC* I, 21), in "La Géante" the very movement of the giant's "Magnifiques formes" spells her grandeur: "J'eusse aimé voir son corps . . . grandir librement dans ses terribles jeux."

As is evident in the preceding passage from *Fusées* and the *Salon de 1859*, large figures are invariably personified, just as, in "La Géante," largeness is conflated with maternity. Moreover, in numerous ocean poems (including "La Chevelure" and "La Musique"), the open sea is seen to rock ships in its sway ("infinis bercements") as a mother does a child (this rocking effect is analyzed in chapter 4 of Bersani's *Baudelaire and Freud*). The mother's body is vast, eurhythmic, with movements and interactions that allow the speaking subject to be delineated, as the sea ("la mer," "la mère") does a ship, as the giant the "je." These specific representations of largeness point to an originary moment, or the "oceanic feeling," as the source of this poetic propensity. In Baudelaire's work, relations between self and other precede and give rise to aesthetic formulations, as a close reading of "La Géante" will suggest.

The Urge to Merge

If the growth and movement of the giant invite us to contend with spatial relations, a second dimension, that of time, is of equal importance in the poem. The sonnet's first short measure—"Du temps"—announces this, one of its major obsessions. The time of lyric narration, mythic time, and psychological time (the palimpsest effect that Freud describes in *Civilization and Its Discontents*) are all in play here—all kinds of time, indeed, except that which is perhaps the most straightforward: historical time.

In his highly suggestive article "Le poétique et le narratif," Laurent Jenny describes a relationship between poetry and narrative that sidesteps historical referentiality while still depending on a chronological progression that begins at point A (the first line of the poem) and ends at point B (its closing line): "Est-ce que les poèmes, si lyriques soient-ils, ne nous racontent pas aussi des 'histoires'? Ce sentiment parfois, à leur lecture, que 'c'est toute une vie' qu'ils narrent en silence, scellée dans le métal de quelques mots. . . . Ce qui fait l'originalité de la temporalité poétique, c'est qu'elle est exclusivement enchaînée à l'énonciation, sans jeu avec un temps référentiel, hors-texte" (440, 448). Jenny calls on readers to see a second order to the poetic text, ruled by contiguity and unfolding, that in no way contradicts the metaphoric architecture usually identified as the predominant characteristic of the lyric. Following his definition of the poetic text, "[qui] narre la succession des états d'une subjectivité" (440), in light of the poem we have before us, we might wonder, who is the subject whose evolution is being traced?

Were we to read this piece as a novel rather than as a sonnet, from start to finish for the story it tells, we would learn: of the giant's birth from mother nature (first quatrain), of her growth and sexual development (second quatrain), and of the enormity of her size (first tercet) and her eventual replacement of her own mother (Nature) as she appears to merge with the natural landscape in sleep or death (second tercet). In such a way the life of the giant after whom the sonnet is named unfolds; this fantastic biography tells a tale of genesis, that not only of the giant but also of the natural landscape at some primordial moment.

And yet a second story intertwines with this first one, that of the speaking subject who, as first person "narrator" of the giant's "biography" (the "sujet de l'énonciation"), becomes implicated in that story (as "sujet de l'énoncé"). I would suggest that the true story of this sonnet, as of the lyric in general, belongs to the speaking subject, whose gradual emergence ("la succession des états d'une subjectivité") follows a specific trajectory. As in a fairy tale, the fantastic setting of "La Géante" serves as a cover for the lyric subject's psychic movement or activity. In this poem about beginnings, the search for origins can be read as an allegorical quest for the vast and amorphous maternal body, which is the starting point for the definition of subjectivity. If this sonnet represents the development of the giant, it can also be said, in its forward movement, to chart the speaking subject's reversion: to inscribe a return to a time preceding the establishment of boundaries between self and other, between subject and object.

It is the slippage from the "sujet de l'énonciation" to the "sujet de l'énoncé" that interests me most here and that I will consider by studying the poem as a progression. "Temps du texte et temps du sujet s'élaborent l'un l'autre dans un geste simultané et indistinct," suggests Jenny (448). I might add that in this poem, the tense as well as the time of the text contribute inextricably to the elaboration of subjectivity. I aim to follow this elaboration through an analysis of verb and tense and by focusing on the interaction between the "I" and the giant, which begins at a distance and moves toward fusion.

The mood and development of the poem are determined largely by its highly structured sentences. With an eye to its syntax, we notice first that two sentences compose the poem and divide it into two parts, a lopsided binary construction. Although of unequal length, the two sentences are grammatically parallel: each has as its kernel the same subject and principal verb ("j'eusse aimé vivre"), followed by a series of infinitives that punctuate the itinerary of the speaking subject. The simpler first sentence with its single infinitive ("j'eusse aimé vivre") gives way to the more complex second sentence, whose infinitives govern others still: "j'eusse aimé (1) voir fleurir . . . et [voir] grandir . . . (2) deviner . . . (3) parcourir . . . (4) ramper . . . (5) dormir."

Baudelaire chose the pluperfect subjunctive, standing for the past conditional, as the mood and tense of his main verbs: "j'eusse aimé." It is surely pertinent that he refused the more conventional past conditional ("j'aurais aimé"), opting instead for this rarer second form. Arguably an appropriate choice, given that the poem is literary, the second form nonetheless leaves the reader hesitating between the conditional and the subjunctive, between the plausible and the imaginary. The conventional past conditional would clearly have colored all the observations of the poem as hypotheses regarding actions not accomplished at a past moment, thus describing events that did not happen but that hypothetically might have. And yet it is perhaps a mistake to consider "j'eusse aimé" a hypothetical, conditional tense, since the past moment is manifestly an imaginary one, belonging neither to a historical time nor even to a realistic but fictional scenario. The use of the subjunctive rather than the conditional places the events of the poem in an unreal, nonreferential, but nonetheless ardently wished-for past. The semantic content of this verb "aimer" ultimately bestows a wishful mood on the poem.

The fantastic central character of the young female giant, along with the optative mood of the poem's main verbs, conspires to set the scene as a mythic, desirable past far removed from the contemporary reality described in such poems as the *Tableaux parisiens*. "La Géante" belongs to what Leo Bersani calls a "nonhistorical past," an idealized past having no relation to referential temporality. He points to "the deliberate unreality of the languid, voluptuous, luxurious past" in "La Vie antérieure" as exemplifying the "atemporal nature of the Baudelairean memory" (30).

The particularity of the infinitive lies in the absence of the markers that are carried by the conjugated verb: person, tense, and aspect. While the implied subject of each infinitive is in most cases clear from the main verb or the context of the sentence ("vivre" and "voir" belong to "je," "fleurir" to the giant's body, and so on), "grandir" stands as an exception, since it is the only infinitive with an ambiguous grammatical subject. Are we to read it as the object of the main verb or as the center of an infinitive clause having "son corps" as subject; as "J'eusse aimé . . . grandir librement dans ses terribles jeux" or as "J'eusse aimé voir son corps . . . grandir librement dans ses terribles jeux"? This ambiguity is telling, since it blurs the lines between the speaking subject and the giant, preceding the moment in the poem where they appear to change roles—a reversal dependent on identification with childhood and "growing up."

Moreover, the infinitives, whose gradual distancing from the main verb begins in the second quatrain, effectively stand independently in the tercets. Their distance from the principal clause shifts the mood of the poem from the subjunctive to the infinitive, thereby stripping the verbs of subjective and temporal markings. Thus the speaking subject is effaced as the grammatical subject "je" recedes, and the time of the action is rendered unclear: the timelessness of the infinitive construction reinstates the possibility that the desire for merger might be realized, since pastness and hypothesis fade as the poem progresses into the tercets, leaving the infinitives of the tercets isolated from the main verb. In fading from the scene, the "je" becomes a less concrete entity.

Considering the semantic content of the infinitives, a progression can be discerned from physical distance to nearness, ending with the final merger of subject and object in sleep. If the lyric narrative of the poem offers a forward-moving scenario, the psychological narrative suggested by this string of infinitives moves steadily backward from a position of distanciation and distinction to interaction and ultimately to fusion. In the first sentence, the sole infinitive clause, "vivre auprès de," places the subject and object in a relation of proximity and yet separation. This passive relation becomes more interactive with the sequence of infinitives attached to the second "J'eusse aimé." In the second quatrain, with "voir," there is sensory contact, beginning with sight, the most intellectual and detached of perceptions. Here the subject watches over the giant, who develops physically and emotionally, growing as she plays ("fleurir . . . et grandir"), almost as an adult does a child. "Deviner" implicates the speaking subject even more, as s/he progresses from simple observation to an interpretive stance.

What is being interpreted here is the giant's burgeoning sexuality. The subject, compared with a "chat voluptueux" (which, although grammatically masculine, is symbolically of equally ambiguous gender), turns her/his interest to the blossoming body and smoldering desire of the giant. Although the vocabulary used to describe the giant's maturation is sometimes menacing (she is one of Nature's "enfants monstrueux" who takes part in "terribles jeux"—these oxymorons both link innocence to a threat), sometimes mysterious ("sombre flamme," "humides brouillards"), the subject's curiosity wins out over the fear of feminine sexuality that assails or sends the "je" running for cover in so many other poems of Baudelaire. In fact, this moment of dark but ardent intensity that evokes a loosening of boundaries precedes a changing point in the poem, for in the tercets the subject runs not away from the fully developed giant but onto its lap.

In the gap between the quatrains and the tercets, the speaking subject and giant might be said to exchange places. The giant, childish and developing in the quatrains, is here fully grown; the speaking subject, first at a detached but watchful distance, here engages in playful activity and seeks shelter and protection from the enormous maternal giant. In the first tercet the rhythm quickens, as does the activity of the speaking subject. "Ramper" comes rapidly on the heels of "parcourir" as the subject roams and climbs the members of the giant: from the distant looking we have arrived at a very sensual touching. For the first time in the sonnet, the physical boundaries between self and other are breached. These action verbs have "I" as their implicit subject, whereas the giant was the subject of the earlier "fleurir" and "grandir." A reversal of sorts takes place at this point, showing the giant receding from action as the speaking subject begins to engage in it.

The final infinitive, "dormir," reflects a slowing both semantically and syntactically. It contrasts sharply in sense with the previous two: the scene is now one of sleep, or merger, rather than activity, as the giant is joined by the subject. Both stretch out in the heat of the sun, whose haze blurs distinctions; the "I" is lost in the shadow of the mountainous breasts. The syntax of the remaining phrase reinforces the sense of this drowsy scene, one of sleep that is the pathway to the unconscious, "l'autre contrée sans limites." (In this happy metaphor, Cixous likens the limitlessness of the unconscious to a geographical terrain without frontiers, similar to the boundless body of Baudelaire's giant.) "Dormir" is suspended for three lines by a subordinated temporal clause made halting by the unusual placement of the adjective "lasse," meant to modify the following direct object, "la [géante]," but suspended instead between commas after the grammatical subject, "les soleils malsains." The reiterated syllable—"lasse, la"—sings like the euphonic but meaningless sounds of a lullaby, and the accumulation of voiced bilabial nasals ([m]) and nasalized vowels ([õ]) in the final two lines suggests a stuttering of maternal sounds: "Dormir nonchalamment . . . ombre . . . / Comme . . . hameau . . . montagne."

Like the giant, the lines of the last tercet finally stretch out without interruption: the caesuras of these three lines are weak, each one occurring at a liaison before a prepositional phrase begun by "à" that situates the giant and speaking subject in space: "à travers la campagne," "à l'ombre de ses seins," "au pied d'une montagne." Finally, the simile in line 14 is inverted from its mirrored partner in line 4, losing its poetic inversion for a more prose-like, linear (horizontal) form: "Comme aux pieds d'une reine un chat voluptueux. . . . Comme un hameau paisible au pied d'une montagne."

The marked parallel formed by these similes, which conclude both sentences, creates a rhetorical frame for the sonnet within which the development of the giant is portrayed and the subject's relation to her takes shape. Each simile describes the proximity of the giant and the speaking subject, whose metaphoric positioning ("aux pieds d'une reine," "au pied d'une montagne") suggests at once hierarchy and protection. Although this parallelism points to repetition and sameness, the chiasmic syntax of the similes once more mimics the giant's and the speaking subject's exchange of roles.

If the first simile is unproblematically positive (the sensuous cat at the foot of its queen), the second is more difficult to interpret. What tone can be ascribed to the final tableau of the sonnet ("un hameau paisible au pied d'une montagne")—one of sincerity or one of ironic platitude? Why does the giant wilt under the rays of the (here hyperbolically pluralized) sun, which surely witnessed her earlier flowering? The danger of the unhealthy suns seems to belie the serenity and security of the scene: a hamlet nestled in the shade of a protective mountain. This ambiguity is much more sinister than the one noted above, where menacing sexual growth is neutralized by the enthusiasm and subsequent involvement of the speaking subject. Here, in this final image, we find the sun laying both the "I" and the giant down to a sleep from which they do not arise. Indeed, Freud points out that the familiarity and security of the "heimlich" (like "hameau," etymologically related to the home, from the Frankish "haim," or dwelling place, translated by Strachey as the "canny") contains its opposite, the hidden secrets of the frightening "unheimlich" (the uncanny). Is this then a nurturing, reposeful sleep or the sleep of death? The shift from the animate ("chat," "reine") to the inanimate ("hameau," "montagne") suggests the latter. Structurally the deadly suns (more dangerous than the "sombre flamme") substitute for the fecund Nature. Symbolically, Mother Nature is replaced by the masculine sun: the subject takes refuge from the heretofore absent paternal principle at the giant maternal breast (evidenced by the oppositional rhyme, "les soleils malsains / l'ombre de ses seins"). The giant thus takes the place of Nature, the speaking subject that of the previously infant giant.

If the multivalenced relationship between the subject and the giant relies on mirroring (both doubling and reversal), there is a second mirroring process at work in the poem. "La Géante" employs self-reflexive language that points to yet another genesis, that of the poem itself. "La Nature" creates by virtue of "sa verve puissante," etymologically, with its powerful word ("verve" is derived from the Latin "verbum"). In the beginning, then, was the word, and from the word are born "[de] magnifiques formes." Magnificent is the form of the sonnet (Donne's "pretty room"), as well as of the giant's "genoux énormes," that maternal refuge for the Baudelairean imagination. Moreover, in the "versant" of these knees so joyous to clamber over hides the poetic "vers": the maternal body becomes a sort of linguistic playground. It is an unexpected surprise to find these words etymologically related: both "vers" and "versant" (the latter a modern derivative of "verser") spring from the Latin "vertere," meaning to turn. "Versus," the nominalized past participle of "vertere," meant a turning of the plow whose furrow gives the image of the line of verse. With a densely poetic language that mirrors unconscious mechanisms, by the creation of "la géante" (and of "La Géante," the poem itself), Baudelaire is able to pass through into a prelinguistic sphere, laying down the giant across the countryside, laying beside her the unspoken subject.

What, then, of this multiple quest for origins: of subjectivity, of language, of form? At best it is a problematic quest, at worst impossible, since a return to undifferentiated being through the structures of language is highly paradoxical. Baudelaire's attempt in "La Géante" to retrieve an era of continuity between the infant and the maternal body through the poetic representation of a mythic, utopian past, could be said to end in the failure that is stasis, so opposed to the "mouvement dans les lignes" that constitutes poetry.

And yet, rather insisting on his failure to realize an elusive desire for origins, let us take this as a starting point for the study of Baudelaire's ambivalent representation of femininity. As I have tried to show, this ambivalence and Baudelaire's exploration of subjectivity are intricately linked in his poetic agenda. Viewed in this light, *Les Fleurs du Mal* calls for an analysis that accounts for its particularly engimatic representation of gender difference.

Chapter 4

"Parfum exotique"

JEANNE THEIS WHITAKER

Quand, les deux yeux fermés, en un soir chaud d'automne,
Je respire l'odeur de ton sein chaleureux,
Je vois se dérouler des rivages heureux
Qu'éblouissent les feux d'un soleil monotone;   (4)

Une île paresseuse où la nature donne
Des arbres singuliers et des fruits savoureux;
Des hommes dont le corps est mince et vigoureux,
Et des femmes dont l'œil par sa franchise étonne.   (8)

Guidé par ton odeur vers de charmants climats,
Je vois un port rempli de voiles et de mâts
Encor tout fatigués par la vague marine,   (11)

Pendant que le parfum des verts tamariniers,
Qui circule dans l'air et m'enfle la narine,
Se mêle dans mon âme au chant des mariniers.   (14)

"Mon âme voyage sur le parfum," declared Baudelaire in his prose poem "Un Hémisphère dans une chevelure" (*OC* I, 300). "Parfum exotique" condenses such a voyage of the spirit in the fourteen alexandrines of a classical French sonnet. Two sentences divide the poem, the first encompassing the two quatrains, the second the two tercets. The main verb in both of these sentences, "Je vois," introduces the visions that communicate the poet's experience to his readers.

The first two lines of the poem lead to this declaration "je vois" by describing the conditions that elicit the vision. What the poet sees is imaginary; "les deux yeux fermés," he deliberately blocks out any view of his immediate external surroundings. Other sense impressions thereby gain importance. He tells us that smell stimulates the visions:—"Quand . . . je respire l'odeur . . . Je vois"—while his tactile sense responds to the warmth of the evening and of his companion's breast. The association with evening and with autumn, however, damps the intensity and the energy of the word "chaud," while the heartiness of "chaleureux" makes "sein" seem more maternal than erotic, as Marie Carlier suggests: "L'intimité amoureuse aboutit à une régression car le bonheur, pour Baudelaire, est toujours lié à l'enfance" (23). The text does not specify, as so many of Baudelaire's poems do, any form of direct physical contact with the woman. Here the man's relaxed, passive position allows his mind to escape to another world, inspired and guided by "l'odeur de ton sein chaleureux."

What he sees at first is an imprecise, vast vista. Baudelaire as a young man sailed down the shore of Africa, an experience to which he often harked back in later years, but these images do not seem to be based on specific personal memories. The notes to the Pléiade edition of *Les Fleurs du Mal* comment, "On dirait que ce sonnet est comme écrit dans le prolongement d'une lecture de *Paul et Virginie*" (*OC* I, 878). The view of the tropics does appear stereotyped: this is an island paradise that may remind a modern reader of the aerial photographs in the generic ads favored by the tourist industry. But these familiar televised views also strike dreams deeper than our plans for our next vacation. Much of what is most dramatic in human experience of our world and in human reflection about it has centered on the shores where earth and sea meet. These two fundamental elements also evoke different aspects of the human psyche—consciousness and the unconscious—that attract us in different directions yet seem most satisfying when they come together. The analogy suggests a sexual metaphor, but both of these elements are generally seen as feminine. In French of course, "mère" and "mer" are homonyms, a fact that only reinforces associations between the sea and femininity. The earth too is usually seen as a maternal symbol.

The moment when a person catches sight of the shore, whether approached from the land or from the sea, is exciting. Sunshine is a common symbol of happiness, of good fortune; "May the sun shine on you" is a blessing. The luminosity of the scene is emphasized by the placement of the verb "qu'éblouissent" and the plural "les feux." Yet "éblouir" has two principal definitions: (1) "Troubler la vue par un éclat trop vif" and (2) "Frapper vivement par sa beauté, fasciner, émerveiller." Both meanings seem appropriate in this context. "Monotone" appears to contradict "vif" and "vivement," evoking an unchanging tone whose regularity and uniformity can lead to boredom. Since monotony has generally negative connotations, a possible limitation of this vision of happiness is thus suggested, yet literally the words tell us only that the sun always shines in the same way along those shores.

The second stanza continues the description, in a series of further complements of the main verb, "je vois." The poet's vision becomes more detailed, but it is still generalized: "une île," "des arbres," "des hommes," "des femmes." The adjectives and other modifiers accompanying these nouns are more evaluative than descriptive. First we are shown this island as a whole, an island where one can be lazy, since Nature, like an all-giving mother, offers sustaining fruit directly from trees. In this vision, the men have attractive bodies, slender and vigorous. The lens focuses more closely on the women's eyes, even, it may seem, on one eye, through the rhetorical use of the singular "œil" to mean "manière de voir, sentiment." The image judges the women's attitude by their frank gaze and finds it surprising. Marie Carlier comments, "A l'apparence physique des hommes répondent les vertus morales des femmes: à la nudité des corps correspond une transparence des âmes. . . . Le verbe 'étonne' montre que cette relation innocente entre les hommes et les femmes n'a plus cours dans notre monde civilisé" (25). The ideal reflected in this vision is based on a generous Nature, men who are attractive and strong, and honest women.

The different aspects of this ideal are all present in "J'aime le souvenir de ces époques nues": a generous, fertile Nature nourishing "ses fils," "L'homme, élégant, robuste et fort," "la sainte jeunesse, à l'air simple, au doux front, / A l'œil limpide et clair ainsi qu'une eau courante" (*OC* I, 12). Though in that poem images of human beauty seem specifically masculine and women are more particularly linked to debauchery and vice in the world "aujourd'hui," it is clear that the main contrast there is between the beauty and purity of ancient peoples and the monstrous corruption of modern nations. One could argue that, in most of "J'aime le souvenir," Baudelaire uses "homme" in the inclusive sense, to designate all human beings. For "Parfum exotique," "hommes" are clearly males whose appearance is attractive *to* others, while the women's appeal is based on how they look *at* others.

The tercets start a new sentence, a new image. The first line again serves as an introduction: "Guidé par ton odeur vers de charmants climats, / Je vois." What the poet now sees is less general—"un port"—but he draws a sketchy outline of this port full of sails and masts, a synecdochic effect, and equally sketchily suggests the travels that their sight evokes, a metonymic effect. The compression of this image is reinforced by a second synecdoche, as "la vague" represents the sea.

In the last stanza a subordinate clause, "Pendant que," brings several shifts in perspective. The subject is now "le parfum des verts tamariniers." This may well be the perfume the woman is wearing, but its scent is now much more clearly identified as that of well-known tropical trees. Their color evokes a quality of the perfume, like the lines from "Correspondances": "Il est des parfums frais comme des chairs d'enfants, / Doux comme les hautbois, verts comme les prairies." This perfume becomes the subject of active verbs. It moves through the air and then moves the poet physically ("m'enfle la narine") and emotionally ("Se mêle dans mon âme au chant des mariniers"). The poem ends in the exaltation not of the visual imagination but of a surge of smell and sound. "Le chant des mariniers" brings a final harmony and the promise of more voyages.

In "Parfum exotique," Baudelaire follows the classical French sonnet rhyme scheme: *abba abba ccd ede.* Théodore de Banville, in his *Petit traité de versification française,* describes this as the perfect model for the sonnet. This poem fulfills the traditional expectations of the sonnet form in interesting ways. What distinguishes a French (or Italian) sonnet is above all its division into two unequal parts, the octave (two quatrains) and the sestet (two tercets). Poets at different periods, and different poets within the same period, have responded to this slight imbalance in various ways, sometimes attempting to raise the six lines of the two tercets to the power of the eight in the two quatrains, sometimes stressing the lighter quality of the second part of the poem.

The sonnet form attracted Baudelaire; not only did he write sixty-eight of them, but he tried to vary the central pattern in many ways, using thirty-four different variations on the fourteen-line form of the poem. With a few exceptions, Baudelaire kept the essential feature of traditional French sonnets, which is the central division into two slightly unequal parts. In his definition of the sonnet, John Fuller writes: "The essence of the sonnet's form is the unequal relationship between octave and sestet. . . . The turn after the octave . . . is a shift of thought or feeling which develops the subject of the sonnet by surprise or conviction to its conclusion" (2–3). Henri Morier, in his

Dictionnaire de poétique et de rhétorique, notes that nineteenth-century poets, in their "besoin d'infini," either abandoned the limited form of the sonnet, or opened it up: "c'est-à-dire que le quatorzième vers, au lieu de prendre un caractère impérieux et définitif, s'élargit vers le ciel ou l'abîme. Le poète lui confère une valeur d'évocation; il y introduit une atmosphère vaporeuse ou sentimentale, voluptueuse ou vibrante, tantôt chargée de nostalgie, tantot de désir ou d'aspiration métaphysique, mais toujours riche en virtualités. En fait, il s'agit de promouvoir l'imagination d'un monde de rêveries, ou d'inviter l'esprit à une réflexion si dense qu'elle déclenche toute une suite de méditations" (385–86).

Baudelaire did often end his sonnets in such a fashion, but when he writes of the form he praises its constraints: "Parce que la forme est contraignante, l'idée jaillit plus intense" (*Correspondance* I, 676). He exploited, in different manners, the complex possibilities afforded by the form's asymmetry. In "Parfum exotique," Baudelaire compensates for the imbalance between the two parts of the sonnet by making the sestet at once lighter and denser. The last line expands and extends the poet's dream.

The two sentences of the poem, both built around the principal verb "je vois," correspond exactly to the octave-sestet division. Each quatrain is syntactically divided into two equal halves; each line, except "Une île paresseuse où la nature donne," which leads to the object "Des arbres singuliers" in the next line, is end-stopped; most are divided by a regular caesura in the middle. This arrangement contributes to the very regular rhythm that flows smoothly as the syntax links the two quatrains, then the two tercets.

When we look at the sound pattern of this sonnet, we notice immediately the elegant sequences of assonances and alliterations in lines such as "*Je vois se dérouler des rivages heureux*" or "*Pendant que le parfum des verts tamariniers,*" in which we also find the near-alliteration of the fricatives [f] and [v] and of the dentals [d] and [t]. In "*Qui circule dans l'air et m'enfle la narine*" we note not only the alliterations of [k], [r], and [l], and the assonances of [i], [ã], and [a], but also the equilibrium due to the repetition of [ã] in corresponding positions on either side of the caesurea and of [ir] and [ri] at either end of the line. Kenneth Burke, in an article entitled "Musicality in Verse," calls this structure "tonal chiasmus." In "Se mêle dans mon âme au chant des mariniers," we are struck by the concentration of [m] and by the balanced near-assonance of "*dans mon âme*" and "*chant des mariniers.*"

We find a striking distribution through the poem of the sounds that are highlighted by the rhymes and by the most common alliterations and assonances. The rhyme sound "eu" occurs five times in the first quatrain, three times in the second (eight times in total in the octave), and not once in the sestet. The sound of the other octave rhyme "onne" is found six times in the first quatrain, four times in the second (for a total of ten times in the octave), only three times in the first tercet, and not at all in the second. In the sestet, the sounds stressed are [a], nasalized [ã], and [m]. These are the three main sounds in the last line: "Se *mê*le d*an*s mon *â*me au ch*an*t des *ma*riniers." These open, warm sounds bring the poem to a resonant end.

The rhymes in this poem cannot be discussed without consideration of the most unusual progression we find in the rhyme words at the end: "mâts," "marine," "mariniers," "tamariniers." Henri Morier, in his *Dictionnaire de poétique et de rhétorique,* contemptuously dismisses "rimes qui remontent de syllabe en syllabe." Baudelaire, however, has done something different here; he has used "le même son comme point de départ" to create "des rimes de richesse croissante" (Cassagne 14–15). The rhymes grow richer, but the rhyme sounds change, allowing concealment of the game. It is concealed further by the fact that the words are not introduced in the neat order of increasing length in which I have listed them. First Baudelaire uses a two syllable word, "climats," then "mâts," then "marine." In the next tercet "tamariniers" comes first, then "narine," and finally "mariniers." Though such effects, once we are aware of them, may seem "confinant aux jeux des Grands Rhétoriqueurs" (Schaettel 99), they are arranged so subtly that they do not seem artificial. On the contrary: they serve Baudelaire's expert handling of the classical sonnet form in this poem.

In the octave, the realistic setting is presented in two lines: "Quand, les deux yeux fermés, en un soir chaud d'automne, / Je respire l'odeur de ton sein chaleureux," and the vision appears as a succession of scenes of a tropical island, its happy shores illuminated by a monotonous sun, its unusual trees, its slender men and its women "dont l'œil par sa franchise étonne." In the sestet, the introduction is condensed into one line and the vision is that of a crowded port. The sea had been evoked by the words "île" and "rivages," but now we see ships that have returned "encor tout fatigués par la vague marine." In the last tercet, movement is no longer past but present as the poet evokes "le parfum des verts tamariniers, / Qui circule dans l'air et m'enfle la narine." Finally this invigorating breath fuses with the song of the mariners. The simultaneous concentration and expansion of the images give the sestet at once greater intensity and greater lightness. In the music of the poem, similarly, both concentration and expansion are created by the use of sounds, and particularly by the clever rhyme scheme, which adds great density to the pattern of repetitions but does so for most readers at a subliminal level.

The ever-increasing poetic density of sounds in the sestet of "Parfum exotique" also serves to bring the sonnet to strong closure, as does the reappearance of the primary sense image, "Je respire l'odeur de ton sein chaleureux," in "Guidé par ton odeur" at the beginning of the sestet. The image of breathing an odor is expanded when "le *parfum* des verts tamariniers / Qui *circule dans l'air et m'enfle la narine* / Se mêle dans mon âme aux chant des mariniers." Unlike the words underlined, the last line does not specifically reinforce the vocabulary of the poem's opening but expands it to other dimensions: to the added sense of hearing, to other types of movement associated with the words "chant" and "mariniers," and finally to a spiritual sphere suggested by "mon âme," a possibility enhanced by the ethereal quality of all the images in the final tercet. Thus, as in a number of Baudelaire's other sonnets, we find a marvelous enlargement of experience at the end of "Parfum exotique."

The date of composition of "Parfum exotique" is uncertain. Claude Pichois, editor of the Pléiade edition of *Les Fleurs du Mal,* suggests that Baudelaire's friend Prarond probably heard the poet recite it in the 1840s; Antoine Adam, editor of the Garnier edition, thinks that it may have been written not too long before the publication of the first edition of *Les Fleurs du Mal* in 1857. There it was placed between "Les Bijoux" and "Je t'adore à l'égal de la voûte nocturne," between a paean of sensual admiration and a cry of sensual and emotional frustration. "Les Bijoux" having been condemned by the court for its eroticism, Baudelaire had to omit it from the edition of 1861. In that second edition "Parfum exotique" appears between "Hymne à la beauté" and "La Chevelure," two of the new poems that Baudelaire created "pour être adaptés à un cadre singulier que j'avais choisi" (*Correspondance* II, 196). Within this new context, "Parfum exotique" gains in significance. "Hymne à la beauté" is the last of a group of five poems that show personified visions of beauty. This group of poems concludes the first section of "Spleen et idéal," which speaks of the poet's vocation and of his ideals. "Hymne à la beauté" asks: "Viens-tu du ciel profond ou sors-tu de l'abîme, / O Beauté? ton regard infernal et divin, / Verse confusément le bienfait et le crime." It answers: "qu'importe . . . Si ton œil, ton souris, ton pied, m'ouvrent la porte / D'un Infini que j'aime et n'ai jamais connu?" (*OC* I, 24–25).

Within "Spleen et idéal," between the poems in which the poet's ideal is considered and the last poems, which express spleen and other forms of inner suffering, we find a large central sequence of love poems. Readers and critics have traditionally seen in the organization of the love poems a progression from a first group, describing a clearly sensual passion, to a second group, which celebrates an idealized spiritual love, and finally to a group showing the reactions of an aging lover, which because of its predominant images and mood may be called the poems of autumnal love. Baudelaire's biography reveals evidence of his different relationships with three different women, who seem to have kindled in him three different kinds of love and whose names are therefore associated with the three groups of poems. Often the sensual poems are called the cycle of Jeanne Duval. She was an actress of mixed racial background, "mulatresse ou quarteronne" (*OC* I, 878), whose stormy affair with Baudelaire lasted for over twenty years, though they lived together only for short periods.

Since "Parfum exotique" is the first of the group of sensual love poems, notes in editions of the 1861 *Les Fleurs du Mal* usually include several pages of information about Jeanne Duval with little other commentary on the poem. Physical descriptions and moral judgments of the historical person are not very relevant to an understanding of this particular sonnet, in which the woman's presence is so ethereal. It suffices to know that Baudelaire loved a woman who reminded him of the tropical landscapes he had discovered when he traveled along the coast of Africa in 1844.

A tangible woman is felt in "La Chevelure," which Baudelaire inserted after "Parfum exotique" in 1861. The new poem expands upon its predecessor and fleshes it out. The poet praises the inspiration of the woman's perfume: "Comme d'autres esprits voguent sur la musique, / Le mien, ô mon amour! nage sur ton parfum." Her hair, however, is now the principal agent of his imaginary voyage. He addresses it: "o toison . . . O boucles . . . Extase," explaining how he intends to use it deliberately: "Pour peupler ce soir l'alcôve obscure / Des souvenirs dormant dans cette chevelure, / Je la veux agiter dans l'air comme un mouchoir!" The poem makes us see and feel the hair, its thickness ("O toison . . . Fortes tresses . . . ta crinière lourde"), its curliness ("O boucles . . . les bords duvetés de vos mèches tordues"), and its darkness. The metaphors of "La Chevelure" are based on those specific physical qualities. The dark, wavy hair can transport the poet like the sea: "Tu contiens, mer d'ébène, un éblouissant rêve / . . . Je plongerai ma tête amoureuse d'ivresse / Dans ce noir océan où l'autre est enfermé." He can discover "La langoureuse Asie et la brûlante Afrique" in the deep aromatic forest of her hair. It even evokes the sky: "Cheveux bleus, pavillon de ténèbres tendues, / Vous me rendez l'azur du ciel immense et rond" (*OC* I, 26–27).

More explicit and tangible also is the poet's feeling of intoxication, expressed not only by direct reference to "ivresse," by "je m'enivre ardemment," and by allusions to drinking in "le parfum, le son et la couleur," and "le vin du souvenir" but by establishing links between kinesthetic sensations that almost prefigure Rimbaud's "Le Bateau ivre." Baudelaire rhymes "Je plongerai ma tête amoureuse d'ivresse" with "Et mon esprit subtil que le roulis caresse" and reinforces this comparison when he begs "Fortes tresses, soyez la houle qui m'enlève!"

"La Chevelure" is not only more colorful, more active, and more complexly metaphorical than "Parfum exotique," it is also more emphatic in many other ways: in seven five-line stanzas there are ten exclamation points, five invocatory "O's," and many poetic inversions of adjectives and nouns, such as "noir océan," "infinis bercements." If the physical basis of the experience is more concrete than in "Parfum exotique," the imagined result is more grandiose: "Un port retentissant . . . / Où les vaisseaux, glissant dans l'or et dans la moire / Ouvrent leurs vastes bras pour embrasser la gloire / D'un ciel pur où frémit l'éternelle chaleur" (*OC* I, 26). If the descriptions of the island and of the port in the first poem seemed sketchy, these appear extravagantly literary.

A third work of Baudelaire's is always compared with "Parfum exotique" and "La Chevelure": the piece from *Petits Poèmes en prose* entitled "Un Hémisphere dans une chevelure." This text is deliberately less poetic, more explicit in its statement of intention and in the unfolding of the metaphors. The poet speaks directly, and quite simply, to the woman: "Laisse-moi respirer longtemps, longtemps, l'odeur de tes cheveux, y plonger tout mon visage. . . . Si tu pouvais savoir tout ce que je vois! tout ce que je sens! tout ce que j'entends dans tes cheveux!" He explains, "Tes cheveux contiennent tout un rêve." One paragraph evokes memories that may seem quite realistic: "Dans les caresses de ta chevelure, je retrouve les langueurs des longues heures passées sur un divan, dans la chambre d'un beau navire, bercées par le roulis imperceptible du port, entre les pots de fleur et les gargoulettes rafraîchissantes." For some readers the text is stamped as unpoetic by Baudelaire's use of as vulgar a word as "gargoulette" and by the final image, which drew ridicule from contemporary critics: "Quand je mordille tes cheveux élastiques et rebelles, il me semble que je mange des souvenirs" (*OC* I, 300–301). Barbara Johnson's essay "La Chevelure et son double" compares "La Chevelure" and "Un Hémisphère dans une chevelure" in detail, noting that "Là où les vers commencent en plein voyage rhétorique, la prose se situe résolument dans la littéralité" (42). She argues that literality itself is a literary device, that the prose poem is a deconstructive reading of the poem in verse.

Comparison with these two thematically similar texts may help us distinguish the particular qualities of "Parfum exotique," whose tone is neither prosaic nor rhetorical but undoubtedly poetic. Ross Chambers uses "Parfum exotique" as an example of "paradigmatic narrative" in which temporal and causal relationships (syntagmatic sequences) are essentially replaced by relationships of similarity and dissimilarity (paradigmatic patterning). There is a clear correspondence between the poet's feelings and his imaginary voyage. He is tired, relaxed, and warm, and he sees "une île paresseuse," des "voiles et des mâts fatigués." By implication "la vague marine" may represent erotic exertion, but there is no overt human action in this poem and almost no bodily presence.

The poet, in this edition of *Les Fleurs du Mal,* placed as the first of the sensual love poems this sonnet, which evokes pure happiness as it fulfills the promise of its ethereal title. Exotic means not only "unusual, having the charm of the unfamiliar," but "something that comes from elsewhere." Perfume is intangible even at its most penetrating: "Il est de forts parfums pour qui toute matière / Est poreuse" ("Le Flacon"). Perfume can float and yet remain, it is pervasive but impossible to locate. Baudelaire is fascinated by these nonmaterial potentialities. He uses perfume to signify transcendence. The words of the poem, however, do not touch readers' sense of smell. They must stimulate our imaginations in other ways. They do so by evoking, more or less directly, perceptions of all the senses, even taste for "des fruits savoureux." All the elements—fire, earth, water, and air—are joined in the poet's sweeping vision. Its very vagueness enhances its suggestiveness; it gains in universality what it loses in precision. Other poems by Baudelaire contain more original, ambiguous, and idiosyncratic images, but none is more lyrical. More indispensable to our experience of poetry than unusual metaphors are patterns of sounds and rhythms, and their effect is more powerful for being mysteriously subliminal. Baudelaire recognized that as perfume transported his imagination, "d'autres esprits voguent sur la musique." "Parfum exotique" creates this music for the poet and for us.

Chapter 5

Immortal Rot: A Reading of "Une Charogne"

WILLIAM OLMSTED

Rappelez-vous l'objet que nous vîmes, mon âme,
    Ce beau matin d'été si doux:
Au détour d'un sentier une charogne infâme
    Sur un lit semé de cailloux, (4)

Les jambes en l'air, comme une femme lubrique,
    Brûlante et suant les poisons,
Ouvrait d'une façon nonchalante et cynique
    Son ventre plein d'exhalaisons. (8)

Le soleil rayonnait sur cette pourriture,
    Comme afin de la cuire à point,
Et de rendre au centuple à la grande Nature
    Tout ce qu'ensemble elle avait joint; (12)

Et le ciel regardait la carcasse superbe
    Comme une fleur s'épanouir.
La puanteur était si forte, que sur l'herbe
    Vous crûtes vous évanouir. (16)

Les mouches bourdonnaient sur ce ventre putride,
    D'où sortaient de noirs bataillons
De larves, qui coulaient comme un épais liquide
    Le long de ces vivants haillons. (20)

Tout cela descendait, montait comme une vague,
    Ou s'élançait en pétillant;
On eût dit que le corps, enflé d'un souffle vague,
    Vivait en se multipliant. (24)

Et ce monde rendait une étrange musique,
    Comme l'eau courante et le vent,
Ou le grain qu'un vanneur d'un mouvement rhythmique
    Agite et tourne dans son van. (28)

Les formes s'effaçaient et n'étaient plus qu'un rêve,
    Une ébauche lente à venir,
Sur la toile oubliée, et que l'artiste achève
    Seulement par le souvenir. (32)

Derrière les rochers une chienne inquiète
    Nous regardait d'un œil fâché,
Épiant le moment de reprendre au squelette
    Le morceau qu'elle avait lâché. (36)

—Et pourtant vous serez semblable à cette ordure,
    A cette horrible infection,
Étoile de mes yeux, soleil de ma nature,
    Vous, mon ange et ma passion! (40)

Oui! telle vous serez, ô la reine des grâces,
    Après les derniers sacrements,
Quand vous irez, sous l'herbe et les floraisons grasses,
    Moisir parmi les ossements. (44)

Alors, ô ma beauté! dites à la vermine
    Qui vous mangera de baisers,
Que j'ai gardé la forme et l'essence divine
    De mes amours décomposés! (48)

More than sixty years ago, T. S. Eliot observed that Baudelaire's "stock of imagery" was less than adequate: "His prostitutes, mulattoes, Jewesses, serpents, cats, corpses, form a machinery which has not worn very well" (*Selected Essays*, 375–76). One might claim, however, that this "machinery" was not meant to last. In offering his list of the outmoded in Baudelaire's poetry, Eliot seized upon precisely those items that characterize *Les Fleurs du Mal* as "modern" in the sense Baudelaire gave it: "La modernité, c'est le transitoire, le fugitif, le contingent, la moitié de l'art, dont l'autre moitié est l'éternel et l'immuable" (*OC* II, 695). Nowhere in

Baudelaire's poetry, perhaps, does the effort to seize the transitory—
"dont les métamorphoses sont si fréquentes"—achieve greater force
and irony than in "Une Charogne." The reader receives a detailed,
dynamic depiction of an animal carcass undergoing decomposition.
The descriptive stanzas by themselves constitute a tour de force in the
poetry of nature, here seen in its most unpleasant yet energetic form
of self-renewal. The carrion amounts to a little cosmos, its activities
producing "une étrange musique / Comme l'eau courante et le vent."
Yet the portrait of the corpse serves none of the rhetorical ends that a
reader might customarily expect. The poem does not use its emblem
of decomposition for the sake of a meditation on mortality or for the
purpose of seduction ("gather ye rosebuds") or to celebrate the cycles
of nature. If, in Michael Jenning's apt phrase, "the corpse is the ulti-
mate allegorical object" (109), Baudelaire's speaker deliberately turns
away from the opportunities for an allegorizing metacommentary in
order to compare the rotting carcass to his beloved: "Et pourtant vous
serez semblable à cette ordure." When the speaker describes in stanza
3 how

> Le soleil rayonnait sur cette pourriture,
> Comme afin de la cuire à point,
> Et de rendre au centuple à la grande Nature
> Tout ce qu'ensemble elle avait joint,

and goes on to instance this productive decomposition by depicting
in stanza 5 how

> Les mouches bourdonnaient sur ce ventre putride,
> D'où sortaient de noirs bataillons
> De larves, qui coulaient comme un épais liquide
> Le long de ces vivants haillons,

the reader's nausea, indignation, and perplexity (or nervous laughter)
signal the presence of what Hugo called the "frisson nouveau" made
available by Baudelaire. This thrill or shock or jolt derives not merely
from a new poetic diction (for example, the introduction of seemingly
unpoetic terms like "exhalaisons" and deliberate clichés like "mon
ange") but more from the reinterpretation of deeply rooted cultural
expectations and beliefs.

The crux of the poem, the rhetorical move that transforms the title
and the opening nine stanzas of description into lethal simile, occurs
when the speaker reminds his companion

> —Et pourtant vous serez semblable à cette ordure,
>   A cette horrible infection,
> Étoile de mes yeux, soleil de ma nature,
>   Vous, mon ange et ma passion!

Star, sun, angel, passion: how utterly depleted of meaning these endearments seem, once the process of putrefaction has been transferred from the carrion to the beloved. And yet the repetition of the word "soleil" in stanzas 3 and 10 suggests that the comparison realigns not just objects (woman will be like decaying animal) but natural forces and relationships (the sun of his nature will become ordure). Whatever the "sunny" woman may once have meant to the poet, inevitably her effect on him will be like the cadaver's, a stimulus for disgust. The universe constructed in this poem displays a process character. Radical transformations and role reversals appear inevitable. These changes will affect nature, the poet and his beloved who was yesterday the poet's sun, tomorrow (and perhaps today) the object of his contempt and loathing.

But does he and will he loathe her? The repetition of terms of endearment in the last three stanzas raises the suspicion that more than irony is intended, that the prospect of her decay excites the speaker and adds a certain zest to his present passion. Leo Bersani includes "Une Charogne" within a Baudelairean project of sadistic sexuality that calls for the woman's immobilization, a deathlike frigidity that cooperates with fantasies of necrophilia (67–89). The poem undeniably fuses images of love and death in its final stanza:

> Alors, ô ma beauté ! dites à la vermine
>   Qui vous mangera de baisers,
> Que j'ai gardé la forme et l'essence divine
>   De mes amours décomposés !

Yet a reading like Bersani's tends to reduce the poem to a symptom-laden fantasy. Instead of using diagnosis as a defense, we need to engage the issue of response. If we are to account for the poem's constructed character and the reader's role in that construction, we must refuse the temptation to take the moral high ground or otherwise pretend we are therapists immune to countertransference. The poem's power depends on its capacity to create an intersubjectivity between the reader and the speaker as well as between the reader and the woman addressed. Operating simultaneously on linguistic and affective levels, this intersubjectivity encompasses and defines not only what Benveniste called the "réalité dialectique" of a poem's discursive poles of "locuteur" and "destinataire" (260) but also the reader who finds him/herself occupying now one and now the other of these poles. While Bersani's reading indicates what it would be like to entertain a fantasy such as the speaker's, we are left with no sense of what it would be like to be the object of such a fantasy, to find ourselves so conceived in the mind of one who calls us "mon ange" and "ma beauté."

Seen from the perspective of the addressee, "Une Charogne" performs several reversals. The theme of death is invoked not for purposes of seduction but to foretell the end of an affair, the decay of the rosebuds the speaker once had gathered. The theme of death is not invoked to celebrate the perpetuity of love-in-death or the lovers' joint metamorphosis and immortality. She will die and rot, but he will have created something immortal, which act would seem to be in the tradition, from Horace through Shakespeare, of the conceit of poetic immortalizing. Yet what has been immortalized is not the addressee as she is or at her best; paradoxically, her decomposed body becomes poetically "aere perennis." The poem's rhetorical structure of question-and-answer ("Rappelez-vous . . . telle vous serez") encourages the addressee to collude in the speaker's portrait of her. The stanzas describing the carrion, since they are framed by the command/invitation for her to recall, assume and reiterate the addressee's revulsion ("La puanteur était si forte, que sur l'herbe / Vous crûtes vous évanouir"); then the concluding stanzas solicit her self-disgust, the application of the images to herself. In this manner Baudelaire reverses the conventional trope of praise, the invitation of the beloved to admire herself in an idealized image. Finally, the imagery of corruption is not invoked for Christian moral considerations but for a peculiar kind of esthetic aim:

> Les formes s'effaçaient et n'étaient plus qu'un rêve,
> Une ébauche lente à venir,
> Sur la toile oubliée, et que l'artiste achève
> Seulement par le souvenir.

This stanza explicitly calls our attention to the way the poem plays off against the tradition of the artistic memento mori. The speaker finds himself intrigued by the unfinished, not yet realized, and sketchlike aspect of the carrion. The analogy between the artistic image and the loved one is arrested at the very point where memory has not yet been concretized in a stable image. To value the blurry sketch over the finished work, much as Baudelaire suggests in the *Salon de 1845* (*OC* II, 390), dematerializes and spiritualizes the artistic process. But in this instance we are concerned less with the ethereal artwork than with a decaying beast whose presently indistinct appearance is likened, by means of the sketch metaphor, to the beloved's future corpse. The speaker, in other words, asserts an aesthetic preference, what Baudelaire praised as "le goût de l'horrible" (*OC* I, 548–49), here manifested in his memory of the carrion and his projected image of the worm-eaten beloved. For the addressee, then, all the tropes that would identify her beauty with permanence are negated and replaced with the oxymoronic figure of perpetual rottenness.

How can putrefaction be immortalized? The question points toward the seemingly contradictory way that Baudelaire handles temporality. Given the poem's intense focus on the transformative aspect of decay, one might conclude that Baudelaire's representation of death agrees with the materialist conceptions of Bayle, Gassendi, and their Enlightenment followers. But the notion of cyclical processes in nature, whereby the corpse enters the food chain, is undercut by the notion of an indefinitely prolonged entombment for the beloved who, to make matters worse, may remain sentient ("ô ma beauté! dites à la vermine"). What ultimately distinguishes Baudelaire's rhetoric from materialist and Christian views of death is the emphasis on arrested development. Descartes and Bossuet alike would have agreed that the body's decomposition precedes its recomposition in some other form, but Baudelaire prefers to prolong indefinitely the time of decay, the moment of transition. What the speaker desires for his mistress is nothing less than a living death, a naturalized and de-Christianized version of eternal suffering.

Clearly the poem not only deploys a novel style of misogynistic rhetoric but exposes in critical fashion the presence of misogyny in the very cultural and poetic traditions it deconstructs. We need to correct, therefore, the view of Erich Auerbach that "corruption of the flesh means something very different in *Les Fleurs du Mal* and in the Christianity of the late Middle Ages" (219). On the contrary, it is the proximity of Baudelaire's decaying animal—"Les jambes en l'air, comme une femme lubrique"—to the images of medieval moralizing that gives "Une Charogne" its relative nihilism, its quite untraditional and un-Christian reduction of the corpse's moral significance. When

Odilon of Cluny preached in the eleventh century on the body's frailty—"filth everywhere"—he did not neglect to conclude how intercourse with women was thus unthinkable: "We, who would be loath to touch vomit or dung even with our fingertip—how can we desire to clasp in our arms the bag of excrement itself?" (Ariès 110). For a theologian like Odilon, the loathsomeness of the medieval (feminine) body would not have been thinkable apart from the idealization of the resurrected body. But in Baudelaire's poem even a secular idealization of physical health or well-being has been removed. By presenting misogyny so nakedly, "Une Charogne" challenges the metaphysical justifications for the privileging of the incorruptible poem (masculine) over the corruptible body (feminine).

Similarly, the poem challenges poetic conventions by inverting the Petrarchan sexual code, exchanging for the celestial the gritty and for the lovely the worm-eaten. A systematic violation of Petrarchan stereotypes (Tucker 892) was bound to offend contemporary readers. Indeed, Gustave Bourdin's review calling attention to the proliferation of vermine in *Les Fleurs du Mal* resulted in the book's prosecution for obscenity (Bandy and Pichois 13). And "Une Charogne" was probably on Sainte-Beuve's mind when he reproached Baudelaire for having "pétrarquisé sur l'horrible" (*OC* I, 890). No doubt Baudelaire's contemporaries would have agreed with a recent claim that the poem "strips poetry of its transcendent power" (McLees 22). But instead of congratulating Baudelaire for having created a new poetic genre (McLees 29), they tended to treat "Une Charogne" as an icon of Baudelaire's effeteness and buffoonery. Nadar's caricature of 1858 or 1859, showing the poet in a state of delectation and surprise over the presence of a fly-blown carcass, drew a somewhat injured response from Baudelaire, who claimed that he found it "pénible de passer pour le Prince des Charognes" (Bandy and Pichois frontispiece, 15; Pichois, *Album Baudelaire,* 162). After all, he objected to Nadar, "Tu n'as sans doute pas lu une foule de choses de moi, qui ne sont que musc et que roses" (*Correspondance* I, 573–74).

In this protest we can glimpse some ambiguities that pervade Baudelaire's poetry and his critical practice as well. A poem like "Une Charogne" stands against many instances of "musk and roses" and of love poems to women whose "chair spirituelle a le parfum des Anges" ("Que diras-tu ce soir") (*OC* I, 43). Likewise, the transformation of woman into carrion would appear to contravene those occasions when Baudelaire the critic abandons his misogyny to appreciate, as when speaking of the poet Marceline Desbordes-Valmore, "l'expression poétique de toutes les beautés naturelles de la femme" (*OC* II, 147). And if "Une Charogne" seems to parody the rhetoric of seduction and its trope of "tempus fugit," a poem like "Chant d'automne" employs this same trope without any undercutting whatsoever. Furthermore, the presence of the trope is presupposed by its very inversion in "Une Charogne." I emphasize these ambiguities to caution against reading the poem as purely the expression of aggression toward women.

Even the rhetorical extremism of "Une Charogne" and the sheer abundance of its images of decay suggest the presence of some obsession more powerful than misogyny. The poem itself is but one of many (most of them adjacent to each other in the 1861 edition) that link images of death and desire. Such images are, of course, omnipresent in Baudelaire's poetry. Here, however, I am referring to images not of death in general ("La Mort des amants" or "La Mort des pauvres") nor of graves and the cemetery ("La servante au grand cœur") but of the sexual and, as Baudelaire seems to indicate, *therefore decomposable* body. In "Je t'adore à l'égal de la voûte nocturne," the speaker characterizes the relation between his erotic fervor and the beloved's coldness in these terms: "Je m'avance à l'attaque, et je grimpe aux assauts, / Comme après un cadavre un choeur de vermisseaux" (*OC* I, 27). In "Le Vampire" (*OC* I, 33) the speaker describes himself as bound to his lover "comme aux vermines la charogne" (now it appears that he is the corpse). And the following poem doubles the corpse image: "Une nuit que j'étais près d'une affreuse Juive, / Comme au long d'un cadavre un cadavre étendu" (*OC* I, 34). The body as corpse foregrounds the instability of flesh, its temporary and only semisolid quality. That this insubstantiality should not be limited to the female body becomes very apparent in a poem like "Un Voyage à Cythère," where the speaker sees himself mirrored in the image of a hanged man being eaten by ravens:

> Les yeux étaient deux trous, et du ventre effondré
> Les intestins pesants lui coulaient sur les cuisses,
> Et ses bourreaux, gorgés de hideuses délices,
> L'avaient à coups de bec absolument châtré. (*OC* I, 118)

The body's vulnerability, its capacity for deformation and rot, and its liability to fragmentation are not restricted to women only, and Jacques Vier suggests the influence of Jansenist theology in the "décomposition généralisée" that links "Une Charogne" to "Un Voyage à Cythère" (48–49). But the decomposition of women in Baudelaire's poetry accompanies anger expressed by a male speaker, whereas the moldering of men accompanies expressions of despair, lassitude, and a self-hatred that the speaker would like to avoid. So concludes the speaker in "Un Voyage à Cythère": "—Ah! Seigneur! donnez-moi la force et le courage / De contempler mon cœur et mon corps sans dégoût!"

Since the deity is invoked, we can hardly deny the speaker a Christian orientation; yet the sentiment expressed, the wish to be delivered from self-loathing, remains opposed to the Pascalian emphasis on the religious efficacy of self-hatred. "Une Charogne" similarly intersects but does not coincide with Christian attitudes toward the body. When Bourdaloue exhorts a "femme mondaine" to scrutinize a cadaver "pour réprimer cet amour infini de vous-même," the misogynistic and moralistic motives of his rhetoric greatly resemble those of the speaker in "Une Charogne." Like the seventeenth-century preacher, Baudelaire also mobilizes images of the cadaver for the sake of destroying narcissism. Yet the context for this attack on self-love is not at all religious. Whatever may have been the historical origins for the hatred of the body as set forth in images of decomposition, a rhetoric that calls attention to the potential decay of the erotic body now aims to subvert contemporary attitudes and cultural values.

Baudelaire's remarks on what he called "L'école païenne" (1852) indicate what may have been the target of the subversions practiced in "Une Charogne." Attacking a resurgent taste for the classical and the mythological in literature, Baudelaire denounced the "malheureux néo-païens" for their affinities with the "sentimentalisme matérialiste" of Heine. Their "déplorable manie" for "les détritus anciens" could only result in sterility and pastiche, in a loss of reason and passion: "Est-ce Vénus Aphrodite ou Vénus Mercenaire qui soulagera les maux qu'elle vous aura causés? Toutes ces statues de marbre, seront-elles des femmes dévouées au jour de l'agonie, au jour de remords, au jour de l'impuissance?" (*OC* II, 47). At issue here is what Baudelaire perceives as the erotic idolatry of the neopagans, their elision of the potential evil caused by their Venuses, their blindness to women's capacity for solace, for devotion, suffering, and remorse. These strictures echo Baudelaire's slightly earlier criticism (in the 1851 review of Pierre Dupont) of the "philhellénisme" that succeeded the "individualité maladive" of the late romantics: "La puérile utopie de l'école de l'*art pour l'art*, en excluant la morale, et souvent même la passion, était nécessairement stérile" (*OC* II, 26). Baudelaire concludes his blast at the neopagans by imagining a poet whose obsession with "le beau, rien que le beau" leads him to rip his friends and vilify his wife. And since the "goût immodéré de la forme pousse à des désordres monstrueux et inconnus," Baudelaire concedes that he understands "les fureurs des iconoclastes et des musulmans contre les images" (*OC* II, 48–49). Is it not plausible to see in these objections to neopaganism the theoretical and critical confirmation of the poetic decomposition of the romantic image of the beloved in "Une Charogne"?

Although the poem may have been composed as early as 1843 (Pichois and Ziegler 185), its ironic attitude toward poetic idealization of the feminine recurs in a much later work, the prose poem "Laquelle est la vraie?" of 1863. The narrator recalls "une certaine Bénédicta, qui remplissait l'atmosphère d'idéal, et dont les yeux répandaient le désir de la grandeur, de la beauté, de la gloire et de tout ce qui fait croire à l'immortalité." But this miraculous woman soon dies, and the narrator buries her. As he gazes at her grave, her double appears, announcing herself as the true Bénédicta: "C'est moi, une fameuse canaille! Et pour la punition de ta folie et ton aveuglement, tu m'aimeras telle que je suis!" In shouting his refusal, he stamps his foot against the ground so violently that "ma jambe s'est enfoncée jusqu'au genou dans la sépulture récente, et que, comme un loup pris au piège, je reste attaché, pour toujours peut-être, à la fosse de l'idéale." The prose poem, rather more explicitly than "Une Charogne," directs attention to what might be called the rhetoric of antiidealism. Here too there is a buried woman and a speaker/narrator who describes her as inspirational. And here too the romantic convention of love-in-death becomes subverted, although somewhat differently. Now it is the failure to immortalize his "decomposed love" that haunts the narrator and condemns him not only to a disillusioned love with "une fameuse canaille" but also to an immobilizing attachment to the grave of the ideal, a grave dug by himself. In sum, "Laquelle est la vraie?" contains a retrospective irony, Baudelaire's admission that he has in fact remained, both in reputation and temperament, "the Prince of the Corpses."

Although I have argued that Baudelaire's antiidealistic treatment of the body presupposes but undermines Christian attitudes, I do not mean to suggest that his stance lacks any spiritual dimension.

Judging from remarks in his critical writings, it seems clear that he regarded the power of imagination to consist in the ability to decompose the world prior to creating it anew. This insistence on the imagination's capacity to radically reshape nature distinguishes Baudelaire's antiidealism from that of the realist painters and writers, who set out the facts of death and dying in a detached, undramatic fashion that emphasized the "sub-heroic banality" of the circumstances (Nochlin 68). Although "Une Charogne" reduces the dead person to the level of an animal, the process of putrefaction is dramatically and energetically rendered. There is no question of representing the dead woman as nonbeing, as a meaningless zero. On the contrary, the poem asserts the persistence of sensation and awareness after death, then compounds this paradox by drawing the analogy between her continued existence and the poem's own immortality. We can make sense of these puzzles if we recognize the extent to which Baudelaire separates form and matter, signifier and signified. As he put it in his journals, "Toute idée est, par elle-même, douée d'une vie immortelle, comme une personne. Toute forme créée, même par l'homme, est immortelle. Car la forme est indépendante de la matière, et ce ne sont pas les molécules qui constituent la forme" (*OC* I, 705). But the spiritualization of the formal in "Une Charogne" accompanies an ethical and not necessarily aesthetic devaluation of the material insofar as the material is subject to decay and evocative of disgust. Furthermore, this devaluation is not neutrally applied to all of creation but is focused rather on the beloved. Accordingly, we need to take a final look at the question of misogyny that "Une Charogne" raises.

Does the poem move in the direction of a cultural conservatism that would enforce the already low status of women by means of a rhetoric that subverts their romantic idealization and identifies them with decaying beasts? Can this be what Baudelaire meant when he claimed that woman is the being "pour qui, mais surtout *par qui* les artistes et les poètes composent leurs plus délicats bijoux" (*OC* II, 713)? Certainly it was by means of a woman, whether actual or imagined, that Baudelaire created "Une Charogne"; yet one would hardly describe the poem as a "delicate jewel." The response that we, as readers, must experience depends not simply on our repulsion at the spectacle of rotting animals and wormy women but equally, if not more powerfully, on our relation to the speaker and his "goût de l'horrible." This taste operates in the service of a final testament to a love that has or will be "decomposed." A love objectified in the body of a woman by metaphors that identify her with the natural world must, like the rest of nature, undergo change. Contrary to Nietzsche's notion of the eternal return, Baudelaire's poem instances a philosophy of the eternal departure. Love will decay, the body of the beloved will decay, and poetry cannot resist these processes. Insofar as we read this poem from the position of both speaker and addressee, we come to inhabit a world where the institution of love and its traditional poetic defenses have failed. Christian or pagan, metaphysical or material, the legitimations of a practice and a discourse that make the body of a woman depend on the soul of a man, on his instruction or adoration or poetry, are exposed by "Une Charogne" as rotten.

Chapter 6

"Le Balcon": The Poetics of Nocturnal and Diurnal Imagery

CLAUDINE GIACCHETTI

Mère des souvenirs, maîtresse des maîtresses,
O toi, tous mes plaisirs! ô toi, tous mes devoirs!
Tu te rappelleras la beauté des caresses,
La douceur du foyer et le charme des soirs,
Mère des souvenirs, maîtresse des maîtresses!   (5)

Les soirs illuminés par l'ardeur du charbon,
Et les soirs au balcon, voilés de vapeurs roses.
Que ton sein m'était doux! que ton cœur m'était bon!
Nous avons dit souvent d'impérissables choses
Les soirs illuminés par l'ardeur du charbon.   (10)

Que les soleils sont beaux dans les chaudes soirées!
Que l'espace est profond! que le cœur est puissant!
En me penchant vers toi, reine des adorées,
Je croyais respirer le parfum de ton sang.
Que les soleils sont beaux dans les chaudes soirées!   (15)

La nuit s'épaississait ainsi qu'une cloison,
Et mes yeux dans le noir devinaient tes prunelles,
Et je buvais ton souffle, ô douceur! ô poison!
Et tes pieds s'endormaient dans mes mains fraternelles.
La nuit s'épaississait ainsi qu'une cloison.   (20)

Je sais l'art d'évoquer les minutes heureuses,
Et revis mon passé blotti dans tes genoux.
Car à quoi bon chercher tes beautés langoureuses
Ailleurs qu'en ton cher corps et qu'en ton cœur si doux?
Je sais l'art d'évoquer les minutes heureuses!   (25)

> Ces serments, ces parfums, ces baisers infinis,
> Renaîtront-ils d'un gouffre interdit à nos sondes,
> Comme montent au ciel les soleils rajeunis
> Après s'être lavés au fond des mers profondes?
> —O serments! ô parfums! ô baisers infinis!   (30)

"Le Balcon" follows a pattern of symmetry and enclosure that is reinforced by the repetition of the opening line at the conclusion of each stanza. The first five stanzas, each containing five lines, are dominated by the themes of spatial concentration, intimacy, and nocturnal appeasement. But the poem's overall tendency toward containment and repose is challenged in the last stanza, where a new dimension, that of a cosmic landscape, and a new time structure, sunrise, suddenly break open and destabilize the established spatiotemporal setting.

My reading of this poem is based on Gilbert Durand's *Structures anthropologiques de l'imaginaire,* in which the author describes the two axiomatic categories of the imaginary, the diurnal and the nocturnal "regimes," in which all other models and structures are contained. "Le Balcon" lends itself well to the type of "archetypal" analysis proposed by Durand. Indeed, the first five stanzas of the poem illustrate the "nocturnal" mode, whereas in the last stanza, the diurnal imagery dominates. At the beginning of *Les Structures anthropologiques,* Durand writes: "There is no light without darkness, whereas the reverse is not true" (69). This seemingly simplistic statement is in fact crucial to our understanding of the nature of the two categories: the nocturnal regime is one of plenary wholeness and autonomy, whereas the diurnal regime is based entirely on duality and antagonism, constantly polarized between Manichaean images of elevation and fall and of light as conquest over negative images of darkness. The aggressive and polemic nature of the diurnal pattern is replaced, in the nocturnal thought, by images of security, intimacy, return, and nurturing. Durand refers to this process as "euphémisation."

The first five stanzas of "Le Balcon" are variations on the theme of reminiscence. According to Durand, memory is far from being a simple (and tragic) awareness of the passing of time, which fills our consciousness with nostalgic longings. Quite the contrary, remembering is a "euphemizing" device that opposes rather than regulates the passage of time. It allows us to "repair" time, to rearrange it, to transform the anguish of its duration into a state of continuity brought about by images of return, of backward motion (Durand 467). Baudelaire qualifies this return as a regression to the very matrix of memory, the image of the mother—"mère des souvenirs"—which opens the poem. In the archetype of the maternal woman, we find the very symbol of the nocturnal regime, as she is the gestational space of the euphemistic memory: the fabric of our adult longing for the golden images of our childhood fantasies.

On the other side of the first caesura, in direct opposition to the mother, is the "maîtresse des maîtresses." This repetition echoes the equivalence found in "mère" and "souvenir." While the words "mother" and "remembrance" are associated through a metaphoric *unity*, with one born of the other, the repetition of the word "mistress" signals a semantic *difference* based on the double connotation of "lover" and "ruler." That which is different is the same ("mère"/"souvenir"), and that which is the same differs ("maîtresse"/"maîtresse"). Between the mother and the mistress, we find yet another binary opposition, in which the "plaisirs" and "devoirs" of the second line refer to both the double meaning of the word "maîtresse" and the duality between mother and mistress. The terms intertwine to form a semantic confusion that forces difference into sameness and binarity into unity while always maintaining the possibility of polarization.

It is worth noting here that most critics of this poem have mentioned this "blurring" of the two feminine identities (the mother and the lover). They have seen in the "toi" of "Le Balcon" the feminine double (mother in the lover and lover in the mother), which, according to Quesnel, is free of the incest barrier (61). It is immediately apparent in the first two lines that in her duality, woman is superlative, she is the sum of all experiences; she is both origin ("souvenir") and outcome ("tu te rappelleras"); she is past and future, although never "present." By positioning the woman beyond any immediacy, and by referring to her throughout the poem in only imperfect and future tenses, Baudelaire also makes this all-powerful, omnipresent figure the paradoxical image of absence.

I would like to suggest that neither the antithetical possibilities that exist within the dual feminine figure nor the dichotomy between inside and outside, past and future, remembrance and projection, are permitted to realize their dividing potentials in the first five stanzas of the poem. A constant compromise is maintained because of the process of euphemization.

How does this euphemistic tendency, perhaps the most consistent and determining quality of the nocturnal imagery, express itself in the poem? We must first note the importance of general and exaggerated statements that, in the first three stanzas, describe a "wellness" of life that is absolute and unconditional. As one critic amusingly noted, eroticism takes on familial values in this poem, and everything at the onset is a "profusion heureuse" (Quesnel 254). The poet lives in a present of generalizations that invites no debate and provokes no anguish: "Que les soleils sont beaux dans les chaudes soirées / Que l'espace est profond! que le cœur est puissant!" Such generalizations, which make up a great part of the poem, are profoundly reassuring, in all of their banality. They express a euphoric well-being, as they encompass past and present and fuse both into an unfocused vagueness. Bachelard, noting Baudelaire's frequent use of such banal images, insists on their soothing effect on the reader, as they suggest "les rêveries du repos" (*Poétique de l'espace*, 52).

There are other forms of euphemization. In its movement toward constriction and closure, the poem suggests an architecture of familiar and securing proximity. If spaces are snug, however, they are never restraining. The openness of the balcony and the vastness of the sunset have the same intimate qualities as the home, the hearth, and the body. We find, in the sharing of descriptive elements, a blurring of the lines that divide inside and outside, for example in the case of warmth and luminosity (whose source is unclear) and in the use of the word "espace" to describe both the universe and the world within. This type of unification of opposites actually becomes the momentum of the entire poem. Along with Jean-Pierre Richard ("Mettons-nous," 120), we see the text as a binary system, in which images alternate between exterior and interior (for example, the hearth versus the evening light and also body versus soul) and between specific and general (for example, "ton cœur" versus "le cœur"). As in the case of the binary representation of woman, spatial structures are based on a figure of compromise in which duality is cohesive and centripetal.

In the poem's spatial structure, the diurnal and nocturnal archetypes form another set of dialectical images. It may appear paradoxical to study space in a poem that focuses exclusively on the themes of time and memory. As the title seems to suggest, however, time can be captured only in its various symbolic and strategic locations. Memory relives its past, not by searching for "time lost," but by constructing its own "spatial stations," of which the balcony would be a privileged observatory. In the words of Bachelard: "Les souvenirs sont immobiles, d'autant plus solides qu'ils sont mieux spatialisés" (*Poétique de l'espace,* 28).

From the very first stanza, three "sites" can be identified. The first is the body, which is not immediately given as a tangible form but is revealed by the "caresses." The second is the "foyer" with its rich connotation of the fireplace and, by extension, the secure and warm environment of the home as shelter (the Bachelardian "maison natale"). The third space, the balcony, is named in the second stanza. It is already present in the first, in which the word "soirs" introduces the exterior element that is later associated with the balcony ("les soirs au balcon").

The three spaces are all, in their grammatical positions, direct objects of the main verb of the first stanza ("tu te rappelleras") and are not syntactically in antithetical positions. For this reason, it could be argued that there is a strategy of alternating motion between inside and outside spaces rather than the dialectical structure of opposition and assimilation that most critics have preferred to discuss. "Le Balcon" can then be said to follow a pattern of repetition. The three spatial references (woman, home, and balcony) appear intermittently in each of the first three stanzas in a movement more circular than progressive. In this pattern, all the qualifiers that identify the three spatial elements may be *exchanged* in the following manner: the "beauty" that is associated in line 3 with the woman's body (through the image of the caress) is later ascribed to the "soleils" (11); the "douceur" of the home (4) is later used to describe the woman's bosom (8); and finally, in a more subtle way, the "ardeur" of the fireplace (6) becomes the warmth of the sunset (11). Similarly, the evening is first "illuminated" from inside ("l'ardeur du charbon"), though the second visual element describes the evening's light as originating from the outside (that is, the sun replaces the fireplace in line 11). In this "shuffling" of predicates, we find a very strong unity between the three thematic areas.

The vastness of "l'espace" is not on the *other side* of the balcony but *within* it. The balcony has the same function as would a window. The balcony, however, because of its volume, becomes an even more powerful symbol of containment. Bachelard points out that, through the window, one discovers the immensity of the universe within the enclosure of the totally secure "centre d'intimité" (*La terre et les rêveries du repos*, 117). From the inside the outside comes to be, and the "charbon" takes precedence over the "soleils," as the poem's origin of light and as its source of warmth. Bachelard has discussed this correspondence between intimacy and infinity: "Chez Baudelaire, l'immensité est une dimension intime" (*Poétique de l'espace*, 177). Throughout the poem, this *intimate* characteristic of space permits the valorization of its nocturnal qualities.

As mentioned earlier, the first symbol of intimacy is the image of the return to the mother's womb. The return is also a reversal, a possibility of turning time back, which cannot be better expressed than in line 22: "[Je] revis mon passé blotti dans tes genoux." This poem is an endless voyage back to intrauterine depths and is a clear example of Durand's "inversion euphémisante." I do not mean that there is no progressive movement in this text. Indeed, as Yves Le Hir points out, the poem clearly recounts "une démarche du crépuscule jusqu'à l'aube" (198). With the approaching nightfall, colors dominate the third and fourth stanzas, giving them the immediacy and concreteness of visual imagery reinforced by a now more specific and intimate representation of the woman's body. Durand points out that "l'attachement à *l'aspect concret* coloré et intime des choses" (319–20) is one of the four main structures of the nocturnal regime. Here the spectrum of colors includes only shades associated with the feminine and the maternal. They range from the pink of "vapeurs roses" to the red coloration of both the sunset and the woman's blood and finally to the thick darkness of the night. Not only do the colors deepen, but they also take on denser consistency as they darken. The vaporous pink thickens into the viscosity of blood and finally solidifies into the heavy matter of the night. The two qualities of the coloration, depth and thickness, eventually find their substance in the "mers profondes" of the last stanza and are associated with the female and maternal principles.

Colors are also sources of light. But light, in this poem, is never bright, cutting, or glaring, qualities all of which belong to a diurnal, white luminosity. On the contrary, the source of light here is paradoxically as dark as the "charbon" and as subdued as the evening sun. These are very important assets of the nocturnal imagery, for without them, the secure and positive valorization of the night might be replaced by the more negative and frightening qualities of the dark "gouffre." According to Durand, "la valorisation de la nuit se fait sou-vent en termes d'éclairement" (307).

In the fourth stanza, there is no light. The "noir" actually forbids all visual contact and allows only a "blind" description of the enclosed surroundings. Critics have unanimously interpreted this stanza as pivotal in the poem. For Jean-Pierre Richard, this is the point at which "l'euphorie de départ tourne manifestement à la constriction et au malaise" ("Mettons-nous," 124). Michel Charles also mentions the opposition between the previous euphoria and the present anxiety that the word "poison" suggests (58). Ivan Barko interprets line 16 as "la dégradation de la vision et l'altération du bonheur" ("'Le Balcon,'" 5). Finally, for Michel Quesnel, this is the place where "la plénitude se fond en inquiétude" (257).

In view of the critical approach I have chosen for my interpretation of this poem, I will consider this stanza not as a break from the first three stanzas but as a continuation of them. Critics have noted a nega-tive change in the fourth stanza, in which the words "cloison" and "poison" have "dysphoric" connotations of separation and death. Yet if we replace them in their context, the two words are themselves sub-ject to the euphemizing process. "Cloison" does not separate the lovers but rather insulates them from the world, creating such prox-imity that the eyes of one can feel (yet no longer see) the "prunelles" of the other, thus eliminating visual distance. In the same way, the poison's deadly potential finds its antidote in the euphemistic epithet "ô douceur" that accompanies it. Moreover, there is a direct link between the "poison" of line 18 and the "blood" of the previous stan-za. In a loose correspondence that is so typical of Baudelaire's poetry, blood is perfume that one can breathe, just as breath is a potion that one can drink. The word "blood" itself is, like poison, associated with the "bad" and impure water, which is a negative feminine image that belongs to the diurnal concept of nyctomorphic terror. Blood, howev-er, is now only a fragrance. It is subjected to the same euphemizing process as in the case of "poison."

I do not mean that negative and perilous elements of darkness are not present here. It is the essence of the nocturnal thought, however, always to favor compromise over polemic opposition. Durand has established this basic difference in the fundamental attitudes that pre-vail in the two regimes. While a diurnal mentality will seek a totalitar-ian goal of conquest and exclusion, the nocturnal thought will assimi-late rather than reject elements of a diurnal nature. Durand reminds us that "les symboles nocturnes n'arrivent pas constitutionnellement à se débarrasser des expressions diurnes" (307). In this poem, all potentially harmful elements of the night are contained and "defused."

The fourth stanza closes with the relaxing scene of the "sommeil" and the interesting image of "feet in hands," a type of "twin" fetal position. This image is taken up again in the fifth stanza, creating the same continuity as the one that we established earlier between the third and fourth stanzas. The poet is "blotti dans tes genoux" in a similar infantlike position that mixes the "fraternel" of line 19 and the "maternel" of line 22. While the fifth stanza introduces a new level of discourse that is a reflection on art, it also concludes the merger of all spatial elements.

By the fourth stanza, the interior space (the "foyer") and the exterior space (the "soir au balcon"), which are the two sources of light and warmth, have been eliminated. The entire space is occupied by the lovers' bodies. Around them, the night closes in. This, however, is not the "vaste comme la nuit" of the poem "Correspondances." In a total reversal of its spatial function, the night in "Le Balcon" has no depth or volume. Rather, it is the "nonspace" of a partition and an indicator of constriction. This reduction of space to the boundaries of the woman's body will last through the fifth stanza.

In the third stanza, the poet's attitude in "me penchant vers toi" (13) alludes to more than an intimate proximity to the woman's body. The main clause, "Je croyais respirer le parfum de ton sang," suggests a sort of vampiric entering of the body that is repeated in line 18 of the fifth stanza ("Et je buvais ton souffle"). This reverse penetration, or process of absorption of the woman's body, is the dominant image of the fifth stanza. Here the act of possession is not only sexual fulfillment but also the exclusive occupation of a uterinelike space that no longer allows the earlier alternating patterns (exterior/interior and so forth).

Although the night is described in terms of its complete opacity ("s'épaississait," "cloison," "noir" [16–17]), the eyes make "blind" vision possible and bring light to the night, if only in a limited way. The eyes of the night are not associated with transcendence and separation, as in the diurnal imagery. Here they spare us the anguish of total darkness and reassure us of the positive value of the night as a protective environment, in which one can fall asleep "in good hands" ("Et tes pieds s'endormaient dans mes mains fraternelles").

Michel Charles, in his study of the poem, offers an interesting comment about the representation of the woman's body: "la femme est représentée d'abord dans sa totalité. . . . Au contraire, à partir de la quatrième strophe, sont énumérées *les parties du corps* de la femme" (60). The critic sees this "fragmentation" as the resurgence of conflict and loss of unity. Rather than a loss of unity, I would suggest that this is a *displacement of centrality,* which far from having a "dispersing" effect, allows for a continued pattern of spatial containment and concentration.

First, the duality sein/cœur (corporeal/spiritual), which Charles views as a representation of totality, does *not* disappear to give way to the multiplicity of body images that we find in the later stanzas. At the end of the fifth stanza, the same image is found that juxtaposes "corps" and "cœur," although the word "corps" replaces the more specific "sein" with its maternal connotation. Second, even though we move away from the "centrality" of the heart and the bosom, which is the preferred focus of the poet's attention until the fourth stanza, our discovery of the woman's body, from head to toes, is far from fragmented. Indeed, every body part participates in the same process of "encasement" ("emboîtement"). The woman's body is actually described only in its relation to the poet's eyes, mouth, and hands and in perfectly "connected" enclosures. The woman is *contained* inside the corresponding body parts of the man. Her eyes, described as the more restrictive "prunelles," are incorporated into the visual field of the poet's eyes. The same image of inclusion is found in "je buvais ton souffle" and "tes pieds . . . dans mes mains."

These repeated images of emboîtement, so important in this poem, are extremely powerful themes of the nocturnal regime. Durand discusses these images in his study of the symbols of inversion and miniaturization—which he calls "Gulliverisation" and which are brought about by various swallowing and digestive processes. Durand sees, in this symbolism of symbiotic absorption, a euphemistic device, "une minimisation inversante de la puissance virile" (241). Indeed, this stanza and the poem in general can be said to represent an "inversion" of functions, a sexual fantasy in which the male is the "contenant" and the woman is the "contenu." This idea is reinforced by the rather obvious symbolism of the woman's feet, a phallic image already noted by Michel Charles, in which the woman represents the male attributes but in a euphemized, nonaggressive version (the feet are "asleep" in line 19). Durand's comments about the sexual significance of the process of emboîtement further enlightens the symbolism of inversion that we have found in this poem: "Cette gullivérisation est une espèce d'infantilisation des organes masculins et dénoterait un point de vue psychanalytiquement féminin exprimant la peur du membre viril et de l'effraction du coït" (241).

In this process of inversion, so typical of the nocturnal imagery, we identify the infantile *regression* toward the "phallico-maternel," as mentioned by Durand. The sexual scenario of the fifth stanza is ambiguous, not only because of the role reversal and the euphemistic quality of the sexual images (the adjective "fraternelles" in line 19 is a good example of a subdued or repressed eroticism), but also because the phallic woman of the fourth stanza inevitably becomes the maternal figure of the fifth. The intercourse described in the fourth stanza continues in the following stanza, although it has lost most of its sexual overtones except for the adjective "langoureuses." This adjective seems to belong to the semantic register of the fourth stanza, just as "fraternelles," with its "familial" connotations, belongs to the imagery of the fifth stanza.

In the fifth stanza, we also find a complete *reversal* of the "contenu/contenant" dialectic. Here the woman's body is no longer the "contained" but the "container." Line 22 is a striking example of this reversal. The cuddly image of "blotti dans tes genoux" is truly the most primal of all positions, in its *incorporation* of the child into the mother's body. It is in this penetration of the woman/mother's body that the "minutes heureuses" can be brought back, that the poet can "relive" his past. In other words, he can repeat the scenario of birth *in reverse*: a birth into the mother.

The grammatical ambiguity of the word "blotti" in line 22 is quite telling, as it modifies either the subject "Je" or the direct object "mon passé." Woman is both the "depository" of the poet's past and the ever-present "activator" of his memory. Time, through the woman, is exorcised of its terror and sheltered in the mother's lap. It can be told only as a cozy vision of primal intimacy and the space of regained osmosis. In the fifth stanza, the word "cœur" reappears, but the dialectical difference between "sein" and "cœur" that we had found in the second stanza is now "leveled." Body and soul have now acquired the same volume, and both have become spaces of containment: "Ailleurs qu'*en* ton cher corps et qu'*en* ton cœur si doux?"

The transformation between the fourth and the fifth stanzas is one in which the male/female roles are *exchanged* but not altered. Yet there are important differences. First, the fourth stanza is a narrative, and in spite of the lack of specificity of the imperfect tense, the verbs used are active and functional. In the fifth stanza, however, the present has supplanted the past tense and the verbs are cognitive: "savoir" and "chercher" have replaced "s'épaissir," "boire," and "s'endormir." Even "deviner" had a performative function (in this case, to "find"), which "revivre" does not have because of the vagueness and generality of its object ("Et revis mon passé"). We then witness a withdrawal of the poet from the dominant role he played in the fourth stanza and a retreat into the depth of erotic memory. The expression "A quoi bon . . . chercher" is clearly restrictive in spatial deployment. Woman is both the source and the object of the search, immobilizing the poet inside a space that has no unilateral direction. Desire ("chercher") is defined as repetition of past intimacies ("revis"), themselves fantasies of future memories ("Tu te rappelleras la beauté des caresses"). Leo Bersani's comment regarding the poem in its entirety is particularly relevant here: "The cradling movements of 'Le Balcon' are almost indistinguishable from the monotonous *jouissance* of sameness" (52).

The second transformation between the fourth and fifth stanzas is in the reference to art: "Je sais l'art d'évoquer les minutes heureuses." Jean-Pierre Richard explains this line as the cry of creativity, resisting, as it may, the force of a "réintégration libidinale" into the uterine space ("Mettons-nous," 125). This "liberating" movement is still, in any case, quite contained, for we cannot ignore the second line: "*Et* revis mon passé blotti dans tes genoux." In other words, the same subject is simultaneously in a state of regression ("revis"/"blotti") *and* invention ("Je sais l'art"). Memory is fantasy and invention. By directly referring to his poetic "skill," and as if to dismiss the possibility of closure, Baudelaire claims, not unlike Ronsard, that art will recreate time. Art, however, is more than an "anticlosure." It is in itself a euphemizing process, through which time, darkness, and closure will lose their negative valorization and their deadly powers. Also, in the "minutes heureuses," we see time not in its merciless linearity but in the rhythmic circularity of its dial. Art, like myth, is a comforting promise of continuity and integration.

Throughout the fifth stanza, the poet settles into a state of complacency. Exterior enticements are no longer possible, and movement is slow, as if in a "digestive" mode ("blotti," "langoureuses"). The first line of the sixth stanza seems to summarize the process of "condensation" that has progressively narrowed the three original spaces into the womblike refuge of the "cher corps"/"cœur": "Ces serments, ces parfums, ces baisers infinis." Indeed, the three elements of this line refer respectively to the third, fourth, and fifth stanzas (the more "narrative" interior stanzas), as if to also present a figure of return, at the poetic rather than the symbolic level.

If the fifth stanza contains a rhetorical question (23–24), the interrogative form of the entire sixth stanza is much more problematic. In the last five lines, the poet does not regain his performative function and is no longer in control of either space or time. Whether his question actually expresses doubt or hope is in fact of little consequence, since he is already removed from the poetic spaces that he has created through the first five stanzas. The lovers and their familiar spaces are noticeably absent from the closing stanza. It is as if the "cher corps," which was so encompassing, so complete, and so confining just moments ago, had suddenly vanished like the vapors on the balcony and with it the poet's desire. Forces beyond the lovers are now at play, and intimate human spaces will be replaced by the cosmic landscape.

In spite of the continuity created by the words "serments," "parfums," and "baisers," the sixth stanza stands in complete *isolation* from the rest of the poem. In the words of Jean-Pierre Richard: "Une cassure a eu lieu" ("Mettons-nous," 126), which I have interpreted as the emergence of a new system of representation. Two new archetypal spaces, the sea and the abyss, now replace the coiled enclosure of the hands and the lap. Also, with its insistence on the theme of rebirth ("renaîtront"," "rajeunis") and elevation ("Comme montent au ciel"), the final stanza clearly stands in opposition to the rest of the poem, which focuses on the movement of descent ("En me penchant vers toi"), and regression ("blotti dans tes genoux"). If we follow the Durandian isotopic classification of images, we find that the sixth stanza represents a "postural" attitude that belongs to the diurnal imagery. This attitude is a departure from the copulative attitude, typical of the nocturnal regime, which is found in the first five stanzas, but represents much more than a "cassure." We are transported into a symbolic mode, with completely different motivations, values, and ends, a mode that, in spite of its antagonism, still allows for continuity.

The balcony is a mitigating element in the spatial duality of the first five stanzas. As Ivan Barko notes, the balcony is an intermediary space, belonging to both the inside and the outside, just as dusk is the intermediate moment between day and night ("'Le Balcon,'" 4). In the last part of the poem, however, we find a much more radical opposition. The "blurring" effect we discussed earlier has been replaced with the sharp contrasting images of the "gouffre" and the "ciel." This verticality is an important function of the diurnal imagery and represents an antagonistic striving to extract oneself from the tenacious grip of time. According to Durand, "Cette symbolisation verticalisante [est] avant tout échelle dressée contre le temps et la mort" (140). In this stanza, the reemergence from the depths of the abyss, as well as the ascent to new life, are primordial images. Time is conquered, no longer through its inversion (as in nocturnal fantasies), but through its transcendence.

It is true that the last stanza is redundant with such images as "fond des mers profondes." The very function of the "profondeur," however, is quite different in the last stanza, in which there is a tendency toward "gigantisme" (Durand 150). This is in exact opposition to the tendency toward intimacy and reduction ("Gulliverisation") that we noted in the other stanzas. Both the archetype of elevation (with its symbols of erection) and the hyperbolic images (which change the intimate surroundings into a cosmic scenery) can be equated with a masculine, aggressive point of view that is typical of the diurnal imagery. We can then interpret the sixth stanza as the striving for *separation* from the feminine and the maternal, now associated with the dangerous opening of "gouffre" and "mers." There is also a desire, in the form of the comparison of line 28 ("Comme montent au ciel les soleils rajeunis"), for masculine domination and celerity.

In the sixth stanza, the sun is no longer the passive provider of the "chaudes soirées." Instead, it is rising, in all its regained energy, toward the celestial substance. It is born from the night yet also soaring *against* it. The rising sun is one of the most powerful symbols of the diurnal masculine archetypes. It is not surprising that, in this poem, the sun is also associated with a baptismal ritual ("Après s'être lavés"), for both sun (as light) and water (as limpidity) are purifying elements. The transformation of the sun from a complementary to a confrontational element, and from the descending to the ascending position, accompanies the changes in the symbolism of water, and more generally, of the liquid substance. The detergent quality that is attributed to the seawater at the end of the poem is in complete opposition to the function of other water substitutes. Two examples of these other liquids are the "blood" and "poison" of lines 3 and 4, respectively, with their stained coloration and their potential for maleficence (athough euphemized in this poem). Water is one of the most ambivalent of all images, as Bachelard points out throughout his *L'Eau et les rêves*. This ambivalence is quite apparent in "Le Balcon." If blood and poison are heavy fluids meant to be contained and absorbed, then the clear water of the oceans is "un milieu dynamique qui répond à la dynamique de nos offenses," as described by Bachelard (225). At the end of the poem, it is a combative rather than a nurturing environment from which the suns emerge, an environment that resists the gravitational pull of the "mers profondes."

If the sea is the great maternal archetype, then it is definitely a fantasy of expulsion from the womb that we witness in the last stanza of "Le Balcon." In this cosmic birth, we find an interesting Oedipal triangle between the three elements: "ciel," "soleil," and "gouffre." Durand writes of a "liaison entre ciel et paternité" (153), and we can then understand the elevation of the sun/son less as a heroic rebirth than as the countermovement against reentry into the uterus. At this symbolic level, the "gouffre interdit à nos sondes" is a rather explicit image of sexual interdiction. In the process of sublimation that takes place in the last stanza, the womb has kept its reproductive function but not its sexual function. The necessary passage through the abyss of the maternal space is one that "washes" and purifies the offspring, as if to "wash away" desire, as Jean-Pierre Richard points out (126).

In its ascetic phase, the diurnal imagination at work in the last stanza contemplates images of light and altitude in order to exorcise the anguish of darkness and fall. At the same time, it is the very product of the nocturnal archetypology that *surrounds* or *contains* the last lines. In a pattern very appropriately called "rimes embrassées," the words "serments," "parfums," and "baisers infinis" take us back to the euphemistic nocturnal imagery just as it is being challenged by the surge of diurnal confrontation. In the association between the nocturnal and diurnal elements, the last stanza suggests a possible *integration* between the two regimes. The scenario implies that the dark territory of the womb may come to light and with the birth of the poem, the son may give life to the mother of memories.

Chapter 7

"Tout entière": A Mystifying Totality
ÉLIANE DALMOLIN

Le Démon, dans ma chambre haute,
Ce matin est venu me voir,
Et tâchant à me prendre en faute,
Me dit: "Je voudrais bien savoir,   (4)

"Parmi toutes les belles choses
Dont est fait son enchantement,
Parmi les objets noirs ou roses
Qui composent son corps charmant,   (8)

"Quel est le plus doux." — O mon âme!
Tu répondis à l'Abhorré :
"Puisqu'en Elle tout est dictame,
Rien ne peut être préféré.   (12)

"Lorsque tout me ravit, j'ignore
Si quelque chose me séduit.
Elle éblouit comme l'Aurore
Et console comme la nuit;   (16)

"Et l'harmonie est trop exquise
Qui gouverne tout son beau corps
Pour que l'impuissante analyse
En note les nombreux accords.   (20)

O métamorphose mystique
De tous mes sens fondus en un!
Son haleine fait la musique,
comme sa voix fait le parfum!"   (24)

When woman's body falls into Baudelaire's lyric hands, it is certain to be examined in its minutest details, to be decomposed the better to be exposed. In fact, Baudelaire's punctilious passion for woman's body has led his poetry on a fetishistic course, a celebration of woman's body parts in a poetic frenzy that the poem itself allows us to call diabolical. "Tout entière" offers a perfect illustration of the tension between the demoniacal fragmentation of woman's body and the poetic effort to keep all of her body parts together in a harmonious unity of fragments. This particular poem will enable us to analyze the way in which the poet aspires to maintain the woman's body in a complete, self-contained form, a complete poem, despite the Devil's injunction for her dissemination, something that would inevitably lead to the incapacitation of the poet himself.

The (thematic) confrontation between satanic and poetic forces on display in "Tout entière" seems to be reflected in the composition of the poem itself. The first three stanzas of the poem appear to be telling a story in a narrative fashion, introducing two characters, the poet and the Devil, placing them in a spatial ("chambre haute") and temporal ("ce matin") situation, engaging them in a dramatic dialogue on the subject of woman's body. The woman's identity remains anonymous, as if to displace the intensity of the scene, shifting it away from her reality and closer to her body, the true subject of the Devil's inquiry. The dramatic pattern collapses by the end of the third stanza, however, and the theatrical dialogue moves into a meditative monologue in the last three stanzas. In this second part, spatial and temporal elements completely disappear, and the poet, left alone in his deepest meditation, is emotionally seized by the powerful complete image of woman's body, which he exposes in poetic figures with which he is familiar. The two distinct sections of the poem, the dramatic dialogue and the poetic monologue, mimic the conflictual situation between the Devil and the poet on the subject of woman's body. Can her body sustain the fragmentation inflicted by the dramatic query of the Devil, or can it be preserved whole by the poet's will? And indeed, are the Devil and the poet distinct characters, or are they one and the same, the double face of a lyric self tortured by its own duality?

"Tout entière" seems to propose a unified feminine body that would satisfy the poet's desire to be ravished—"Lorsque tout me ravit"—literally "When everything ravishes me," "ravishes" evoking both ecstatic spiriting away and violent enrapturing by the "tout," referring to the totality of her body rather than to seduction by any particular part of her. This ravishing totality cannot be trusted, however; it is a lure evoking the integrity and the harmony of the beloved body, a poetic trap in which the poet falls under the intoxicating influence of his confused senses: "O métamorphose mystique / De tous mes sens fondus en un!" Here we encounter once again the confusion of senses characteristic of Baudelairean poetics, most strategically exposed in the poem "Correspondances." As in the latter poem, synesthesia pervades the lines of "Tout entière": "Son haleine fait la musique, / Comme sa voix fait le parfum!" The perfume of the woman's breath creates musical harmony, and in the music of her voice a perfume can be sensed. A chiasmic displacement occurs from her breath and her voice to the music and the perfume invading the poet's senses.

In *L'Exposition universelle*, Baudelaire refers to a similar displacement of the senses in the case of the intellectual—"un homme du monde, un intelligent" (*OC* II, 576)—who is imaginatively transported from his everyday world to a faraway and unknown country. In the exotic land the intellectual discovers the mysterious power of the senses as they encounter new forms, colors, and tastes: "Ces fruits dont le goût trompe et déplace les sens, et révèle au palais des idées qui appartiennent à l'odorat, tout ce monde d'harmonies nouvelles entrera lentement en lui, le pénétrera patiemment, comme la vapeur d'une étuve aromatisée" (577). In this stimulative process, the taste of fruit not only displaces the intellectual's senses but also deceives them, replacing taste with smell. The word "trompe" adds a mystifying dimension to the simple metonymy that makes possible the passage from material objects (fruits) to sensations (palate, smell). "O métamorphose mystique / De tous mes sens confondus en un" suggests that there is an undeniable analogy between the mystificatory displacement of the intellectual's senses and the mystical metamorphosis of the poet's senses. The importance of this identification lies in the duplicitous quality that the word "mystique" acquires from the reading of the intellectual's synesthetic experience as it resembles the experience of the poet in "Tout entière." The mystification of the senses identified by the intellectual is similar to the mystical sensual experience of the poet. The poet, whose desire is to solve the mystery of woman, is doomed to be mystified by his own displaced senses.

In "Tout entière," the mystery of woman lies in the mystery of her body, a harmonious and exquisite whole: "Et l'harmonie est trop exquise / qui gouverne tout son beau corps." The whole body of the woman is too exquisite, too refined for the rational and analytical mind to seize. Thus the condition for capturing the harmonious wholeness of her body entails apprehending its beauty with chaotic senses and exposing oneself to the mysterious powers of the aesthetic feminine other. The poet defies "l'impuissante analyse" in order to locate the particular and numerous affinities that create the wholeness of her body. If the analytical and rational mind cannot conceive of the wholeness of the body, it is the task of the chaotic and passionate mind to do so. In fact, there is no vision of her body as a whole other than that created by an illusion of the senses.

The possibility of representing in a poem the totality of woman's body is as mystifying as the possibility of representing, in the title "Tout entière," the grammatical gender of the adverb "tout," which modifies the feminine adjective "entière." Regardless of gender and number, adverbs in French do not modify; they remain neutral. The adverb "tout," however, stands outside of the grammatical norm, and it has its own special set of rules, as if the incommensurability connoted in its seme were reflected in its exceptional grammatical treatment. "Tout" is a signifier of totality, of limitless totality. It modifies the space occupied by its accompanying adjective with a sense of boundlessness. The unrestricted nature inscribed in its seme clashes with the restrictive nature of formal gender marking. Does not "tout" represent a semantic field too vast to be encompassed and comprehensively apprehended by any strict grammatical order? In fact, it can be argued that grammar breaks its pattern of adverbial neutrality when it is faced with the immensity of "tout." When it is juxtaposed with a feminine adjective, "tout" adds an "e" to its neutralized signifier; it feminizes itself and becomes "toute," as in "toute petite," for example.

But if grammatical rules can be broken once to accommodate exceptions, they can be broken twice, and when the feminine adjective starts with a vowel, as "entière" does, the written "e" disappears, at least from the visible world of letters. It is necessary to clarify our position on the status of the rule and its interaction with the exception in the grammatical order. The existence of the grammatical rule may be justified in conjunction with the existence of the exception(s) to that rule. Following this perspective, we may understand the exception less as a diverging element to the general rule than as its existential part, its marginal limits. If the purpose of the exception is to define the strict encapsulating of grammatical rules, the exception also hints at the idea of exclusion as indicated by the Latin matrix of the word *exception*— "excipere"—which means to exclude from, to withdraw. If, indeed, the exceptional element to the grammatical rule stands as an excluded rule that has broken free from the central rule and operates according to its own set of rules, the reason for the separation of the exception from the central rule could arguably be the result of an intentional desire— on the part of the psychologically and culturally diverse speakers—to break the strict pattern of a grammatical order that appears unsatisfy-ing, as it attempts to represent gender categories.

When grammar strikes the "tout" of "Tout entière" by cutting off the "e" from its expected feminine ending, it eliminates the feminine gender marking the "whole" less than it makes this gender invisible. Only oral French allows "tout" to be pronounced "toute," thus restor-ing the feminine sound that the written form excludes. Indeed, pho-netically, the "e," the mark of the feminine, can still be heard less as an ending than as a link—a liaison—between "tout" and "entière." This liaison is a dangerous liaison for orally allowing the gender con-nection that the written juxtaposition of "tout" and "entière" breaks into a masculine and a feminine form. There is a feminine voice bring-ing together male totality ("tout") with female entirety ("entière"); "tout" and "entière" appear to reiterate notions of wholeness and may sound redundant. The function of "tout," however, is to enhance the idea of wholeness intimated in "tout entière"; "tout" is the guar-antor of absolute thoroughness as it modifies "entière." The abso-lutism reflected in the title foreshadows the poet's absolute desire to describe the woman's whole body in the poem. Her body is not just entire but completely entire, that is, more entire than the wholeness that each predicate alone can signify. It surpasses the delimited mag-nitude that the mind can conceive.

This ungraspable and magnificent femininity inscribed in the phrase "tout son beau corps" presents its chaotic immensity to the comprehensive writing of the poet; poetic language appears as a medium of representation too scant to encompass the figure of femi-ninity and too prescribed to represent the imprescriptible nature of the female subject. In "Tout entière," the immense and imprescriptive femininity of the poem must remain veiled, private, like a dangerous liaison. Nevertheless, as we have noted, femininity punctuates the title of the poem. It neutralizes the modifier "tout," strips it of its mas-culinity. Indeed, "tout" in "Tout entière" has the appearance of a masculine form, while it really responds to the neutrality conferred upon all adverbs. In fact, this neutralization/neuterization of "tout" is the reason that femininity must remain invisible on the scene/seen of writing. It is the feminine power of emasculation in language that leads grammatical dictatorship to bend rules, to go out of its way to reestablish the signifiers of male discourse, even if elements of this male discourse, like "tout," have in writing the same morphology as the neutral form of adverbs ("tout" as a masculine adjective is spelled the same way as the adverb "tout"). "Tout" in "Tout entière" could pass for a masculine form, when it really is a neutral adverb, a "neutered whole." The feminine totality signified by the title of the poem can be read as an attractive chaotic field that the curious poet wishes to enter, not without feeling threatened in his masculinity. For the poet to reach out for the wholeness of femininity might result in the writing of impotent verses—castrated poetic language—as indicated in the poem by the mention of "l'impuissante analyse."

"Tout" is the representation of an impossible dream of totality—a dream about figuring feminine "wholeness"—a dream whose realization presents too great a risk for the poet's masculinity. For him to want a full representation of her body may result in the giving up of his pen(is), which he may do by feminizing himself and by accepting the oral feminine liaison that narrows the gap separating gender differences in his poetic language.

The poet's desire to capture the totality of the woman's body as recorded in the title of the poem emerges in the poem itself. The poet does not put his masculinity on the line, however, and his desire to possess her whole body remains as unrealized as his desire, implied in the written title, to capture a feminine totality that can be only phonic. The "métamorphose mystique" that makes his writing possible is the illusory effect that allows him to cross over to the sensual and physical wholeness of the woman's body; it is also a safe way to preserve the undivided masculinity of his senses/signification ("tous mes sens fondus en un"), and the undefined meaning of "sens" stresses the undivided masculinity inscribed in his poetic sensations as well as his poetic meaning.

In this poem, we may say that Baudelaire takes for the whole body of woman the object of an illusion created by his mystified poetic senses. In fact, the illusiveness of his senses is clearly marked at the beginning of the poem by the presence of the mystificatory figure par excellence: the Devil. The Devil deliberately throws the poet into a state of confusion. One night, he comes into the poet's bedroom and asks which part of the woman's body the poet prefers: "Parmi les objets noirs ou roses / qui composent son corps charmant, / Quel est le plus doux?" The Devil's query brings into play the fragmented body of woman as he speaks of her black and pink body parts.

In "A une madone," the poet's desire to envelop the wholeness of the female body is associated with her dress, and her fragmented body appears at this time in shades of white and pink, as opposed to the black and pink suggested by the Devil in "Tout entière":

> Ta Robe, ce sera mon Désir, frémissant,
>
> Onduleux, mon Désir qui monte et qui descend,
>
> Aux pointes se balance, aux vallons se repose,
>
> Et revêt d'un baiser tout ton corps blanc et rose. (*OC* I, 58)

On the one hand, by referring to the woman's black body parts, the Devil in "Tout entière" could have in mind the representation of the modern woman seen in "Le Chat," who also has a brown body. On the other hand, the white body of the Madonna, whose color recalls the white body of the statue in "La Beauté," can be read as the ideal woman who will soon be violated by the demoniacal poet ("Je mettrai le serpent qui me mord les entrailles / Sous tes talons") and who finally turns black ("volupté noire"). It is important to note that whether ideal white ("A une madone") or modern black ("Tout entière"), both women still retain the pink color of their flesh, the color associated with the intimate and sensual female body. The white Madonna and the black Devilish woman have in common the pleasure of the flesh signified by the pink body parts that they both display to the male's gaze. Whether created by God or by the Devil, the woman manifests herself in Baudelaire's poetry as a voluptuous body, a body caught between the ideal and the modern, respectively symbolized in the text by a contrasted schematic of colors.

The Devil's question in "Tout entière" can be reformulated in the following terms: of all the fragments of the woman's body, which one do you prefer? It is the Devil's question that introduces the idea of fragmentation into the poet's impossible desire to possess its fullness. His inquiry about fragmented woman is immediately answered by the poetic denial of her fragmentation, and the assertion of her totality: "Puisqu'en Elle tout est dictame, / Rien ne peut être préféré."

In fact, the poet's desire to bring together all her fragments in a totalizing form is so strong that he endows the woman with the power of "dictame," an herb that was traditionally used as a soothing balm for all cuts and pains. Everything—"tout"—about the woman is "dictame," a healing poetic ointment created by the poet to alleviate what we identified in the title of the poem as the effect of castration that she inflicts on his poetic body. The notion of castration makes explicit the threat on the poet's body, his fear of being unable to conserve his sexual identity unharmed, to protect it from a menace that he cannot ignore. According to Leo Bersani, the threat of castration posed by woman, the idea that, as artist, the poet must also accept the risk of impotence, is part of Baudelaire's poetic experience. The poet sees in the figure of woman his own "unanchored self" (Bersani 15), his own feminine side that he must violently repress, with crude and obscene sadistic gestures of his own applied to her body in response to the threat of castration that she poses to his body. In other words, he counteracts his imminent loss of virility by creating a fantasy of dislocation of her body. This dislocation becomes the core of his poetic enterprise.

In "Tout entière," the poet sets up an imaginative play between his sadistic masculine self, embodied in the Devil, who presents woman in terms of her body parts, and his feminine self, embodied in the female healer who rehabilitates the body, recovers all scattered body parts, and offers a patched-up image of the full body. Woman then appears as the healer of all cuts, including the cut of castration symbolized in the neuterization of the "tout," a poetic operation phonetically performed by the feminine liaison restoring the graphically absent "e." When the poet creates woman's image to fulfill his wish to possess the totality of her body, even if it means a complete collection of body parts, he also creates the possibility that he might not emerge unscarred from this dream of feminine totality. I would like to reinforce this statement on the menace that woman, as a person made of "scattered discontinuities," presents to the poet's desire invested in his writing by recalling Bersani's final remark concerning the poem "Les Bijoux." According to Bersani, the image of the fragmented woman brings the fear that the poet may lose the integrity of his masculine desire and become sexually divided. In fact, we see traces of this separation at work in "Tout entière."

In a strange turn of events, the woman/healer—the dictame—of "Tout entière," while protected from the Devil's incisive question by the poet's affirmation of her totality, turns against the latter, protector of her integrity. As restored totality, her body causes the poet's self to be divided. Indeed, the poetic consciousness refers to itself as a divided subject; in the first two stanzas the narrator refers to himself in the first person until he has to answer the Devil's question. Then he uses the second person: "Tu répondis à l'Abhorré." This sudden separation of the "I" and the "you," of the poet and his soul, occurs at the very moment when, to fight the suggestion made by the Devil about the fragmented body of the woman, the poetic self asserts her totality. In other words, the poetic self separates into an "I" and a "you"—a self and an other, perhaps a male self and a female soul—as it faces the possibility of a whole woman's body. It would appear that, as a whole, she demands the division of poetic consciousness; she forces the poet out of his dream of undivided pleasures with her body. The condition for the representation of her full body is the dissemination of poetic identity. Her illusory unification necessitates his fragmentation.

"Tout entière" names an illusory condition for the body of the woman and the loss of masculine subjectivity at stake behind this illusion; it subverts the promise behind its title by referring to a fragmented poetic consciousness, the victim of its desire to cross over gender boundaries. The Devil thus appears less as a separate figure fighting the imagination of the idealistic poet than as a calculated and controlled interference of no real threat staged by the poet trying out the Devil's position for his unanchored self. The poet in "Tout entière" is, so to speak, the Devil's advocate. As such, he embodies on the one hand masculine desire commanding his cutting of the female body. On the other, he fulfills his feminine role as a powerful "healer" capable of repairing the dissemination of her body, now his body as a result of his phantasmatic experience with the other sex. I have shown how this double play of sexual identity in "Tout entière" becomes problematic for the poet who fears emasculation. The impending loss of virility is confirmed when by the end of the poem he qualifies his enterprise as impotent: "l'impuissante analyse." To fight masculine impotence while conserving his femininity, Baudelaire redefines the concept of totality first in "Tout entière" and then in his *Journaux intimes,* in which he claims: "Tout est un nombre. Le nombre est dans tout" (*OC* I, 649). According to Baudelaire, "tout" is not just an indivisible entity, a number, a body, but also composed of numbers, of body parts. "Tout" points to its own inner ambiguity; that of simultaneously representing two opposite ideas: an unbroken entirety and an infinite number of fractions. Such ambiguity is reflected in the double sexual role played by the poet, who, as a lyric poet, traditionally male, sides with the Devil and divides the female body and who, as a modern poet, sides with the woman and gathers her disseminated body parts in an eclectically composed poetic whole.

Chapter 8

Fur in My Brain: "Le Chat"*

MARGARET MINER

I

Dans ma cervelle se promène,
Ainsi qu'en son appartement,
Un beau chat, fort, doux et charmant.
Quand il miaule, on l'entend à peine,   (4)

Tant son timbre est tendre et discret;
Mais que sa voix s'apaise ou gronde,
Elle est toujours riche et profonde.
C'est là son charme et son secret.   (8)

Cette voix, qui perle et qui filtre
Dans mon fonds le plus ténébreux,
Me remplit comme un vers nombreux
Et me réjouit comme un philtre.   (12)

Elle endort les plus cruels maux
Et contient toutes les extases;
Pour dire les plus longues phrases,
Elle n'a pas besoin de mots.   (16)

Non, il n'est pas d'archet qui morde
Sur mon cœur, parfait instrument,
Et fasse plus royalement
Chanter sa plus vibrante corde,   (20)

Que ta voix, chat mystérieux,
Chat séraphique, chat étrange,
En qui tout est, comme en un ange,
Aussi subtil qu'harmonieux!   (24)

* I thank Mary-Kay F. Miller and Brian Hyer for their valuable suggestions.

II

De sa fourrure blonde et brune
Sort un parfum si doux, qu'un soir
J'en fus embaumé, pour l'avoir
Caressée une fois, rien qu'une. (28)

C'est l'esprit familier du lieu;
Il juge, il préside, il inspire
Toutes choses dans son empire;
Peut-être est-il fée, est-il dieu? (32)

Quand mes yeux, vers ce chat que j'aime
Tirés comme par un aimant,
Se retournent docilement
Et que je regarde en moi-même, (36)

Je vois avec étonnement
Le feu de ses prunelles pâles,
Clairs fanaux, vivantes opales,
Qui me contemplent fixement. (40)

In his preface to Baudelaire's posthumously published *Œuvres complètes,* Théophile Gautier wrote at some length about the poet's love for cats. In fact, declared Gautier, "Baudelaire était lui-même un chat voluptueux, câlin, aux façons veloutées, à l'allure mystérieuse, plein de force dans sa fine souplesse, fixant sur les choses et les hommes un regard d'une lueur inquiétante, libre, volontaire, difficile à retenir, mais sans aucune perfidie et fidèlement attaché à ceux vers qui l'avait une fois porté son indépendante sympathie" (35). Whether or not this description would have fit Baudelaire in person, it certainly fits one of his poems. It might almost serve as a prose summary of "Le Chat," the poem numbered fifty-one in the 1861 edition of *Les Fleurs du Mal.* This poem starts out by evoking a cat's supple strength, ends up by picturing its penetrating stare, and insists along the way on the intimate relation between this cat and the poet.

The poem and Gautier's description of Baudelaire do not quite match, however. Whereas Gautier speaks of Baudelaire as a cat, the poem says instead that the poet *contains* a cat. More specifically, the poet's brain contains a cat, a mobile cat that walks around in his head much as a thought turns over in his mind. As the first line clearly announces, then, the poem is about poetic consciousness, about creative projects and processes as they take shape inside the poet. But as the first stanza makes equally clear, the poem is also about a cat, a real, fur-coated cat, meowing softly for attention, rather like the brownish blond kitty who is padding across my desk as I write this essay. Words like "appartement" and "miaule," everyday words that did not belong to the poetic vocabulary of Baudelaire's time, strongly suggest that the cat in this poem is to be taken literally; it is an actual household pet, four-footed, given to pacing the floor. The word "cervelle," also nonpoetic, heightens this tension between literal and figurative understandings of the first stanza. As an anatomical term, "cervelle" too evokes the physical reality of creatures with organs and limbs. Yet "cervelle" is the crucial word that links the cat with the poet's mind, thus implying that the prowling feline should be taken as a sort of warm, fuzzy metaphor representing the poet's mental activity.

Already in the first four lines, therefore, readers must confront a question that will remain pertinent throughout the poem: should the cat, the poem's central image, be read literally or figuratively or (if this is possible) both? Either kind of reading by itself seems incomplete, but if one tries to combine the two, the result is a nonsensical, almost disturbing representation of the poet, poised diligently over his work while a furry feline strolls around the furnished interior of his skull.

A number of critics, among them Jacques Crépet, Georges Blin, Antoine Adam, and Felix Leakey (partially summarized in Claude Pichois's notes to Baudelaire's *Œuvres complètes* [I, 925]), have raised a similar question. These critics did not for the most part use the terms "literal" and "figurative," however, and they were primarily interested in an angle of the problem that does not concern me here: they wanted to decide specifically whether the poem was a figurative evocation of Marie Daubrun, one of Baudelaire's mistresses, or whether the poem was merely a fanciful depiction of a real cat (possibly, as Claude Pichois suggests, Marie Daubrun's own pet). Their debate necessarily remained inconclusive, since it uncovered no evidence either in the poem itself or in surrounding documents, such as letters and memoirs, to prove that "Le Chat" was really about either Marie or her cat. The debate did not take into account the possibility that the poem constitutes an investigation into relations between the literal and the figurative in poetic language as such, which is the possibility that I want to consider.

The problem, moreover, is not simply how to choose among different ways of interpreting the cat image. It also involves discerning the relations between the *inside* of the poet's head (where ideas and images are conventionally believed to circulate freely, unencumbered by substance) and the *outside* of that same head (where cats take on mass and volume and where poems, laboriously inscribed on paper, circulate with difficulty). At first glance, a cat would appear to be the perfect vehicle for exploring these relations between the inside and the outside: cats are proverbially unwilling to stay on any one side of a door or wall, and they might well serve as emblems for the restless, always incomplete movement of images from the abstraction of the mind to the concrete reality of the page, as in T. S. Eliot's "The Rum Tum Tugger":

> The Rum Tum Tugger is a terrible bore:
> When you let him in, then he wants to be out;
> He's always on the wrong side of every door,
> And as soon as he's home, then he'd like to get about. (*Cats*, 17)

But—also proverbially—cats' reasons for going out and coming in are inscrutable, and the poem is similarly enigmatic with respect to the connections between what is inside and what is outside the poet's brain. The rest of my chapter addresses these connections. It aims in particular to look at the difficulty or the uncertainty involved in representing links between brain and world, and it shows how the poem's narrator hesitates not only between figurative and literal language but also between (so to speak) his indoor and his outdoor cats.

"Le Chat" is divided into two numbered sections, which are in many ways distinct from one another. The first and longest section gives, or at least appears to give, a fairly straightforward answer to the question of what connects the cat in the poet's brain with the rest of the poet's world. The cat, according to this section, acts like a muse: it inspires the poet, playing on his heart like a bow on a string, so that the music pent up inside the poet's mind may eventually be released and heard by others. In fact, since violin strings were still made of catgut in Baudelaire's time, it seems clear that the cat controls not just the bow but the poet's whole heart instrument. The cat furnishes not only the means for making the heart resonate but also a vital part of the resonating substance. Thus invested with the powers traditionally attributed to muses, this "chat séraphique" is more divine than mortal, and it manipulates the poet with superhuman skill. On the one hand, the cat's music is "harmonieux" enough to make the poet's heart vibrate in tune, like a harp accompanying an angel. On the other hand, the cat's song is "subtil" enough not to let its own angelic harmony drown out the poet's individual music, which must be toned down for frail human ears. With perfectly measured authority, the cat-muse alternately soothes and stimulates the poet ("s'apaise ou gronde"), providing him with the ideal conditions for producing and disseminating poetry.

As with more traditional muses, a good part of the energy that this cat-muse transmits to and through the poet is erotic, designed to awaken and sublimate desire. To do this, the cat increasingly identifies itself as female: despite the masculine form "chat" that appears in both the first and the sixth stanzas, the feline becomes an increasingly feminine presence in section 1. This happens, however, not as a direct result of the male poet's desire for the cat but rather as an indirect result of the cat's transformation into a disembodied voice. The "beau chat" of the first stanza is fully ambulatory and three-dimensional, but this creature quickly dematerializes in line 4 into a barely audible meow. Thereafter the cat appears only as the feminine word "voix" (6 and 9) or the feminine subject pronoun "elle" standing for "voix" (7, 13, and 16), so that one tends to lose sight of the original, presumably male animal announced in the poem's title. The longer the poet continues to describe the cat's lovely voice, the more the cat appears to be lovingly feminized. It even comes as something of a shock to encounter, in line 21, the sudden juxtaposition of the feminine "voix" with the masculine "chat": one wonders momentarily whether the voice still belongs to the cat or whether it has taken on a separate, erotically charged life of its own. This split between voice and cat is reinforced, moreover, by a clash between the sensual attributes of the feminine voice ("qui morde") in stanza 5 and the more abstract, cerebral qualities of the masculine cat ("mystérieux," "séraphique," "étrange") in stanza 6. As an "ange," the cat represents an eerie blend of masculine charisma with feminine eroticism.

The cat-muse's voice is remarkable for other reasons as well. The poet insists that its power is magical but also at least partially hidden:

because of "son charme et son secret," the voice will probably remain inaudible or incomprehensible to everyone except the poet, whose task is to transmute it into recognizable poetry. Thus concealed and protected, the voice ("qui perle et qui filtre") attains both extreme clarity and extreme purity. All possible imperfections are filtered out of it as the voice flows in delicately rounded pearl drops through the murkiest tangles of the poet's consciousness. Paradoxically, its absolute purity seems to give the voice its erotic power, since the rhyme in stanza 3 suggests that the *filtered* voice is particularly potent as a love-inspiring *philter*. This superlative purity also confers additional powers on the voice: in stanza 4, the poet declares that the voice is so perfectly precise that it can adapt itself equally well to the most exaggerated or contradictory passions, and he further asserts that the voice is somehow pure enough to dispense with words, speaking in tones purged even of language.

This last assertion is important. Without using a single word, claims the poet, the cat-muse's voice can make itself understood as clearly as it would by using conventional syllables clumped together in long sentences. What is more, the wordless voice is able not only to calm the most violent pains but also to contain—that is, to subdue and/or to foster (the French "contient" can mean either)—every sort of ectasy: "Elle endort les plus cruels maux / Et contient toutes les extases." In the absence of language, that is, the voice can both express and manipulate the most extreme conditions likely ever to arise in the poet's consciousness; bereft of words, the voice gains literally unimaginable powers of unmediated expression and unlimited persuasion. If this is the case, however, the poet must surely find himself in an uncomfortable position. His own poem, composed of words and sentences in the usual manner, can hardly do justice to the miraculous voice it is meant to evoke; the rhyming association of "mots" with "maux" suggests the poet's anguish at his inferior, language-bounded condition. Moreover, since the poem is clearly no match for the cat-muse's voice, one begins to wonder whether the poet can in fact understand that voice as well as he has indicated. It would seem much more probable that the poet, accustomed to listening for ordinary sentences and encumbered by his need to use words, has neither heard the voice clearly in his head nor written about it accurately in his poem.

There are, in fact, some hints in section 1 that the poem cannot really convey the power and beauty of the cat's wordless voice, hints that when the poet wants to exteriorize that voice in his poem, his language shows itself to be unwieldy and inadequate. Some awkwardness is already apparent in line 4, which unbalances the first stanza by launching a new, incomplete proposition rather than rounding off the three preceding lines, as French poetic tradition would require. Line 4 also introduces the incongruous verb "miaule," which is followed by other discordant verbs such as "gronde" and "morde": a surprising number of the active verbs that refer to the cat's voice indicate strident discomfort. Further uneasiness makes itself felt in line 5, the poet's first attempt to find adjectives to describe the feline voice ("Tant son timbre est tendre et discret"). Instead of flowing syllables that might imitate the cat's lustrous, filtered pearl drops of sound, this line is crammed with staccato consonants; the [r] that rasps among the initial explosions of "Tant," "timbre," "tendre," and "discret" suggests that, in the next line, the harsh term "gronde" will describe the voice much better than the gentle "s'apaise." And when the poet maintains that this voice fills him "comme un vers nombreux," there is reason to doubt that the sensation is unequivocally pleasant. In the much-quoted poem "Au Lecteur" that opens *Les Fleurs du Mal,* the "vers" that swarm around the poet's brain are not harmonious verses of poetry but rather a wormlike "peuple de Démons" that lives there, "Serré, fourmillant, comme un million d'helminthes" (*OC* I, 5). Similarly, in the fourth of Baudelaire's "Spleen" poems, the poet's brain is overrun by "d'infâmes araignées" that are closer to worms than to poetic verses (*OC* I, 75). These famous echoes from other *Fleurs* make it likely, then, that despite its singular indefinite article ("un vers" in line 11 is a verse, not a worm), the "vers nombreux" filling the poet's brain in "Le Chat" has as much to do with vermin as with poetry.

In other words, various disturbing glitches or dissonances in section 1 intimate that the poet's language is not fully under his control. He would apparently like to share with readers the marvelous sound of the cat-muse's voice, or at least a reasonable approximation of it, but treacherous words keep interfering. It is of course possible that the poet deliberately distorts the cat's voice with certain words, if only in order to prove his creative independence, but in that case there is nothing to show that he has truly heard and understood the voice in all its unimaginable expressiveness. Perhaps the clearest indication of the poet's predicament comes in line 14, another line joltingly punctuated by explosive [t]: "Et contient toutes les extases."

Etymologically, "extase" comes from the Greek "extasis," which refers to the condition of being outside oneself; to be in ecstasy is to be figuratively beside oneself, separated from self-awareness, as well as literally incapable of reasoned communication. But in line 14, the cat-muse's voice is said to "contain" within itself these "extases," just as the poet's brain holds within itself the cat. The situation is thus confusing, maybe impossibly so: how can the poet contain *inside* himself the same cat whose voice contains precisely the ecstasies that must necessarily force the poet *outside* himself? Even if the cat "contains" by repressing rather than releasing them, this overwhelming swarm of repressed ectasies is bound to return, eventually driving the poet out of his own head. Centered around these troubling "extases," then, section 1 of "Le Chat" makes it very difficult to know exactly how the narrating poet can relate the cat inside his brain to the outside world of his readers. When he turns inward to the cat-muse's voice, he is likely to be ecstatically moved outside his own mind; when he turns outward, speaking to readers in his own voice, he is not only cut off from the inspiring, interior cat but also betrayed by elements of the poetic language he is obliged to use. Therefore, however closely bound together they may appear to be, the poet is in some crucial ways alienated from the cat that ostentatiously inhabits his own brain.

The nature and the extent of this alienation become clearer in the course of section 2. To begin with, the break between sections 1 and 2 signals a change in the poet's manner of presenting the cat, particularly in view of the possessive pronouns that frame the break on either side. In line 21, almost at the end of section 1, the poet addresses himself directly to the cat, hyperbolically praising "ta voix, chat mystérieux." This is the first and only time that the poet uses the second person singular, apparently hoping to establish a dialogue with his muse. In the rest of the poem, he uses only the first and third persons singular; most notably, he returns to the third person with "sa fourrure" in line 25, right at the beginning of section 2. From then on, the poet avoids any form of direct communication with the cat, as if he now considers it impossible. Described in the third person, like an inert object or a stranger kept at a distance, the cat comes to seem much more like a household pet than an inspiring muse. Even during the poet's sole attempt at conversation, in stanza 6, the cat is given no opportunity to answer or to acknowledge the poet's presence, and all hope of dialogue evaporates when the poet returns definitively to his third person evocation.

Section 2 also demotes the cat from muse to animal in other ways. There are in this section no references at all to the cat's voice: either the voice has fallen abruptly silent, or else it has suddenly lost its power to hold the poet's entire attention. He is much more preoccupied in this section by the cat as a corporeal entity, by the look of its eyes and by the color, texture, and smell of its fur. As a result, relations between the cat and the poet seem less intimate than before, even though the contact between them is more concrete; the feline voice heard earlier (one should remember that "entendre" in French means both "to hear" and "to understand") belonged more immediately to the private recesses of the poet's mind than the cat now perceived with senses other than hearing. In the absence of the cat's voice, moreover, the poet's own words grow increasingly enigmatic. When he claims to have been "embaumé" by the odor rising from the cat's fur, for example, his meaning remains unclear. The French "embaumé" can apply either generally to something filled and permeated with fragrance or, more specifically, to a dead body preserved with fragrant substances. It is hard to guess, then, whether the scent of the fur has merely bathed the poet in sweet perfume or whether it has actually killed and embalmed him. It is more conventional to suppose that the cat has only perfumed the poet, but given that the "extases" in the cat's voice have already threatened to drive the poet out of his mind, one cannot discount the more radical possibility that an odor in the fur has driven him all the way to a mummified death. In any event, the ambiguous "embaumé" emphasizes the danger involved in either caressing the cat or writing about it.

Once the cat is no longer constituted primarily by its voice, its predominant femininity begins to fade as well. The "fourrure" of stanza 7 shares the feminine character of the voice, especially since the poet strokes the fur as he would the dark blond hair of a woman. But in stanza 8, the cat turns into an "esprit" whose essential masculinity is made clear by the pronoun "il," repeated five times in only three lines. It might at first seem that despite its new, fully masculine identity, the cat returns in this stanza to its former functions as muse, appearing once more as a godlike, disembodied being with the power to inspire. This being is more likely to inspire fear than creativity, however: it not only presides over everything within its "empire" but also acts as judge with full authority to approve or condemn. Faced with this masterful entity, the poet does not dispute its right to rule his mind. On the contrary, he comes close to renouncing all his own authority (or author-ity) when he cannot even decide just what the entity is, helplessly asking "est-il fée, est-il dieu?" Moreover, since the term "esprit familier" usually applies to a soul that, embodied in an animal, has returned from the dead, one wonders exactly what sort of entity the poet himself has become. Is his head the haunted "lieu" of a dead spirit now incarnated in a cat? If the poet has in fact died, as suggested in the previous stanza, then perhaps his emptied and embalmed brain has been taken over by a stranger's soul. Or perhaps the cat spirit represents a part of the poet's own half-dead soul, a part now totally alienated and bent on terrorizing the mind to which it formerly belonged. In either case, the poet's brain is no longer a comfortable "appartement" amicably inhabited by his resi-dent muse. It is instead a scary place, an empire under the absolute jurisdiction of someone or something else, a space where the poet himself is not at home.

The poet's near-exclusion from his own mind is confirmed in the last two stanzas of the poem, which offer an image even more unnerving than the fur-filled brain of the first stanza. As if deter-mined to make readers understand that neither his brain nor the cat in it are mere figures of rhetoric, the poet describes how he literally looks inside himself: his eyes turn irresistibly inward ("Se retournent docilement"), like well-oiled ball bearings rotating 180 degrees under the steady pull of a magnet ("Tirés comme par un aimant"). This movement is both machinelike and involuntary, beyond the poet's control; although he claims in line 33 to love the cat, he makes no con-scious decision to look at it. And considering his supposed familiarity with the cat, he is unaccountably surprised by what he sees:

> Je vois avec étonnement
> Le feu de ses prunelles pâles,
> Clairs fanaux, vivantes opales,
> Qui me contemplent fixement.

The poet's "étonnement" seems to come partly from the pale but fiery shine of the cat's eyes, as if he had never before seen the bizarre gleam of feline eyeballs in a dark room. But he is more astounded by the strange fixity of the cat's gaze. Coming from eyes that resemble "Clairs fanaux," this gaze would appear to hold out the promise of meaning, like lighthouse lamps signaling to ships or inn lanterns beckoning to travelers. Yet this promise is never fulfilled: the poem abruptly ends before the gaze has been deciphered, as if the poet cannot bring himself to admit that the cat's message to him—rendered first with its voice and now with its eyes—is still incomprehensible. Describing these enigmatic eyes as "vivantes opales," the poet cannot seem to decide whether their light comes from the intelligence of a live, communicative being or rather from the blank, meaningless surface of a stone. So although he is now glued eyeball to eyeball with the cat, the poet can find no way either to understand the creature inside his brain or to write about it adequately for the readers outside. If there is a message, it cannot be understood and will never be transmitted.

In the course of "Le Chat," then, relations between the poet and his inner cat seem to change considerably but never become completely clear. Portrayed in sequence as a harmonious voice, an overpowering perfume, a haunting judge, and a fixed gaze, the cat nonetheless remains a perpetual enigma: always apparently on the point of understanding one another, the poet and the cat never quite achieve a meaningful rapport. As a result, it grows more and more difficult to tell which of the protagonists involved in this poem is more frustratingly trapped. Is it the cat, imprisoned in the poet's mind and unable to penetrate its shadowy depths ("mon fonds le plus ténébreux") even with its miraculous voice and its burning eyes? Or is it the poet (and, by extension, interested readers who depend on him), bizarrely unable to communicate with the creature that makes its home in his head, rubbing its furry sides along his brainpan? What looked at first like a playful picture of the poet and his muse now looks instead like a fruitless confrontation between two prisoners of a misunderstanding.

To feel more fully the strangeness of this misunderstanding, it may be helpful to compare it briefly with a less troubled, more straightforward representation of the rapport between a muse and a poet. In his well-known "Nuits," a group of four loosely related poems published between 1835 and 1838, Alfred de Musset explores the mutually supportive intimacy between a romantic poet and his inspiring muse. However unlikely the comparison may appear, some of the situations evoked in the "Nuits" and in "Le Chat" are—superficially, at least—very similar. Musset's muse is a blond-haired, feminine, goddesslike being who exercises magical powers over the poet's mind. Like Baudelaire's pair, Musset's poet and muse relate to one another in the manner of perfectly tuned and harmonious instruments; the muse famously begins "La Nuit de mai" by demanding, "Poète, prends ton luth et me donne un baiser," while the poet reciprocates in "La Nuit d'octobre" by saying, "Prends cette lyre, approche, et laisse ma mémoire / Au son de tes accords doucement s'éveiller." Also in this latter poem, the last of the four "Nuits," the poet's attention ultimately shifts from the sound of the muse's lyre to the scent of a "pelouse embaumée" and then to the sight of a "premier rayon du soleil," thus following the same sensory progression from hearing to smell to sight as in "Le Chat." Furthermore, "La Nuit de mai," "La Nuit d'août," and "La Nuit d'octobre" all focus on the comings and goings in the poet's "cabinet d'étude," just as "Le Chat" centers on the brain/apartment/empire that forms the place of poetic production (Musset 35, 52, 59, 53).

These similarities are striking enough to suggest that perhaps "Le Chat" and the "Nuits" embody—with individual variations—a similar, romantic understanding of inspiration in the same basic image of the muse. But the differences between the two works are even more striking, which implies instead that if "Le Chat" meets the "Nuits" on common ground, it does so more to challenge or subvert the romantic tradition than to join with it. The first difference to note concerns the purely nonlinguistic powers of expression and persuasion attributed to the muse in "Le Chat." In sharp contrast, the muse of the "Nuits" seems almost verbose. Her long speeches, in precisely calculated alexandrine verse, could hardly be more unlike the wordless, ecstasy-filled utterances attributed to the Baudelairean cat-muse and reported secondhand in a few laconic, octosyllabic quatrains. In addition, Musset's muse enters consistently into genuine communication with his poet; except for "La Nuit d'octobre," all the poems are formally structured as dialogues between "La muse" and "Le poète," an arrangement that diverges markedly from the single abortive attempt at conversation between the poet and his cat-muse in Baudelaire's poem.

Not only does Musset's muse remain articulate throughout her association with the poet, but she also retains her unambiguously feminine identity. Whereas the cat-muse's femininity is never fully established and evaporates toward the end of "Le Chat," the "Nuits" muse wields feminine charm to growing advantage. She does so partly by necessity, since this muse is obliged to compete for the poet's love with a human woman whose attractions are more concrete. By the "Nuit d'octobre," however, the muse has won the contest, proving herself more faithful than any mortal lover and thereby seducing the poet back to work on his poems. At the same time, this persevering muse manages to lure the poet once more into his study, the hearth to which he must return in order to receive new inspiration. In "La Nuit d'août," the muse at first laments her beloved's prolonged absences from his study, claiming that "Ton cabinet d'étude est vide quand j'arrive" and that in consequence "Rien ne réveille plus votre lyre muette" (47–48). When the poet breezily hints that he has been spending all his time with another lover, the muse warns him that his poetic talent is vitally rooted in his study—the "home" ("demeure") where she is accustomed to meeting him (47)—and that the way back into this center and source of his creative power may not always be open to him:

> Crois-tu qu'en te cherchant tu te retrouveras?
> De ton cœur ou de toi lequel est le poète?
> C'est ton cœur, et ton cœur ne te répondra pas. (49)

The poet does not listen to this warning until "La Nuit d'octobre," by which time he has been betrayed by his human mistress and is glad to be reunited with the muse at the heart of his poetic domain: "nous voilà seuls, assis près du foyer" (52). And once their reunion has taken place, the poet and the muse are once again free, as they were at the opening of "La Nuit de mai," to explore the countryside surrounding the "cabinet d'étude," thus drawing inspiration from both the domestic comfort inside their "foyer" and the beautiful scenery outside it.

This is the most crucial difference between Baudelaire's poem and Musset's. The "Chat" muse is contained within the strange "appartement" of the poet's brain, unable to send reliable messages to the poet or, via the poet, to readers. One might even say that this feline muse is trapped inside the limits and confusions of the poet's words: like a house pet meowing to be let in or to be let out, in endless alternation, this brain cat always feels itself caught on the wrong side of either a mind filled with abstractions or a room filled with fur; half muse, half animal, it paces skittishly along the divide between the figurative and the literal. The "Nuits" muse, in contrast, enjoys much greater liberty. She freely meets the poet in his homey "cabinet d'étude" and just as freely goes with him outside it; the two of them engage in long, wordy exchanges untroubled by language barriers. Musset's poet, moreover, serenely accepts the division between his own concrete existence and his muse's abstract status. Content to understand her as a "spectre" (40) that figuratively walks into his head when he literally walks into his study, the poet feels no serious anguish at the task of moving linguistically from the muse inside his mind to the world outside it. Therefore, when his muse warningly questions him about this task ("Crois-tu qu'en te cherchant tu te retrouveras? / De ton cœur ou de toi lequel est le poète?"), he has reason to be confident: however far he may wander into the outside world, he will soon be reconciled with his inside muse, that is, with his own heart, with himself. It is precisely this reconciliation that never happens in "Le Chat." Baudelaire's poet is never united with his muse, inside or outside his head; the poem ends with a final, mutually uncomprehending clash of eyes as the poet gazes simultaneously into and out of himself. Breaking with romantic tradition as well as with the poet's desire, Baudelaire's "Chat" stares straight at the difficulty (the impossibility?) of representing either the nature of poetic inspiration or the workings of poetic language.

Chapter 9

"L'Invitation au voyage"

K A R E N   A .   H A R R I N G T O N

> Mon enfant, ma sœur,
> Songe à la douceur
> D'aller là-bas vivre ensemble!
> Aimer à loisir,
> Aimer et mourir
> Au pays qui te ressemble!   (6)
> Les soleils mouillés
> De ces ciels brouillés
> Pour mon esprit ont les charmes
> Si mystérieux
> De tes traîtres yeux,
> Brillant à travers leurs larmes.   (12)
>
> Là, tout n'est qu'ordre et beauté,
> Luxe, calme et volupté.
>
> Des meubles luisants,
> Polis par les ans,
> Décoreraient notre chambre;
> Les plus rares fleurs
> Mêlant leurs odeurs
> Aux vagues senteurs de l'ambre,   (20)
> Les riches plafonds,
> Les miroirs profonds,
> La splendeur orientale,
> Tout y parlerait
> A l'âme en secret
> Sa douce langue natale.   (26)
>
> Là, tout n'est qu'ordre et beauté,
> Luxe, calme et volupté.

Vois sur ces canaux
Dormir ces vaisseaux
Dont l'humeur est vagabonde;
C'est pour assouvir
Ton moindre désir
Qu'ils viennent du bout du monde. (34)
—Les soleils couchants
Revêtent les champs,
Les canaux, la ville entière,
D'hyacinthe et d'or;
Le monde s'endort
Dans une chaude lumière. (40)

Là, tout n'est qu'ordre et beauté,
Luxe, calme et volupté.

Much of Baudelaire's poetry is framed by ambiguities and paradoxes that immobilize and confine the poetic self to a deterministic world. No teleologic vision guides and moves the self forward. On the contrary, his position is analogous to Mallarmé's portrayal of the swan in "Le vierge, le vivace et le bel aujourd'hui," which, though foreseeing potential freedom, remains trapped in the ice.

The figure of the self as "déjà condamné" stems from a Manichaean perspective that Baudelaire attributes to the fall of Adam and Eve. Analyzing the nature of laughter in *De l'essence du rire*, he espouses this dualistic stance: "le rire humain est intimement lié à l'accident d'une chute ancienne, d'une dégradation physique et morale. . . . Dans le paradis terrestre . . . c'est-à-dire dans le milieu où il semblait à l'homme que toutes les choses créées étaient bonnes, la joie n'était pas dans le rire" (*OC* II, 527–28). Whereas joy expresses wholeness, laughter is contradictory and corresponds to the duality of human nature. Baudelaire's view of laughter as a sign of both superiority and weakness (*OC* II, 530) informs the irreconcilable ironic stance of the poetic persona in his poetry.

Yet sparks of hope, sporadically strewn throughout Baudelaire's works in the form of poetic reverie, point to the retrieval of the Edenic paradise as a possible way of overcoming this inherent duality. Reverie should not be confused with dreams in general. In *La Poétique*

de la rêverie, Gaston Bachelard argues that dreams and dream imagery
are aimed at the real, often as a response to a particular event or per-
son: "Le rêve reste surchargé des passions mal vécues du jour" (13).
Reverie, on the other hand, releases us from our connection to the
real: "on voit bien qu'elle est le témoignage d'une *fonction de l'irréel,*
fonction normale, fonction utile, qui garde le psychisme humain, en
marge de toutes les brutalités d'un non-moi hostile, d'un non-moi
étranger" (12). In reverie, the subject turns away from the real and is
free to give shape and meaning to his own conception of the imagi-
nary. When Baudelaire's poetry mirrors this view of reverie, it points
forward and involves expansive movement through which the figure
of the self breaks loose from worldly confines. In the realm of the
imaginary, the retrieval of the Edenic ideal becomes a potential, albeit
rarely successful, endeavor.

Reverie is not, however, merely a rhetorical figure that Baudelaire
intersperses in his poetry: it also reflects his desire to seize and trans-
form the world to offset the devastating effects of his "spleen." Unlike
irony, which undermines or destroys the object or person being
embellished, while distancing the self from the object of desire ("A
une madone"), reverie favors transfiguration as the poetic self mimet-
ically identifies with the object of embellishment, thus reducing the
distance between self and other.

In "L'Invitation au voyage," Baudelaire transfigures the image of
the woman by associating her with the scenery of the exotic country
that is the aim of his voyage. The poem highlights an expansive move-
ment animated by the relation between the sensory perceptions and
the interaction of the woman's absence and presence. Calling on the
woman to join him, the poet views her presence as the springboard
initiating his reverie. But visual light and color imagery paradoxically
emerge to overshadow her presence, revealing the predominance of
the sensory associations in prolonging the poet's reverie.

To illuminate this interplay, I shall turn to Baudelaire's critical writ-
ings concerning the depiction of imagery through sensory perceptions.
Those poems in which sensory perceptions minimize the self-other
conflict and contribute to a sense of harmony and well-being ("Parfum
exotique," "La Chevelure," and "Le Serpent qui danse," to name a
few) point to the external force that Baudelaire's theory of correspon-
dances imposes on the work. Espousing this concept in *Richard Wagner
et Tannhäuser à Paris,* Baudelaire advances the notion that synesthetic
associations can elicit similar responses in different people:

> La véritable musique suggère des idées analogues dans des cerveaux différents. D'ailleurs, il ne serait pas ridicule de raisonner *à priori*, sans analyse et sans comparaisons; car ce qui serait vraiment surprenant, c'est que le son *ne pût pas* suggérer la couleur, que les couleurs *ne pussent pas* donner l'idée d'une mélodie, et que le son et la couleur fussent impropres à traduire des idées; les choses s'étant toujours exprimées par une analogie réciproque, depuis le jour où Dieu a proféré le monde comme une complexe et indivisible totalité. (*OC* II, 784)

Baudelaire then shows the common thread running through his reverie and the reverie of Wagner and Liszt as they listen to *Tannhäuser*. Similarly, in "L'Invitation au voyage" visual imagery fuses with the portrayal of the woman, showing that sensory associations overshadow her presence and, as we shall see in the second stanza, give rise to cosmic and universal reverie.

"L'Invitation au voyage" also accentuates poetic reverie as a departure from reality, thus setting it apart from those poems ("La Cloche fêlée," "L'Héautontimorouménos," and the "Spleen" poems, for example) in which the poetic self is unable to escape the ironic self-awareness of his status as "déjà condamné." More specifically, it is an escape from the city (Paris), which so often heightens Baudelaire's sense of stagnation, paralysis, and doom. Paris is a paradoxical symbol of excitement and vitality coupled with debauchery, sloth, and vice, all of which Baudelaire portrays with much fervor. John Johnston comments on this intensity: "What we see of Paris is created mainly in terms of the poet's imaginative intensification, but it lacks the moral overtones that one finds in his poems about the city and posits, instead, an ideal to counteract the moral decay of the large city." At the same time, as Johnston points out, the image of Paris remains an intrinsic backdrop to "L'Invitation au voyage" (13), for it is a constant reminder of the need to construct an ideal to escape from reality.

The implied intrusion of the city's harshness does not, however, diminish the intensity of the poet's dream world. On the contrary, as in "Parfum exotique" and "La Chevelure," imaginative intensification aims at attenuating the exigencies of reality and is enhanced by the intermediary role of the woman. In all three poems the poetic self projects a form of the ideal upon an idyllic setting by invoking the presence of the woman. But unlike the tropical paradise that "Parfum exotique" and "La Chevelure" evoke, "L'Invitation au voyage" describes an exotic country that attracts us with its oriental and mysterious characteristics. Many critics have suggested Holland as the poem's setting, citing both the exotic charm that it exerted on the French at that time and the influence of Dutch painters. According to Jacques Beauverd, "C'est là une Hollande lointaine et fabuleuse telle que le poète pouvait l'imaginer à travers les souvenirs de l'escale qu'il avait faite au Cap de Bonne-Espérance, terre à la fois hollandaise et exotique" (746–47). Unlike those who emphasize the correlation between the woman and the scenery as the impetus for the poet's reverie, Beauverd suggests that "L'Invitation au voyage" was inspired by a museum painting: "Dans 'L'Invitation au voyage,' le poète et son amie sont *physiquement en train de regarder des tableaux hollandais dans un musée, ou d'en feuilleter un album de reproductions. Et c'est la peinture précise et réelle que l'un et l'autre ont sous les yeux que désigne et invoque comme support de rêverie le poète à son amie.* De plus, il ne s'agit pas seulement, comme dans 'Les Phares,' d'une série *rêvée* de 'transpositions d'art': on devine que le poète et son amie *se déplacent* devant les tableaux (ou tournent les pages d'une série de reproductions). . . . Quoi qu'il en soit, nous avons, *strophe à strophe,* une rêverie sur une série de tableaux successifs" (747). The amorphous features of this country are shrouded in the mystery of their haziness ("les soleils mouillés de ces ciels brouillés") and provide an ideal frame of reference for the foreground work of the poet's intensification. "L'Invitation au voyage" celebrates the haziness of the land as the junction where reality gives way to reverie.

The poet's dream begins when he calls on the woman to join him in his journey. Immediately, we note the platonic or even fraternal relationship between the poetic self and the woman ("Mon enfant, ma sœur"). Though ambiguous, this line nonetheless establishes the woman's nonthreatening role. She is also closely associated with the description of the landscape as the poet takes care to show that her enticing charms interact with those of the countryside. Through her, he envisions an escape to a "never-never" land. The prose poem of the same title, though different in tone and tenor, refers to such a land of make-believe: "Il est un pays superbe, un pays de Cocagne, dit-on, que je rêve de visiter avec une vieille amie" (*OC* I, 301), reassuring us that it does indeed exist. Using the woman to usher in his reverie, the poet expresses his desire to communicate and share this experience: "Mon enfant, ma sœur, / Songe à la douceur / D'aller là-bas vivre ensemble!" The verb "songer" intensifies the poem's dream mode because, through memory, imagination, or an association of ideas, it conveys the power to evoke or to conjure up images and imagery. The poet's reverie is also extended by the infinitives ("Aimer à loisir / Aimer et mourir") that connote the timelessness that characterizes expansive reverie. Fear of death is absent from this tranquil setting, as the verb "mourir" neither suggests negativity nor imparts a sense of finality as it does in so much of Baudelaire's poetry. Roger Bauer argues that Baudelaire's dream vision "est le fruit d'une fantaisie désireuse d'atteindre l'absolu et ne craignant pas pour cela d'affronter la Mort et Satan. Désormais le rêve signifie l'aventure et point seulement l'attente et l'espoir" (57).

Ordinary limits of time and space have no importance in reverie, thus creating a temporal and spatial vacuum. For example, the country the poet evokes remains nameless, but it certainly becomes central to his project of fleeing the noxiousness of the city and the constraints of reality. Georges Poulet captures the amorphous nature of Baudelairean reverie when he says:

> Le rêve de bonheur qui le transporte dans une Inde ou dans une Hollande imaginaire, le transfère idéalement dans un lieu où il lui semble loisible de se retrouver tel qu'il était ou tel qu'il devait être, avant la faute, dans l'état que les théologiens qualifient de pure nature. Néanmoins, sans insister dès à présent sur ces voyages qui ont pour destination un pays allégorique, il convient de remarquer que le voyage baudelairien, s'entend le voyage mental, manque aussi bien de destination que de terme: car 'les vrais voyageurs sont ceux-là seuls qui partent pour partir.' Ils vont ils ne savent où. Et si, en fin de compte, comme but de leur course, ils choisissent la mort, c'est que celle-ci n'est pas une destination positive. Elle n'est pas un *lieu* déterminé ou déterminable. Elle est simplement un *là-bas*, aussi différent que possible de l'*ici* détesté. (22)

Thus timelessness and indefiniteness, where boundaries between life and death are diminished, form the essence of Baudelairean reverie, with the accent on a state of vagueness. Spatially, we witness the fusion of the woman and the scenery ("au pays qui te ressemble") to the extent that one recalls the other in the poet's imagination. Visually, the synesthetic pleasure the poet derives from his reverie occurs through the woman's presence, which conjures up visual images of the new and enchanting country. Though olfactory images are predominant in most of Baudelaire's poetry, "L'Invitation au voy-

age" highlights, instead, visual imagery that fashions the poet's rever-
ie. It reflects the strength of the poet's imaginative faculties as he por-
trays a beguiling and captivating landscape intricately associated
with the woman's presence.

Overcast skies also blur temporal and spatial restraints, allowing
one to delight in reverie's seductiveness. They combine with the sun
and exert their own fascinating charm, to which the poet compares
the woman's eyes. The adjective "mystérieux" bonds her presence to
the visual landscape and creates an uncertain though nonetheless
enticing atmosphere with a touch of doubt, and perhaps even of dan-
ger, creeping into this symbiotic relation as the poet refers to her
"traîtres yeux." A few words need to be addressed to the ambiguity
in the adjectives "mystérieux" and "traîtres," for it would appear that
they threaten the harmony suggested by the poem. Women in
Baudelaire's poetry often pose a threat to the well-being of the poetic
self. They are to be feared, distrusted, and at times, even hated. One
must avoid placing one's hopes, dreams, and desires in them,
because, as Baudelaire says in several poems, they are cruel, cold, and
indifferent.

The context of "L'Invitation au voyage," however, does not war-
rant such an explanation. Though Baudelaire often uses the adjective
"mystérieux" to describe the uncertainty of women and cats, it does
not have an inherent negative connotation. In "Ciel brouillé," for
example, "mystérieux" underscores the ambiguity in the color of the
woman's eyes: "Ton œil mystérieux (est-il bleu, gris ou vert?)" (*OC* I,
49). As in "L'Invitation au voyage," "Ciel brouillé" emphasizes these
resemblances between the woman and the surroundings. With her
alluring manner, she attracts the poet and compels him to wonder if
he will discover within her "plaisirs plus aigus que la glace et le fer"
of the implacable winter. Similarly, in "L'Invitation au voyage" the
poet is drawn to the mysterious and unknown charm of the
woman's eyes, not knowing whether danger awaits, for in her
"traîtres yeux" lies the potential to betray. If any danger is implied
in the adjectives "mystérieux" and "traîtres," however, it owes more
to the unknown nature of the voyage itself. Yet the poet never ques-
tions the step into the unknown. In "Chant d'automne," "mys-
térieux" has a comparable effect ("ce bruit mystérieux sonne comme
un départ"), revealing that though the journey to the unknown
could entail possible danger, it could also be an auspicious invitation
to follow (*OC* I, 57).

Along with the evocative force of "mystérieux" and "tes traîtres yeux," the word "charmes" has the power to draw both reader and poet into this voyage of the unknown. In its etymological definition, "charme" is analogous to a magical spell capable of exerting considerable influence over its subjects. In "Un Fantôme," Baudelaire refers to particular fragrances whose "charme profond" casts a spell that transforms the past into the present. "L'Invitation au voyage" parallels "Un Fantôme" in that the charm of the woman's eyes, symbiotically linked to the charm of the countryside, casts a spell over both reader and poet. Through this association, not only does Baudelaire transfigure and embellish the description of the woman, he also minimizes her potential danger and is thus able to flee momentarily the devastating effects that one finds in his "Spleen" poems.

At the same time, we are reminded that the trip's destination is less important than what it affords the poet (Poulet 22). Taking leave of the status quo, he searches for an ideal, for something new or different. That Baudelaire has a conception of this ideal runs consistently throughout his poetry, and we note its link to the past: "Rien de plus rigoureusement conçu par Baudelaire que ce système des deux passés, d'un passé radieux et paradisiaque, suivi d'un autre passé, celui-ci ténébreux et irréparable" (Poulet 16). In "Le Voyage" the poetic voice refers to the ultimate voyage, death, as a longing to find what is missing in his life: "Au fond de l'Inconnu pour trouver du *nouveau!*" Though this poem is a desperate realization that no hope remains in this worldly life and that both past and present are filled with dark shadows, "L'Invitation au voyage" still envisions the former, radiant past transposed upon the present as an alternative to the drudgery of daily life. The exotic land thus becomes a refuge and a prelude to the personal and intimate reverie that we find in the second stanza.

No longer focusing on the woman, the poet's reverie leads us from the outside to the inside, to the bedroom where the poet celebrates the splendor and charm of the hearth. Whereas the first stanza links the woman to the new and enchanting land, the visual imagery now consumes her presence. Emphasis is placed instead on the intimacy that emanates from the room and fills the poet's senses. Though the shift from the exterior to the interior restricts our vision, it does not suggest an obstructive enclosure. On the contrary, the room's various objects (shiny furniture polished by time, elegant ceilings and mirrors, rare flowers that combine with the hint of exotic fragrances) are filled with expansive movement and communicative harmony that intensify and extend the poet's reverie. Recalling the poem's title, these objects invite us to enjoy the luminous and gleaming effect they exude. The reflective play of the mirrors and the polished and shiny furniture reverberates to create a kaleidoscopic impression of an endless expansion. Olfactory imagery is also instrumental in securing the poet's reverie. The fragrances of rare flowers and amber recall the last two stanzas of "Correspondances":

> Il est des parfums frais comme des chairs d'enfants,
> Doux comme les hautbois, verts comme les prairies,
> —Et d'autres, corrumpus, riches et triomphants,
>
> Ayant l'expansion des choses infinies,
> Comme l'ambre, le musc, le benjoin et l'encens,
> Qui chantent les transports de l'esprit et des sens. (*OC* I, 11)

Amber is one of those fragrances ("riches et triomphants") also capable of provoking an infinite feeling of expansion. In "L'Invitation au voyage" it plays a similar role: the furniture, mirrors, rare fragrances, and amber combine to create a spiritual accord of which Baudelaire says, "Tout y parlerait / A l'âme en secret / Sa douce langue natale." This serene harmony reaches beyond spatial and temporal boundaries to overcome the exigencies of the present, with the visual and olfactory sensations enabling the poet to pass from the real to the imaginary. Emmanuel Adatte emphasizes the crucial role of imagination in allowing the poet to surpass the real:

> L'imagination permet ainsi à Baudelaire de s'assurer une victoire imaginaire sur le monde, en surmontant l'opposition entre le réel tel qu'il est vécu par lui et le réel tel qu'il voudrait qu'il fût. Cette tension permanente entre être et vouloir être, existence vécue et existence rêvée suscite dans l'âme de Baudelaire le besoin absolu de recréer et de restructurer le monde de telle manière que le réel, dépassé, coïncide avec le monde qu'il a intérieurement désiré. C'est ainsi que Baudelaire peut écrire: "La Poésie est ce qu'il y a de plus réel, c'est ce qui n'est complètement vrai que dans *un autre monde*." (14)

"L'Invitation au voyage" is thus an example of how Baudelaire transfigures the woman and country (first stanza) to recreate a world that conforms to the ideals of his dream (second stanza). His reverie takes full shape and transports us to this "autre monde" of "splendeur orientale" (23). The hint of Orientalism, with its accent on the exotic, adds the finishing touches in the transition to this place where the notions of time and space are suspended. The timelessness of this poem diametrically opposes the spleen poems, which are anchored to the here and now. In "L'Invitation au voyage" Baudelaire's reverie underscores the retrieval of a paradisiacal past as a potentially attainable ideal. The first two stanzas point to this step out of time: the infinitives of the first stanza eliminate a specific time reference and give rise to the conditional verbs in the second stanza, thereby opening the way to a move beyond time, to the world of the unreal. The conditional mode complements poetic reverie by establishing the unreal as the frame of reference within which the poet can explore the possibilities of the expansive and unrestrained movement characteristic of reverie.

Paradoxically, the expansive reverie of the second stanza does not actively include the woman. Though she initiates the poet's dream, her presence here has been overshadowed. Leo Bersani shows that Baudelaire's impression of women accounts for the problematic status of their absence and presence: "The woman exists for Baudelaire, not in order to satisfy his desires, but in order to produce them" (39). Bersani is speaking specifically of "La Chevelure," but one can similarly argue that the woman in "L'Invitation au voyage," vital in inaugurating the poet's dream, does not, however, sustain it. Through her, he envisions a move beyond the real, but she loses her identity. The only reference to her comes in the form of "notre chambre." Even this mention has only a minimal effect, for it is the room, not the woman, that becomes the object of the poet's reverie.

The third stanza begins by ambiguously evoking the woman's presence and showing that, within the poet's reverie, her desires are satisfied. Referring to the peaceful setting of ships harbored in the canals, Baudelaire says, "C'est pour assouvir / Ton moindre désir / Qu'ils viennent du bout du monde." Though she may not directly satisfy the poet's desires, her embellishment and transfiguration lead to the cosmic reverie of this stanza and create a state of well-being.

The tranquillity of the lines "Dormir ces vaisseaux" and "Le monde s'endort dans une chaude lumière" further underscores the harmony of the poet's reverie. Yet Baudelaire writes that the ships' immobility goes against their nature ("Dont l'humeur est vagabonde"), for they are now enclosed in the limited confines of the canals instead of traveling freely on the open seas. Does this dormancy threaten reverie's expansive momentum? Ivan Barko contends that, on the contrary, the immobility of "L'Invitation au voyage" has a peaceful effect that allows the poet's reverie to flourish fully: "La force du mouvement est enfin dominée et maîtrisée, sans être pourtant abolie, et le poème se termine sur le spectacle d'un paysage lui-même médiateur d'une nature humanisée ('champs,' 'canaux,' 'ville') et d'un soleil couchant qui incarne le grant moment médiateur du crépuscule du soir, où le jour se joint à la nuit" ("La méditation," 186). This junction marks the culmination of Baudelaire's reverie as it resolves two contradictory tendencies, "le désir du mouvement et le désir du repos" (185). Far from inhibiting reverie's movement, the calm and stillness of both land and sea allow it to dissipate "dans une chaude lumière."

Such peaceful quiescence is infrequent in Baudelaire's poetry and is primarily associated with dreams or reverie. More often than not, however, immobility designates an undesirable and negative state. In "Je suis comme le roi d'un pays pluvieux," for example, it sets in as ennui. Though the poem is filled with movement and action, it contrasts with poet's sense of futility. He is compared to a rich but lethargic and bored king. All the people surrounding the king cannot draw him out of his lassitude. Even the alchemist's remedy is insufficient to revive him, for his blood has been replaced by the green waters of the river Lethe, which saps him of all vitality.

From the beginning, the poet is already incapacitated by his defeated position. We do not know how he arrived at such a helpless state, which makes the poem all the more pathetic. It is almost irrelevant to question how he got there, however, for we sense that he has no hope of overcoming his immobilization.

Like many other poems in *Les Fleurs du Mal* showing the paralyzing effects of immobilization, "Je suis comme le roi d'un pays pluvieux" contrasts strikingly with the immobility of "L'Invitation au voyage," in which immobility, synonymous with tranquillity and rest, does not inhibit the free expression of reverie. Those poems that illustrate the positive features of immobility point to quiescence as a move from the real to the unreal. The first two stanzas of "La Vie antérieure," for example, possibly evoke the distant world of the imagination or perhaps the hazy memories of a former time blurred by the merging of waves and sky to form the "tout-puissants accords de leur riche musique." Immobility is especially linked to quiescence in the third stanza: "C'est là que j'ai vécu dans les voluptés calmes" (*OC* I, 17–18). The "voluptés calmes" convey a sense of serenity that transcends the real and revitalizes memories. Suggestive of the calm and harmony in "L'Invitation au voyage," the tranquility of the scene contributes to the poet's expansive reverie with its suspension of time.

Both "La Vie antérieure" and "L'Invitation au voyage" thus represent a triumph over the pernicious ennui of the spleen poems. In the third stanza of "L'Invitation au voyage," Baudelaire's theory of imagination is vital in warding off any potential paralysis: nature, dream, and city join in a conciliatory manner to attenuate and transform the harshness of the real ("Les soleils couchants / Revêtent les champs, / Les canaux, la ville entière, / D'hyacinthe et d'or"). Though nature and city are often antagonistic in Baudelaire's poetry, they dwell peacefully here "dans une chaude lumière." The warm light acts like a blanket to protect and nurture the serenity of the landscape; however, unlike a blanket, which conceals its contents, the light's force radiates outward to illuminate and expand the poet's reverie. (This opposes the "Spleen" poem "Quand le ciel bas et lourd pèse comme un couvercle," which closes in and traps the poet's ennui.)

The harmony of the poet's reverie is further highlighted by the structure of the three stanzas: the alternation of two lines of five syllables and one line of seven syllables produces a steady and continuous rocking that prolongs the infinitude of the moment. As Jean-Pierre Richard says, "Le bonheur du bercement, que chante Baudelaire en termes inoubliables tient à sa paix, à son harmonie, à son accord profond avec l'être qui l'accueille en lui. Son mouvement de va-et-vient équilibre et balance la vie autour d'un pivot fixe" (*Poésie,* 142). The poem's anchored structure tempers any dangerous and unbridled movement and makes possible a solid and expansive reverie wrapped ever so gently in the blanket of "chaude lumière."

The refrain, "Là, tout n'est qu'ordre et beauté / Luxe, calme et volupté," tops off the poet's reverie; repeated after each stanza, it has a stabilizing effect as an affirmation of Baudelaire's belief that a place of order and beauty is possible. The reference to the indeterminate "là" is an antidote to the stark reality of our mundane existence; it is a place of calm, beauty, and opulence without discord. The pairing of "calme" and "volupté" reminds us of "les voluptés calmes" of "La Vie antérieure": it signifies the felicitous accord between two potentially threatening emotions, excessive pleasure ("volupté") and tedious boredom ("calme"), in which each adjective neutralizes the negative potential of the other, thereby creating an atmosphere of contentment. This harmony echos Baudelaire's appreciation of time and space, which intensify an ecstatic awareness of living: "Il y a des moments de l'existence où le temps et l'étendue sont plus profonds, et le sentiment de l'existence immensément augmenté" (*OC* I, 658). "L'Invitation au voyage" is a testament revealing such privileged, though rare, moments when the triumph of will and the reconciliation of the *coincidentia oppositorum* prevail over all obstacles.

"Le Cygne" of Baudelaire

GÉRARD GASARIAN

I

Andromaque, je pense à vous! ce petit fleuve,
Pauvre et triste miroir où jadis resplendit
L'immense majesté de vos douleurs de veuve,
Ce Simoïs menteur qui par vos pleurs grandit,   (4)

A fécondé soudain ma mémoire fertile,
Comme je traversais le nouveau Carrousel.
Le vieux Paris n'est plus (la forme d'une ville
Change plus vite, hélas! que le cœur d'un mortel);   (8)

Je ne vois qu'en esprit tout ce camp de baraques,
Ces tas de chapiteaux ébauchés et de fûts,
Les herbes, les gros blocs verdis par l'eau des flaques,
Et, brillant aux carreaux, le bric-à-brac confus.   (12)

Là s'étalait jadis une ménagerie;
Là je vis, un matin, à l'heure où sous les cieux
Froids et clairs le Travail s'éveille, où la voirie
Pousse un sombre ouragan dans l'air silencieux,   (16)

Un cygne qui s'était évadé de sa cage,
Et, de ses pieds palmés frottant le pavé sec,
Sur le sol raboteux traînait son blanc plumage.
Près d'un ruisseau sans eau la bête ouvrant le bec   (20)

Baignait nerveusement ses ailes dans la poudre,
Et disait, le cœur plein de son beau lac natal:
"Eau, quand donc pleuvras-tu? quand tonneras-tu, foudre?"
Je vois ce malheureux, mythe étrange et fatal,   (24)

Vers le ciel quelquefois, comme l'homme d'Ovide,
Vers le ciel ironique et cruellement bleu,
Sur son cou convulsif tendant sa tête avide,
Comme s'il adressait des reproches à Dieu!   (28)

II

Paris change! mais rien dans ma mélancolie
N'a bougé! palais neufs, échafaudages, blocs,
Vieux faubourgs, tout pour moi devient allégorie,
Et mes chers souvenirs sont plus lourds que des rocs.   (32)

Aussi devant ce Louvre une image m'opprime:
Je pense à mon grand cygne, avec ses gestes fous,
Comme les exilés, ridicule et sublime,
Et rongé d'un désir sans trêve! et puis à vous,   (36)

Andromaque, des bras d'un grand époux tombée,
Vil bétail, sous la main du superbe Pyrrhus,
Auprès d'un tombeau vide en extase courbée;
Veuve d'Hector, hélas! et femme d'Hélénus!   (40)

Je pense à la négresse, amaigrie et phtisique,
Piétinant dans la boue, et cherchant, l'œil hagard,
Les cocotiers absents de la superbe Afrique
Derrière la muraille immense du brouillard;   (44)

A quiconque a perdu ce qui ne se retrouve
Jamais, jamais! à ceux qui s'abreuvent de pleurs
Et tettent la Douleur comme une bonne louve!
Aux maigres orphelins séchant comme des fleurs!   (48)

Ainsi dans la forêt où mon esprit s'exile
Un vieux Souvenir sonne à plein souffle du cor!
Je pense aux matelots oubliés dans une île,
Aux captifs, aux vaincus! . . . à bien d'autres encor!   (52)

From the very first reading of "Le Cygne," one is struck by a blatant disproportion. Obviously, there is more in the text than meets the eye in the title. Unlike other poems (such as "Correspondances," "La Vie antérieure," "L'Invitation au voyage," and so forth) in which the main theme follows from the title, "Le Cygne" is not simply about a swan. And what it is also about becomes all the less simple as we attempt to ascertain it. From the ever more complex critical responses it elicits, this poem looks all the more difficult to read as our critical scrutiny increases. The complexity of "Le Cygne" has to do in large part with its central, most puzzling ambiguity. Unanimously perceived as the poem of melancholy, it is seen also—often by the same critics—as the poem of modernity. In order to account for this paradoxical view of the poem, most critics have sought to reconcile Baudelaire's *melancholic* sense of loss (mediated in the first part by the opening figure of Andromache) with his *modern* curiosity for the present (triggered in the second part by the transformation of Paris). For Victor Brombert, "Le Cygne" is a successful attempt to turn a painful memory into a modern artifact. For Ross Chambers ("'Je'") also, the poem manages to turn mourning into writing, bile into ink. Instead of wasting his mental energy in such acts as regretting or rebelling, the poet uses it to create works in which his opposition to the reactionary politics of his time is expressed in allegorical disguise. But the very attempt to harmonize and synchronize these two opposite postures is called into question by the poem itself. While empathizing with the swan and other melancholic figures that are sunk in their memories, Baudelaire is looking to the present in order to resist and escape their deadly depression. This dual experience is the experience of a duel, of an endless inner conflict between two opposite drives. And this conflict—behind and beyond the romantic figure highlighted in the title—may be seen as the dominant yet hidden theme of the poem.

In an initial apostrophe that seems to be consistent with traditional modes of lyric expression, the poet claims to be inspired by Andromache, a powerful literary figure who has captured his mind. Exiled from Troy after the death of Hector, Andromache wept over her dead husband above a false, "empty" tomb that she had built on the shore of an artificial river (the "Simoïs menteur"), in order to be reminded of the original, true Simoïs flowing through her native city. The way he thinks about her, however, is more intellectual than sentimental, less lyrical than analytical. Far from being obsessed by her as "la dame de ses pensées" (a traditional object of platonic love), he is "oppressed" by her as "la dame de sa pensée," taken in the most literal sense. Instead of simply expressing his feelings for her, he reflects on her as she instigates a coherent chain of thoughts leading from her to the swan (in the first part) and then from the swan back to her (in the second part), before veering toward other, more human types in the last three stanzas. The thought of Andromache, consistently expressed in the present indicative, is not simply a memory. Although she is remembered by Baudelaire as having once aroused his memory of a swan encountered earlier in his life, "jadis," before the transformation of Paris by Baron Haussmann, her image seems to be always present in his mind. As a permanent source of inspiration, she initiates and sustains the process of writing while also initiating and sustaining, as a fertile memory, the process of recollecting. In other words, she is tied to the act of writing the poem while being also related to a past experience recounted in the poem.

This dual, ambiguous status of Andromache is quite evident in the first two stanzas. On the syntactic level, these stanzas are clearly connected: "ce petit fleuve" (1) is the subject of "a fécondé" (5), which is rejected at the beginning of the second stanza. If we bracket lines 2–4 (a mere apposition providing a description of "ce petit fleuve") and lines 7–8 (a parenthetical comparison between cityscapes and human hearts), the syntactic backbone stands out as follows:

> Andromaque, je pense à vous! Ce petit fleuve (1)
> A fécondé soudain ma mémoire fertile, (5)
> Comme je traversais le nouveau Carrousel. (6)

In line 1, "ce petit fleuve" stands for Andromache, both as a metonymy (the river is part of her saga) and as a mirror image (the river is a "pauvre et triste miroir" reflecting her sorrow). Through this river with which she blends also by adding her tears to the flow, Andromache irrigates and "fecundates" the memory of the poet. But it happens in the past only (as he was crossing the "nouveau Carrousel"), not in the present (as he is writing and thinking about Andromache). The syntactic unity of the first two stanzas is both underlined and undermined by a temporal disjunction between present and past, thought and memory. Between line 1 and line 5, there is a surprising shift from a thought expressed in the present tense ("je pense") to a memory expressed in the past tense ("a fécondé"; "je traversais"). This temporal discontinuity is also highlighted by the exclamation mark of line one. Punctuating a present thought, this mark isolates it from a past recollection.

For most of the first part, the poem fluctuates between two competing, parallel perspectives that do not intersect before line 24. On the one hand, the thought process elicited by Andromache leads to an awareness of change (7–8) immediately followed by an epistemological discovery (9–12). In thinking of Andromache, for whom Troy is lost, the poet realizes that Paris also has changed ("Le vieux Paris n'est plus"). But instead of being overwhelmed with nostalgia, the poet reacts with a positive insight into his own art. The elegiac "hélas!" does not refer to the disappearance of the old Paris. It is interjected to lament the fact that human feelings do not change as fast as the shape of cities. Moreover, by simply saying "le vieux Paris," and not "mon vieux Paris," Baudelaire manages to remain emotionally detached from his own statement. He discovers that everything he envisions while writing, present or past, is seen in the same way: in the mind's eye ("Je ne vois qu'en esprit"). In this "tableau parisien," the city turns into a "bric-à-brac confus" where scenes of the past ("ce camp de baraques") coexist with contemporary sights ("ces tas de chapiteaux ébauchés et de fûts"). On the other hand, the second theme of the first line ("ce petit fleuve") leads not to a series of general observations but to a chain of personal memories. More precisely, it leads to the memory of an involuntary memory; it evokes a time in the past when the poet, crossing the construction site of the "nouveau Carrousel," suddenly remembered a still earlier time when, instead of "ce Louvre," he came face to face with a swan who had escaped from a zoo. Ironically, the swan was not better off for having freed itself from its cage, since the urban environment of its newly conquered freedom was even worse, more unnatural than the zoo. Still more ironically, the *new* environment of the swan was the *old* environment of the poet (his "vieux Paris"). If the latter identified with the swan's struggle for life, which he could do now that they shared the same surroundings, he could not help but feel estranged from his own familiar milieu.

As a powerful personal memory ("Là je vis . . . Un cygne"), the swan provokes a movement of sympathy allowing it to be seen by the poet as a self-metaphor. As a result, most critics are justified in perceiving the swan's distress as analogical to the poet's melancholy. If we substitute the "vieux Paris" for the "ménagerie," the condition of the swan can be seen to reflect that of the poet. But the analogy is made problematic by what makes it possible. In regretting the old Paris, the poet proves to be very much unlike what he is like, since he cannot help but long for what causes the swan's distress. The analogy, then, is invalidated by the very irony it entails. Irony works here to prevent the poet from losing himself in his analogical reflection. In that sense, it prepares the sudden shift from past to present in line 24. By affirming "Je vois ce malheureux," the poet returns to the present and retrieves his "présence d'esprit." In the light of the present indicative, the swan is no longer an object of longing but instead an object of thinking; it stops being a memory to become a myth; it escapes a personal past (that of the poet) to reach a universal, permanent present.

With the present tense of line 24, the swan turns out to be seen as a "myth," exactly like Andromache at the beginning. The first part ends where it began, with a vision no longer tied to a personal memory but relating instead to a universal myth. As it becomes a myth ("mythe étrange et fatal"), the swan escapes from its cage in the poet's memory to be seen instead in the mind's eye, like Paris and Andromache before. This return to a broader, more universal mode of vision is confirmed and completed at the beginning of part 2, when the swan is itself seen as a thought object leading back to the thought of Andromache ("je pense à mon grand cygne . . . et puis à vous, / Andromaque"). The writing process, one discovers in "Le Cygne," is governed by a "strange and fatal" tendency to move away from actual memories toward universal myths. The poet's memory of "*his* great swan" turns into a timeless representation (a "myth") and ends up being presented as a full-blooded allegory ("Un vieux Souvenir") whose poetic presence resonates only in the poet's mind, not in his memory: "Ainsi dans la forêt où mon esprit s'exile / Un vieux Souvenir sonne à plein souffle du cor!" The horn that blows at the end of the poem has lost the soft, distant, and sad sound it traditionally has in French lyric poetry (as in Vigny's "Le Cor" or Apollinaire's "Cors de chasse"). By raising the volume of the horn, which is blown here full blast, Baudelaire deliberately drowns the melancholic overtones of this romantic instrument. With its first letter capitalized, moreover, the old "Souvenir" turns into a timeless allegory that is disconnected from the poet's personal *souvenir*. As a universal abstraction, this "Souvenir" does not relate any longer to a particular individual experience, and the melancholic feelings it elicits, as a result, are no longer personal.

In the last stanza, where a final lesson follows logically (after the adverb "Ainsi") from the poem, the poet articulates a fundamental difference between himself and those who inhabit his thoughts. If "Andromaque," "le cygne," "Ovide," "la négresse," and so forth live in exile, they do not do so by choice. For them, exile is an existential ordeal that is not self-imposed. For the poet, on the contrary, exile is a deliberate intellectual experience. As he chooses to write, his mind takes off ("s'exile") to a "forêt" planted with symbols and other rhetorical figures (such as the allegorical "Souvenir" of line 50). This "forest of symbols" is itself metaphorical of a literary space where "everything turns to allegory." This crucial observation is made by the poet well before the end, at the beginning of part 2:

> Paris change! mais rien dans ma mélancolie
> N'a bougé! palais neufs, échafaudages, blocs,
> Vieux faubourgs, tout pour moi devient allégorie,
> Et mes chers souvenirs sont plus lourds que des rocs.

This crucial stanza is read by most critics as a clear, lyrical expression of Baudelaire's personal feelings. For Victor Brombert, this "pivotal stanza" leads to a second part "which confronts the preceding themes of evanescence with a proclamation of [the poet's] immutability" (101). For Jean Starobinski, it is the "symmetrical axis" of the poem, the dividing line between two parts designed to mirror each other (*La mélancolie*, 61). At the very center of the poem, Baudelaire's own melancholy is highlighted as a dominant, enduring mood motivating an endless production of self-reflexive figures. In Bernard Weinberg's words, "the swan is only one of several 'persons'" who are "analogized to the speaker," that is, who are introduced by the poet to mirror his situation, which is "a change in time from a happy past to an unhappy present" (32, 35). According to these views, the many personae of the poem are as many analogical figures reflecting the poet's own sense of loss and alienation, which is imputed to the destruction of the old Paris under Baron Haussmann. As a result of this widely shared interpretation, the opening exclamation of part 2—"Paris change!"—is traditionally read as an implicit "j'accuse!," an outcry denouncing the drastic changes that have caused the pulse of Paris to beat faster than the poet's heart. In this light, the whole stanza can be seen as a personal variation on the general theme parenthetically exposed in lines 7–8. But what is deplored by the elegiac "hélas" of line 8, as we have seen, is not the urban transformation per se. It is, instead, the asynchronic relation between human hearts and cityscapes. Similarly, what is lamented here, at the very beginning of part 2, has less to do with the change of Paris than with the poet's inability to adjust to it.

This existential lag has not escaped the scrutiny of Starobinski, who writes that "le mélancolique sent qu'il retarde dans sa réponse au monde" (*La mélancolie*, 64). In falling behind, the "lyric subject" falls into a deep depression for which Paris is blamed. As an accusation, "Paris change!" charges the chaotic city-in-transition for the poet's melancholic sense of entrapment. The worst depression, for Starobinski, comes from feeling trapped in the chaos of Paris, unable to escape the "bric-à-brac confus" of the modern city: "La pire des mélancolies, c'est alors de ne pouvoir passer outre, de rester captif du bric-à-brac" (65). This interpretation, which is shared by many critics, rests on a problematic assumption that the poet rejects urban change. In line 29, however, urban dynamics are seen as a positive (albeit chaotic) process before which the poet, unable to move, has no one to blame but himself, nothing but his own melancholy: "Mais rien dans ma mélancolie n'a bougé!" In light of this negative picture of melancholy, presented here as a burdensome curse holding the poet back (in a backward dis-position), "Paris change!" can be read, retrospectively, as a self-accusation. Whereas the Paris of the 1850s—here personified—engages in a bold, dramatic transformation leading to a new urban look, the poet remains dreadfully inert, timidly ensconced in the past, placidly attached to his "memories." In "mes chers souvenirs," moreover, "chers" may be read as an ironic qualification emphasizing the stifling, oppressive nature of memories simultaneously described as "heavier than rocks." In contradistinction to the poet's timid, petrified attitude, the personified capital dares to change. By its example, it challenges the poet to exchange his outdated melancholic pose for a more dynamic existential stance.

To better understand the first stanza of part 2, we may tamper—ever so briefly—with the text and permute two crucial sentences (here underlined) so as to underline their mutual opposition:

> Paris change! *tout pour moi devient allégorie,*
> Palais neufs, échafaudages, blocs, vieux faubourgs,
> *Mais rien dans ma mélancolie n'a bougé!*
> Et mes chers souvenirs sont plus lourds que des rocs.

This interchange helps to show that allegorical expression (tied to the change of Paris) is opposed to melancholic depression (linked to the old Paris). The dynamic city challenges the poet to see everything ("tout") in a new allegorical light, no longer in the melancholic shadow cast by old memories. Contrasting with a melancholic gaze fixated on the past only, the allegorical outlook encompasses old *and* new Parisian sites. As "everything for (him) turns to allegory," the poet envisions "vieux faubourgs" and "palais neufs"; his mind simultaneously pictures "le vieux Paris" and "le nouveau Carrousel." More precisely, allegorical vision enables him to see "old boroughs" *turn into* "new palaces," as if "everything" appeared not *in its being* but *in its becoming,* as an allegory of change itself.

As we begin to see, Baudelaire's fascination with the allegorical process stems from a desire to escape his depression by emulating, in his style, a city that is constantly changing. In "Paris change!" the universal present clearly indicates that the city's change extends beyond the historical transformations of the 1850s. Consequently, Paris appears as the embodiment of a permanent "devenir" that is also inherent in the mode of writing chosen by Baudelaire in this "tableau parisien." In addition to turning memories into myths, as we have already seen, this mode of writing also transforms every allegory into another allegory, ad infinitum. Under the sign of Victor Hugo, a living allegory of exile to whom the poem is addressed, "Le Cygne" takes us through an endless chain of composite figures sharing the same melancholic pose. This metamorphic chain is a "bric-à-brac confus" of literary characters (Andromache, Ovid's man, the swan), poets (Victor Hugo, Ovid), and persons (negress, orphans, sailors, prisoners, vanquished, and so forth) of all times and conditions. As it leads from one myth to another myth, the allegorical style answers the challenge of Paris by matching with rhetorical figures the evolution of the city's architectural shapes. In other words, the organic growth of the city is emulated by the poem's own progress.

In this poem, "mythe" and "allégorie" are more or less interchangeable. Originally, a "myth" is a narrative endowed with symbolic meaning. The story of the swan, which is symbolic of Man's metaphysical rebellion, fits this definition very well and provides a bitterly ironic parallel to the literary story of "Ovid's man." In Ovid's *Metamorphoses,* man raises his head to be distinguished from other creatures, according to God's will. Baudelaire's swan also looks heavenward but only to ridicule the noble posture of Ovid's man. Unlike Ovid's man, the defiant swan turns its frustration against God and blames him for its exile, in a series of rhetorical questions that do not so much demand an answer as much as question divine justice. In the modern sense of the word "mythe," however, it is nearly impossible to tell the protagonist from the plot. Here, for instance, the swan itself is a myth, not only the story in which it appears (as if the swan were an allegory of the myth it stands for). The same could be said of such literary characters as Andromache or "Ovid's man" but also of more human *persons* such as the "negress," the "orphans," the shipwrecked "sailors" trapped on a distant island, the "prisoners," the "van-quished," and "so many more."

Being a "tableau parisien" in its own right, "Le Cygne" reflects some of the disparate elements of a Parisian scene (a swan, old and new buildings, and so forth). The "bric-à-brac confus" is even greater in the poem than in Paris, where one may by chance encounter a swan but not Andromache. This legendary figure of the past appears in a contemporary urban setting staged by the poet, in a style that is itself a medley of old and new expressions. One of these new expressions—"bric-à-brac"—not only describes the modern chaotic city but also designates the poem itself as the scene of allegorical writing. Just as the old Paris turns into a new city, "Andromaque" (1) leads to "Paris" (29). As we turn from the first to the second part, the antique figure of melancholy gives way to the modern figure of change. This passage, however, should not be construed as a linear move away from the past. The return of Andromache, in the second part (36–37), attests that the initial image of melancholy has not disappeared from the allegorical scene of change. Conversely, signs of a changing Paris are already present in the first part, among static figures paralyzed by their memories. As we can see, the "tableau" abounds in disparities that are much more than realist depictions of Parisian scenes. The poem does not simply reflect urban contrasts but deflects them in its own style, which is richer in shocks than Paris itself. In his own effort to move forward, the poet surpasses the progress of the modern city. His style does not simply capture, it creates a modernity that includes rather than precludes the enduring *presence* of the past. Although it seems to suggest a linear progress from antiquity to modernity, the symmetrical position of "Andromaque" and "Paris" in the poem serves instead to emphasize their permanent confrontation. Constantly face to face, these two allegories contrast sharply with one another, a contrast that itself represents a struggle, in the poet's mind, between melancholy and change.

In writing "Le Cygne," Baudelaire is leaning over melancholic figures lost in their memories. Instead of mourning a personal loss, he meditates on losses suffered by others, in a sympathetic gesture apparently devoid of self-interest. But his fixation on melancholic figures is constantly disrupted by the perpetual motion in which they are caught. As these figures turn in the poet's mind, they also turn into other figures, at an increasing speed, as indicated by the ever more frequent recurrence of the verb "je pense." In the second part alone, "je pense" is repeated three times (34, 41, 51) and is implied seven times before the preposition "à" (36, 45, 46, 48, 52), as if thoughts were turning ever faster in the poet's mind—as on a carousel. This fast-forward motion, moreover, keeps revolving around the pivotal, self-allegorical figure of Victor Hugo, to whom the poem is addressed. Through this alter ego in exile, Baudelaire discovers that the various exiles he creates are self-allegories. What these allegories display *and* disguise, however, is not Baudelaire's biographical self but rather his poetic persona, who he becomes when he turns into endless allegories of his own literary exile. In a dizzying style inducing a kind of existential vertigo, Baudelaire moves away from a stable personal self toward ever-shifting identities that compose his poetic persona. The Parisian "bric-à-brac" in "Le Cygne" turns out to be a metaphor, not only for the style in which the poem is written, but also for the way in which the poet is transformed by his own style.

Chapter 11

The Role of Structural Analysis: "Les Sept Vieillards"*

MARIE MACLEAN

Fourmillante cité, cité pleine de rêves,
Où le spectre en plein jour raccroche le passant!
Les mystères partout coulent comme des sèves
Dans les canaux étroits du colosse puissant. (4)

Un matin, cependant que dans la triste rue
Les maisons, dont la brume allongeait la hauteur,
Simulaient les deux quais d'une rivière accrue,
Et que, décor semblable à l'âme de l'acteur, (8)

Un brouillard sale et jaune inondait tout l'espace,
Je suivais, roidissant mes nerfs comme un héros
Et discutant avec mon âme déjà lasse,
Le faubourg secoué par les lourds tombereaux. (12)

Tout à coup, un vieillard dont les guenilles jaunes
Imitaient la couleur de ce ciel pluvieux,
Et dont l'aspect aurait fait pleuvoir les aumônes,
Sans la méchanceté qui luisait dans ses yeux, (16)

M'apparut. On eût dit sa prunelle trempée
Dans le fiel; son regard auguisait les frimas,
Et sa barbe à longs poils, roide comme une épée
Se projetait, pareille à celle de Judas. (20)

Il n'était pas voûté, mais cassé, son échine
Faisant avec sa jambe un parfait angle droit,
Si bien que son bâton, parachevant sa mine,
Lui donnait la tournure et le pas maladroit (24)

* My special thanks to Jenni Brown, not only for transcribing the original seminar, but also for several original suggestions, and to my colleague Philip Anderson for some fine points of analysis.

D'un quadrupède infirme ou d'un juif à trois pattes.
Dans la neige et la boue il allait s'empêtrant,
Comme s'il écrasait des morts sous ses savates,
Hostile à l'univers plutôt qu'indifférent. (28)

Son pareil le suivait: barbe, œil, dos, bâton, loques,
Nul trait ne distinguait, du même enfer venu,
Ce jumeau centenaire, et ces spectres baroques
Marchaient du même pas vers un but inconnu. (32)

A quel complot infâme étais-je donc en butte,
Ou quel méchant hasard ainsi m'humiliait?
Car je comptai sept fois, de minute en minute,
Ce sinistre vieillard qui se multipliait! (36)

Que celui-là qui rit de mon inquiétude,
Et qui n'est pas saisi d'un frisson fraternel,
Songe bien que malgré tant de décrépitude
Ces sept monstres hideux avaient l'air éternel! (40)

Aurais-je, sans mourir, contemplé le huitième,
Sosie inexorable, ironique et fatal,
Dégoûtant Phénix, ·fils et père de lui-même?
—Mais je tournai le dos au cortège infernal. (44)

Exaspéré comme un ivrogne qui voit double,
Je rentrai, je fermai ma porte, épouvanté,
Malade et morfondu, l'esprit fiévreux et trouble,
Blessé par le mystère et par l'absurdité! (48)

Vainement ma raison voulait prendre la barre;
La tempête en jouant déroutait ses efforts,
Et mon âme dansait, dansait, vieille gabarre
Sans mâts, sur une mer monstrueuse et sans bords! (52)

I f we subscribe to the view that, in poetry, form *is* meaning, any sig-
nification can only spring from the workings of the signifier or con-
crete printed text. We must recognize that, in the first instance, the
signifier is our only certainty, since the signified differs in different
possible contexts of reception. It follows that any interpretation *must*
be based, in the first instance, on the formal properties of the text. A
formal analysis is not an end in itself, but it alone can give validity to
our readings. "Les Sept Vieillards" has many possible readings, but

they are all dependent on its highly stylized structure, and this struc-
ture is in its turn an integral part of the architecture of the new section
"Tableaux parisiens" that Baudelaire incorporated into *Les Fleurs du
Mal* in the second (1861) edition. For the details of the wider social
and literary contexts to which the poems belong, I will refer my read-
ers to other authorities, Richard Burton in particular, in order to con-
centrate on the textual analysis of "Les Sept Vieillards" itself.

Formally, the "Tableaux parisiens" depend on metamorphosis and
modernity. They might have as an epigraph "Le Vieux Paris n'est
plus (la forme d'une ville / Change plus vite, hélas! que le cœur d'un
mortel)" ("Le Cygne"). In their strategic sequence, Ross Chambers
("Are Baudelaire's . . . ?") contends, the poet examines first the Paris
of the daytime and then the Paris of the night, together with the fan-
tasies bred by his urban wanderings. The first poem of the section,
"Paysage," inscribes this diurnal preoccupation; then follow eight
poems inspired by the streets of the great city. The central and turn-
ing point is the linking poem between night and day, street and
home, "Crépuscule du soir." Next come eight poems of the night, a
section that finishes with "Crépuscule du matin." Thus the whole
eighteen poems form a complete cycle of their own. Another possible
indication of textual structure comes from *Le Spleen de Paris*, as the
experiment with the prose poem was contemporaneous with the
"Tableaux parisiens." Baudelaire divided the prose poems into three
categories: "Choses parisiennes," "Symboles et moralités," and
"Oneirocritie" (interpretation of dreams). "Les Sept Vieillards"
belongs to both the first and the last of these categories.

Written in 1859, it is the fifth poem of the "Tableaux parisiens" and
the second of its three longest and, many say, greatest poems ("Le
Cygne," "Les Sept Vieillards," and "Les Petites Vieilles"), which are
dedicated, and not just for reasons of self-interest, to Victor Hugo, the
acknowledged doyen of nineteenth-century poetry. It is a poem built
on, parodying, and yet going beyond a certain baroque style of
romanticism or, one might even say, the style of Victor Hugo himself.
Of this hijacking of the old in the service of the new, Baudelaire says
himself, when sending the manuscript to its first publisher in June
1859, "C'est le premier numéro d'une nouvelle série que je veux ten-
ter, et je crains bien d'avoir simplement réussi à dépasser les limites
assignées à la poésie" (*Correspondance* II, 583).

I will use a method of formal analysis that owes its existence to
Jakobson's theories of the two axes of language: the syntagmatic, or
horizontal, which governs syntax and prosody as conditions of

sequence, and the paradigmatic, or vertical, which governs the forma-
tion of semantic and phonetic sets and their relative dominance in the
text. Levin has developed this approach into a theory of poetic *cou-
pling* that stresses the coincidence in key expressions of at least two
levels of repetition (or redundancy). Thus we must make an initial
analysis of the four levels of the poem—semantic, syntactic, phonetic,
and prosodic—and carefully chart the redundancy that a good poem
establishes between them. The advantage of this detailed examination
of the poetic signifier is that it is extremely suggestive and can then be
teamed with any of the traditional (for example, thematic) or more
recent (for example, psychoanalytic) methods of approach to produce
an interpretation. We must always stress that any interpretation is
provisional and partial, and inevitably dependent on the context of
the reader as well as that of the author.

The title needs to be borne in mind throughout, as it not only has
prosodic priority but is also a vital clue to the dominance of certain
semantic and phonetic paradigms. "Les Sept Vieillards" already con-
tains in "sept" not only a number but also an archetypal figure of
magic and mystery (see Tucci; Burton, "Baudelaire and Shakespeare";
and Rollins). The "old man" is also archetypal, paradigmatic of both
the positive and (as here) the negative father in Jungian terms. The
phonemes of the two words will also prove of vital importance in fur-
ther coupling.

Composed of alexandrines with alternate rhymes, and four line
stanzas, of which the last rhyme is always masculine, the poem con-
tains five main divisions. We identify these divisions by shifts in time
and space, marked adverbially and by tense changes, and/or by the
appearance or disappearance of actors on the stage of the text.

> Stanza 1: Invocation to the city
> Stanzas 2 and 3: The foggy setting and the narrator
> Stanzas 4–7: Description of the first old man
> Stanzas 8–11: Appearance of the six others (one finds here many
>   stylistic variations, minor divisions)
> Stanzas 12 and 13: The double vision and distorted reason.

One already notices the structural symmetry of the stanza sequence
1/2/4/4/2 and also the fact that there are thirteen stanzas. Thirteen is
the archetypal number of death, so both title and prosody indicate
that we are in the realm of magic and the occult.

Stanza 1

Stanza 1 is set apart by the fact that it is an invocation, initially timeless and averbal. When a verb appears, it is in the present tense, separating the time of narration from the narrated event. We can perhaps best appreciate the workings of coupling by looking at line 1. The word "cité" is marked syntactically by its position on either side of the comma, prosodically by the parallel relation to the caesura and its incorporation in the chiasmus: "fourmillante" (A, qualifier, 4 syllables) "cité" (B, noun, 2) / "cité" (B, noun, 2) "pleine de rêves"(A, qualifier, 4). It is marked semantically as belonging to the paradigm of the urban (serially redundant), and phonetically it also provides redundance with the [s] [t] of "sept" and the coming "spectre" and "mystères." Thus it is not only coupled but, as it were, quadrupled, so that its importance is highlighted. The city, in the "Tableaux parisiens," is a place of diversity, indeed of "polymorphous perversity" and hence of metamorphosis. Here it is also a place of doubleness, "spectre" having the second meaning of juxtaposed image. It is anthill, the architectural yet living giant, the "colosse puissant" in whose veins (the narrow canals) runs the "sève" of mystery. A semantics of liquidity dominates the beginning and end of the text. The "passant" is embroiled by the day/nightmare, the "rêve" (phonetically coupled with "vieillards"), and becomes acted upon rather than acting. Caught up in the dream, he ceases to be an impartial observer, like the usual Baudelairean flaneur. The enjambment of line 4 and the alliteration of the [k] both emphasize the image of the "canaux" that will develop further in the following stanza. The present tense of the verb of invocation will give way to the past tense in the story of the meeting. This stanza is far from completely analyzed, and it will be clear that space does not permit an exhaustive study of all four levels of the poem. Nevertheless, salient features of the signifier will be discussed.

Stanzas 2 and 3

Stanzas 2 and 3 shift the narrative to a specific setting, in a time—"Un matin"—in the past and in a place, "la triste rue." There is an effect of suspense due to the reduplication of the subordinate clauses ("cependant que," "Et que"). We are left waiting for the principal verb ("je suivais") for five lines. The "coupe" after the third syllable in line 6 draws attention to the distortion of the houses by the "brume" and renews the simile of line 4 ("deux quais d'une rivière accrue"), thereby recreating both the reality of the city's running gutters and the illusion ("simulaient") of a setting: the streets, "canaux étroits" full of "brouillard" and "mystères," become a "décor." The poet is at the same time both actor, a paradoxical hero on the set likened to his melancholy soul, and narrator, which allows the intimacy of the first person account. Melancholy is, by tradition, yellow like "le brouillard" and "les guenilles" and later, like the "fiel," the only touch of color in the whole poem. In line 10 the two "coupes" of the ternary alexandrine—a Hugolian specialty—"je suivais / roidissant mes nerfs / comme un héros" heighten the tension by the broken rhythm and add emphasis to the paradigm of rigidity in "roidissant." The oxymoronic fluidity of the apparently static "faubourg" is heightened by the chiasmic assonance of the long syllables of line 12—"Le *faubourg* se*coué* par les *lour*ds tombe*reaux*"—with this last word also providing the link between water and death.

Stanzas 4–8

With "Tout à coup" there is a syntactically marked shock effect, as the old man appears in line 13, followed by suspense, due to the coupling of the long subordinate clauses "dont" and "Et dont." The verb that belongs to the subject "un vieillard" must wait for an entire stanza and, by a very daring Hugolian enjambment, appears all alone, as a "rejet" at the beginning of the fifth stanza. "Les guenilles jaunes" echo "sale et jaune" and the enjambment at line 14 accentuates "imitaient." There is a constellation of words paradigmatic of illusion: "simulaient," "décor," "imitaient," "aspect." Both spatial and phonetic continuity exist between "le brouillard," "le ciel," and "le vieillard." Semantically, all are yellow, formless, and threatening, and they are also linked by the internal rhyme of "brouillard," "vieillard," and aural reinforcement in "pluvieux." Then the redundancy of pleu*voir* leads into the concentration of emotion in "yeux," as so often with Baudelaire. This is strongly syntactically and prosodically marked, since "luisait dans ses yeux" ends the stanza but does not end the sentence. The conflict between the prosodic rule—that a stanza be self-contained—and the syntax places the emphasis on "yeux" and "apparut" and, with them, the all-important activity of the "regard."

The text uses the semantic tripling of "yeux," "prunelle," "regard," the simile "On eût dit . . . trempée / Dans le fiel," and the remarkable metaphor "aiguisait les frimas" to accentuate the paradigm of vision. But note also the two parallel enjambments of lines 17–18 and lines 19–20, with the repeated shock of the second "rejet" in two lines: "Dans le fiel." This "rejet," which forces the "coupe" after three syllables, leaves the caesura before "regard," while the fact that it would be expected to follow "regard" causes hesitation. The harsh sounds [p] [f] [i], linked with the semantic sharpness of "trempée," "aiguisait," intensify the menacing paradigm of stiffness in the synecdoches and simile that figure the old man: "barbe," "poils," "roide," "épée." In line 20, the unexpected "coupe" of 4/8, and the alliteration ("projetait," "pareille"), reinforce one another. The stressed reference to Judas (the thirteenth man at the Last Supper) leads into the extended metaphor of the mythological Jew.

The sixth stanza continues the tableau, the design, the geometry. The two "coupes" in line 21—"vouté, / mais cassé, / son échine"— break the line, so that the sound is coupled with the meaning. "Parfait angle droit" brings both geometrical severity and an equivalent harshness of sound. Note the consonance of "pareille," "parfait," "parachevant," and "pas," the echoes giving a sort of interior rhyme. It is impossible to follow all the phonetic play, but binary rhythm, as in "la tournure" and "le pas maladroit," is one example and foreshadows the semantic emphasis on doubling that is central to the text.

The enjambment between the sixth and seventh stanzas couples with the use of the imperfect to accentuate the archetype of doomed recurrence. Line 25 also seems to limp. The animal raises a wounded leg. The man supports himself with a stick. He represents human age itself, since he portrays the enigma of the sphinx (what goes on three legs at evening?). The Jew leaning on his stick is reminiscent not only of Judas the betrayer but also of the myth of "le juif errant," who laughed at Christ and was eternally condemned to wander all over the world without being able to stop or to die, a myth that spawned many fashionable variants in the nineteenth century. "La neige" and "la boue" combined again suggest a dirty yellow, just as the implacability of "il allait s'empêtrant" prefigures the unending hostility between the man and the world. The inversion of lines 27 and 28 gives force to the simile, another figure of death: "Comme . . . savates." "Hostile" seems to belong to a semantic paradigm encompassing coldness, hardness, stiffness, angularity. Both syntax and prosody bring out the superb contrast between the beginning and the end of line 28. One expects the poor creature to be apathetic but instead he imposes himself, he threatens.

Stanzas 8–12

Now the development begins; to the paradigms of coldness, hardness, and hostility are added those of hell and persecution. The repetition becomes obsessive. Note the metonymy in line 29, which deliberately echoes Hugo. Here we see a cortege of solitary words that follow each other as do the old men: "barbe, œil, dos, bâton, loques." The parallel elements become more marked to add emphasis to the repetition. With "Son pareil," and "Ce jumeau," for instance, there is syntactic, semantic, and metric parallelism. The coupling that is normal in poetry is heightened to an obsessive thematic reduplication. In lines 30 and 32, "du même enfer venu" and "Marchaient du même pas"—one after the "coupe" and followed by the verb, the other before the "coupe" and preceded by the verb—give a chiasmic balanced effect. The consonance of the [ny] links "Nul" to "inconnu."

In the ninth stanza there is a major syntactic and semantic change. The two rhetorical questions, followed by a two-line exclamation, stress the persecution complex betrayed in "complot infâme," "méchant hasard," "m'humiliait." Note the resurgence of the narrator as victim (from lines 2 and 10) with the return of the first person pronouns. In line 35 the first repetition of "sept" from the title stimulates the reader's search for meaning in the text. The coupling of the temporal paradigm with the alliteration of [m] in "sept fois," "de minute en minute," "multipliait," is accentuated by the [s] of "sept," "ce," "sinistre," "se," which adds a note of menace.

In the tenth stanza there is a change of tone and of syntax. The exclamation becomes an injunction, an imperative using "que" and a main clause subjunctive. The narrator appeals to the reader; he speaks in the present but to the third person. Despite the "frisson fraternel," he does not say "tu," thus maintaining the solemn tone of a moral tale. There is an echo effect and further parallelism in the two subordinate clauses "qui rit" and "qui n'est pas." The enjambment and the "coupe" in line 39 place the emphasis on "Songe," creating a semantic link with the initial "rêves." The magic connotations of the recurrent "sept" are extended in "monstres," which also belong to the paradigm of doubleness, since a monster has a double nature, human and divine, human and animal, or divine and animal. A monster is also, polysemically, something that is *shown* to us, a warning, seen, as it were, from line 1 and the first chiasmus onward. The paradigm of recurrence and, with it, the archetype of the eternal return derive syntactic and prosodic force from the position of "éternel," which applies equally to hell, to the "juif errant," to death.

In the eleventh stanza there is another syntactic change. We return to the past but in the conditional (which can be used to threaten) and to the rhetorical question that, by inversion, allows the prosodic stress on the hypothetical "huitième." This last rhetorical question consists of three lines and three metaphoric variations on the theme of obsessive repetition. "Sosie," semantically another double, is syntactically stressed by the ternary rhythm of its three succeeding qualifiers. The archetype of self-procreation, the "Phénix, fils et père de lui-même," another symbol of the eternal return, is also marked by the alliteration of "fatal," "Phénix," "fils." By this stage, self-respecting readers must be panting to interpret the "Sept vieillards" themselves, especially as the poet has encouraged an allegorical reading with the words "tout pour moi devient allégorie," in the preceding poem "Le Cygne." Many have tried, and any may be chosen. For Alison Fairlie and Yvonne Rollins, the spectres represent the seven deadly sins. To Burton, they are intertextually linked to Macbeth's vision of Banquo's ghost and the seven succeeding kings. To me, and also to Nina Tucci to some extent, they represent the seven days of the week. In Baudelaire's works overall, "le temps" is "inexorable" and "fatal" (one must compare this poem with "L'Horloge"), but the week also repeats itself indefinitely, and each day has twenty-four hours and is therefore a "sosie" of all the others. The last line of stanza 11 shows the defeated poet turning back on himself from this recurrent vision of hell. He takes refuge in his own space, behind a closed door, and inside himself, but of course, the nightmare of the city and of time originated there in the first place.

Stanzas 12 and 13

In the conclusion of the poem the key word is "double." All the components of the lines are doubled to respond visually to the first comparison with the drunkard, "l'ivrogne qui voit double," who, like the "passant" of line 2, is hooked by the images he creates. The passé simple of lines 44 and 46 endeavors to reinstate singularity instead of the obsessive and terrifying recurrence. The striking chiasmic effect of lines 45 and 46—"Exaspéré . . . double" and "Je rentrai . . . épouvan-té"—is highlighted by the fact that the two participles are coupled on all four levels. The disorder of the narrator's mind is echoed in the two ternary alexandrines of lines 45–46 with their uneven "coupes" (4/5/3 and 3/5/4), which are also syllabically chiasmic. Stressed by the reduplication are words paradigmatic of wounding ("malade," "fiévreux," "blessé") and of madness ("morfondu," "trouble," "absur-dité"). "Morfondu" provides a good example of characteristic Baudelairean polysemy; its synonyms are "enrhumé," "refroidi," "ennuyé," and "déçu," but if we read deconstructively, we can also see that it is overdetermined by its phonetic link with "mort" and with "fondu," liquidity.

Throughout these stanzas, not only is the mind/spirit "brouillé," but the phonemes of the title, the [s] [t] of "sept," and the [v] [i] [e] [j] [a] [r] of "vieillards," recur in every possible combination, phonetic play that, by fragmentation and "befogging," has a latent connection with the "brouillard" of line 9. The alliteration of the [m] sound in "comme," "fermai," "ma," "mystère," "tempête," "mon âme," "mâts," "mer," and "monstrueuse" is important because it reinforces the key word—"monstre"—which is a metaphoric version of "colosse." Both are paradigmatic images of the hellish vision of the modern city itself, the city that breeds a population of clonelike mon-sters, the "sept vieillards." At another level, irrationality and the unconscious are the "monsters" that threaten to overwhelm rationali-ty and consciousness. Monstrous too are the meaninglessness of life and the sameness of the meaningless images, against which no door can be closed.

The thirteenth stanza, that of death, is in effect a remarkable extended nautical metaphor. It begins with "prendre la barre," as the spirit of the narrator becomes "une vieille gabarre" that "raison" can-not control. "La tempête" is the tempest of madness and of terror, echoing the wintry fog of lines 9–18 but also "playing the game" of frustrating the narrator just as the poem itself frustrates any attempt at closure. The last two lines are a "tour de force" of suggestion and rhythm. One notices once again the splintering effect of the "coupes" (6/2/4 and 2/7/3) in lines 51–52. Most startling, but also exactly com-plementing the chiasmic opening line of the whole poem, are the visual and phonetic effects of the final multiple chiasmus (see table). Baudelaire was so satisfied with this ending that he drew a sketch below it of the boat on the sea (see figure).

mon âme	metaphoric equivalent		vieille gabarre
	dansait, dansait		
	ans	ans	
sans ———>		<——— sans	
a	b	b	a
Sans mâts,	sur une mer	monstrueuse	et sans bords
adjectival phr.	[s y m]	[m y s]	adjectival phr.

This section of manuscript raises another vital issue in textual analysis to which I can only allude here. The study of variants is a major guide to the development of the signifier, and for "Les Sept Vieillards" we have perhaps the most complete set of variants in the whole Baudelairean corpus. These have been given in full by Leakey and Pichois in the aptly named "Les sept versions des 'Sept

Vieillards.'" It remains to study the full textual implications of the many modifications, particularly the phonetic variations that improved the harmony of the text. One can see, for example, in the sample given, the dramatic intensification of the metaphor but also the phonetic shifts. For instance, in line 51, "vieille gabarre" was originally the flat "comme un navire." This wording was improved to "pauvre gabare" (*sic*), and the poet finally hit on the perfect solution with "vieille gabarre," coupling the boat metaphor with phonetic and semantic feedback to the title.

Let me stress again that a textual analysis must precede an interpretation. The insights it provides are at once an impetus to creative readings and a "garde-fou" against abusive readings. From the evidence available, one could try, for example, a Freudian interpretation based on the Oedipus complex ("fils et père," 43), starting with the hostile father figure (at line 13!), and showing the progressive threat of castration, from "aiguisait" (18) to "blessé" (48). Tucci has already done a quite impressive Jungian study, and Burton and Cellier have looked at intertextuality, but how about an autobiographical approach, reading the text in conjunction with Baudelaire's laudanum addiction and chronic depression? Then, of course, we can use the phonetic overdetermination and polysemy of the poem as the basis for our own deconstructive flights, "jouant" on the stage of the text. The main thing is to remember that there are always two levels in a poem, the conscious and unconscious. On the one hand, in "Les Sept Vieillards," we have the poetic virtuoso, apparently flattering the master but really showing off his effortless control of textual strategies and the startling metamorphoses he could impose on an old theme. On the other hand, we have the unconscious drives and repressions, the traces of the world of nightmare, and the obsessions inscribed in the lines by the chiasmic mirror images of repressed fears. No worthwhile reading can afford to work on one level alone.

Chapter 12

Order and Chaos in "A une passante"

WILLIAM THOMPSON

La rue assourdissante autour de moi hurlait.
Longue, mince, en grand deuil, douleur majestueuse,
Une femme passa, d'une main fastueuse
Soulevant, balançant le feston et l'ourlet;   (4)

Agile et noble, avec sa jambe de statue.
Moi, je buvais, crispé comme un extravagant,
Dans son œil, ciel livide où germe l'ouragan,
La douceur qui fascine et le plaisir qui tue.   (8)

Un éclair . . . puis la nuit! —Fugitive beauté
Dont le regard m'a fait soudainement renaître,
Ne te verrai-je plus que dans l'éternité?   (11)

Ailleurs, bien loin d'ici! trop tard! *jamais* peut-être!
Car j'ignore où tu fuis, tu ne sais où je vais,
O toi que j'eusse aimée, ô toi qui le savais!   (14)

In the midst of a bustling, noisy street scene, the poet crosses paths with a woman in mourning, who immediately captivates him. They apparently exchange a brief glance before being separated by the crowd and by their own paths in opposite directions. The poet regrets the brevity of this encounter and laments the impossibility of recapturing this moment in the anonymity of the large city. He even accuses the woman of having intentionally caused him great suffering. Reprising several familiar Baudelairean themes, "A une passante" is undeniably one of the great "Tableaux parisiens," an extraordinary poem of the city, a superb evocation of the anonymity of the modern urban setting and of the impossibility of pursuing a chance encounter or of halting the passage of time. Such occurrences are a regular feature of city life; strangers often exchange glances, knowing that little, if anything, will result of these encounters. But for the poet, apparently uncomfortable in these busy surroundings, one such meeting can have considerable consequences.

"A une passante" has been a particularly popular subject for Baudelaire scholars, who have brought to the interpretation of this poem a variety of perspectives, such as the erotic (Raser, Humphries), the biographical (Quesnel, reading the poem as an evocation of Baudelaire's mother), and the comparative (Heck, setting Baudelaire alongside Proust; LeBoulay, alongside Constantin Guys; Häufle, alongside Nerval; and Godfrey, alongside Lamartine); others have viewed the poem as street poetry (Chambers) and as an urban poem (Aynesworth; Benjamin, *Baudelaire: A Lyric Poet*). Indeed, one could devote an entire study to an overview of the critical exegeses of this poem (many of which appear in the bibliography).

The present analysis will focus on the fundamental opposition in "A une passante" between order and chaos, an opposition that makes difficult any exact interpretation of the poem. I will demonstrate how the tone of the poem shifts frequently and dramatically, from the chaos and seeming torment of both the street scene and later the poet's inner self, to the attempt on the poet's part to establish some sort of order, both in his own mind and in the syntax, vocabulary, and overall structure of the poem, as manifested in particular in the orderly depiction of the passerby and in his final comments on the impact of this woman on him.

For the purposes of this analysis, "A une passante" has been divided into six segments, each corresponding either to an atmosphere of disorder/chaos or to one of order/harmony in the development of the poem. That six possible divisions may be found in a poem of only fourteen lines demonstrates already an inherent instability in the structure of the poem (although I do not mean to argue that the poem must be segmented in this fashion). We will see that there is neither a gradual progression from one state to the other (chaos to order, order to chaos) nor a clear resolution of the consequences of this opposition. The poet never manages to escape completely the chaos introduced in the street scene described in the first line, since the most orderly element in the poem—the woman who appears in the street—will in turn cause his mental turmoil, another chaos. In this poem, chaos may lead to order, just as order leads to chaos. This uneasy opposition appears all the more remarkable if we attempt to hypothesize and

reconstruct the process through which the poem has been composed:
the poet undergoes this experience in the street, an event he will
remember and later put on paper in the form of a sonnet. Yet even in
this poetic creation, the chaos of the scene persists. In spite of the time
that we assume elapses between the encounter and its commemora-
tion on paper, the poet is not capable of recalling this experience and
its impact in a uniformly clear and logical fashion. My analysis will
proceed according to the following divisions:

l. 1: *disorder* of the street
ll. 2–5: *orderly* description of the woman
ll. 6–7: *disorder* of the poet's reaction to the woman
l. 8: *order* of his interpretation of this reaction
l. 9–12: *disorder* of his hopelessness
ll. 13–14: *order* of his final accusation and summary of the situation

The first line does much more than simply provide a physical set-
ting for what is to transpire; it establishes the atmosphere of chaos
that will reign over much of the remainder of the poem. The state of
confusion is immediately evident in the opposition of the linearity
suggested by the "rue" to the sense of disorder and confusion of
"assourdissante" and "hurlait." The street is neither physically nor
thematically a means of arriving at an end. On the contrary, the poet
seems transfixed, incapable of movement or clear thought. The oppo-
sition between chaos and order is clear in the relationship of the poet
to his surroundings. As Remacle notes, the street is described as
"autour"—around—the poet (in itself a disorienting description), and
the source of the noise, the grammatical subject of "hurlait," is the
street itself. In addition, the two terms that qualify the street literally
surround the poet in the first line: "*assourdissante* autour de moi
hurlait." But the lack of detail about the precise sources of this noise
(Benjamin notes that the crowd, if not mentioned, is implied) would
seem to indicate that something—or someone—else will be the exclu-
sive focus of the poet, who appears immobile, as if at the center of a
whirlwind, the passive spectator of the action surrounding him. In
fact, the title—"A une passante"—makes the mention of "la rue" vir-
tually redundant, or at the very least predictable, as we can assume
that the woman concerned is not an acquantaince and could only
have been encountered in an anonymous public sphere.

The initial qualifier—"assourdissante"—is a key element in the
poem. Not only does it establish the relationship between the poet

and the street; it creates a mood that will color the poet's depiction of the woman and, later, of his own mental state. One of his senses—his hearing—has been rendered ineffective from the beginning, and one might suggest that his ability to see (far more important in this poem) has been greatly impaired as well, as the constant, chaotic movement of the crowd impedes a clear or prolonged view of the individual passersby. The setting in which the poet finds himself overwhelms him in a potentially frightening and certainly incapacitating manner. In fact, the verb of the first line—"hurlait"—seems to evoke a bestial or monstrous imagery, reminiscent of the reference in "Au Lecteur," the introductory poem of *Les Fleurs du Mal,* to "Les monstres glapissants, hurlants, grognants, rampants" (*OC* I, 6).

The effect of the setting on the poet is unpleasant, unlike that in another poem, "Les Aveugles" (the poem that immediately precedes "A une passante"), in which the poet says of the street: "tu chantes, ris et beugles." But the poet in "Les Aveugles" was also "hébété," overwhelmed by his environment, just as in "A une passante" the deafening street causes an initial disorder in the poet's thoughts. Ross Chambers, however, suggests that "A une passante" "is not out of control, like a howl; nor does it imitate a howl: its topic, indeed, is not lack of control but the subtle alliance of control . . . and disorder . . . in the one conjoined experience of beauty and death" ("Baudelaire's Street Poetry," 257). The importance of the initial line, then, is not to describe the street nor, for that matter, to establish an atmosphere of chaos but to set the (disordered) stage for, and to establish a contrast with, the subsequent description of the woman.

Lines 2–5

After the first, chaotic (albeit superbly constructed) introductory line, the focus shifts immediately to the exact, orderly description of the woman passing by. From the rapidity and chaos of the "rue assourdissante," we progress to the slow, relatively peaceful movement of the woman: "longue, mince, en grand deuil." She stands in stark contrast to the hustle and bustle of the surrounding street, as if part of an idealistic dream in the midst of the harsh reality of urban life. The movement from the general to the specific in the first stanza, from the crowd to the woman, also functions as a progression from disorder to order, from the chaotic goings-on in the street to the deliberate, careful (and quite specific) manipulation by the woman of her clothing in the fourth line ("Soulevant, balançant le feston et l'ourlet").

Ironically, the woman, before she is specifically mentioned, resembles the street. As both "rue" and "femme" are feminine, the two adjectives at the beginning of line 2 could very well be describing either (the street being the only noun in the poem thus far). If everything else around the poet is deafening confusion, the woman, like the physical street, is depicted as possessing a linear form ("longue"), and her progression (or the poet's focus on her progression) is distinct. But the woman and the street scene are far from identical, as Jean-Claude LeBoulay stresses: "Cette passante n'est pas un élément parmi d'autres de cette multitude, elle en est la négation" (25). While everything else around the poet provokes a confused aural response, the woman is described in clear, visual terms: tall, slender, and dressed in mourning.

Yet if the first hemistich of line 2 is marked by visual clarity, the second—"douleur majestueuse"—is ambiguous. At first glance, the majestic pain would appear to be that which the poet assumes the woman experiences in her mourning. If we allow for this interpretation, this line recalls the third line of another poem in the "Tableaux parisiens"—"Le Cygne"—in which the poet, speaking to Andromaque, refers to "L'immense majesté de vos douleurs de veuve." Yet if one reads to the end of "A une passante" and realizes in what state the seductive passerby will leave the poet, this "douleur" might well be the poet's own, an initial, violent "coup de foudre" when confronted with this apparition. At the moment when the poet attempts to understand the woman, to penetrate her exterior, we witness his lament. One might even suggest that, as the woman passes by him, the poet assumes the pain that he believes she feels. (It is worth noting the prominence and reverence accorded to "douleur" in Baudelaire's poetry; the word appears frequently and in *Les Fleurs du Mal* is capitalized on three occasions.) In whatever manner we interpret this word, "douleur" does certainly introduce, in the midst of a physical description of the woman, an element of unbearable emotion.

The first actual reference to the woman is strikingly straightforward—"Une femme passa"—especially in comparison with the "majestic" language that makes her stand out in the previous line and in comparison with the minuteness of the detail that will be devoted to her in the description that follows. The brevity of this initial reference undoubtedly parallels the brevity of the moment at which the poet catches sight of the woman (and subsequently loses sight of her). Yet following this key encounter, the poet seems capable of recalling every detail of this "tableau parisien." Indeed, the information in the latter half of line 3 (and later in line 4) is remarkably precise: from the woman in her entirety we pass immediately to the detail of one hand. Not only is a specific body part the focus of attention (which in itself is could hardly be considered unusual), but it is qualified in an extraordinary manner. What is the reader to make of "fastueuse"? Rich, sumptuous? Is this qualifier intended to reflect how the hand is perceived by the captivated poet, indicating his nearly obsessive (or fetishistic) point of view? Or is this an indirect reference to the woman's social standing (Aguettant points out that these lines describe "détails de costume d'un goût bien bourgeois," 157)? From this might we imply that part of her attractiveness lies in her social standing? The subsequent lines would justify either interpretation, as they too focus on the details of the woman's clothing, yet from the perspective of an entranced male gaze. The precise vocabulary of this line is all the more striking in that it describes a woman who, chronologically speaking, is already a part of the past. She has, in fact, "passed by," the passé simple indicating that her action is complete and that she has already disappeared or is on the verge of doing so. In addition, as she disappears into the deafening, bustling activity of the street, any accurate description of her apparently becomes more problematic.

I have already stated that the description of the woman (in lines 2 through 5) is orderly, precise in opposition to the chaos of the street. This is particularly evident in the fourth line, where the two participles of the first hemistich—"soulevant, balançant"—suggest the rhythmic, flowing movement of the woman's skirts (in stark contrast to the general disorder of the street). That they are both composed of three syllables is hardly a coincidence, "balançant" in particular providing the line with both rhythmic and semantic equilibrium. This "balance" continues, in terms of the poetic structure, with the 3/3 syllabic division of the second hemistich (making the pattern for the entire line a perfectly orderly 3/3/3/3).

The most specifically descriptive elements in the poem are, in fact, the references to the woman's outfit at the end of the first stanza: "le feston et l'ourlet," the lace border and the hem of her dress or skirt. (Again, as with her hand, the focus is on the details concerning the

woman's extremities, those parts of her body that the poet can perceive when she makes any movement.) The orderly description of the
woman, however, does not conclude at the end of the first quatrain,
as one might expect. If lines 2 through 4 provide a physical description that one could probably perceive during a brief glance, the information in line 5 (which *is* the last line of the physical portrayal) is
clearly more interpretive of the preceding lines and introduces a dramatic change in tone, moving beyond the objective (or quasi-objective) depiction by the poet and toward an obsessive preoccupation
with the woman (this woman? any woman? all women?—yet another
question left unanswered and perhaps unanswerable). Among the
descriptive elements in this line, only "noble" would seem to coincide
with what has preceded, falling within the same register as
"majestueuse" and "fastueuse." It is the remaining elements that
require further investigation, as they formulate a confusing depiction
that troubles the apparent order that the woman has represented so
far and stand as a transition point between the physical description of
the woman (lines 2–4) and the reaction of the poet (lines 6–8).

"Agile," according to the *Petit Robert,* connotes "de la facilité et de
la rapidité dans l'exécution de ses mouvements." Although, to be
sure, the poet's exclusively visual encounter is brief, the description in
line 2—"longue, mince, en grand deuil"—would appear to describe
anything *but* quick, physically light movement. We have no indication of the woman's age, but perhaps Baudelaire means to suggest
relative youth—although a widow, she might still be young, attractive, desirable. This qualifier also sets the woman in contrast to the
poet who, for his part, will be described as "crispé," incapable of
flowing movement. The brief, enticing, exhilarating glimpse of an
ankle or foot, even one in mourning, is cause for an intense reaction.
This woman—"agile et noble"—has perhaps both the physical attributes and the social position that the poet finds desirable.

Yet the description of the woman's leg, the ultimate point of focus
in fact—"avec sa jambe de statue"—leaves another indelibly ambiguous impression. The poet captures only a brief view of this leg. But
this leg—agile, if it too can be qualified by the preceding adjective—is
also that of a statue: fixed and immobile. This ultimate orderly depiction renders the animate inanimate, the living immobile. The implications of this description are various: does the woman exemplify a perfect beauty, one that could be, or is worthy of being, immortalized in
the form of a statue? If such is the case, is this a positive qualification,

one that elevates the woman to the status of idealized being? Or is this description, in fact, the source of some degree of alienation between the woman and poet, a strange alienation indeed, considering that they do not know each other? Is the woman's beauty artificial, her leg (like the white leg of a statue) an unreal but stable presence in the hectic city scene in which this encounter takes place? At another level, one might see this immobile "jambe de statue" as an inevitable reflection of the brevity of the moment during which the poet catches a glimpse of the raised hem and what it dissimulates. Although the woman herself is "agile," this agility allows for only one excruciatingly brief view, so that what lies underneath appears motionless. Yet the brevity permits, ironically, a more ordered although less reliable description. It is relatively simple for the poet to describe what little he has seen. By focusing on one aspect or feature of one "isolated" individual, he escapes the chaos of the entire landscape. Perhaps there is an advantage to depicting what one sees in one brief moment, rather than over a prolonged period of time.

Lines 6–7

After the four lines devoted to description of the woman, the sixth line introduces a shift in focus from the seen to the seer, from the object to the subject of the gaze. The "moi" of the first line reappears, once again in a state of motionless disorder—"crispé comme un extravagant." "Crispé" itself may denote a variety of mental states causing tension, anguish, impatience, irritation, or pain, any of which we might offer to characterize the poet's state of mind in this case as he reacts to the woman. But more important, this adjective reflects the disorder in the poet's mind. His precise description of her physical appearance leads not to understanding but to upheaval on his part: "Significantly, the narration begins to break down at the moment when the man returns to himself and refers to his reaction . . . to the passante" (Aynesworth 330). We see that the chaos of the first line has not been eradicated or counteracted by the woman's brief presence but has been displaced into the mind of the poet, leading to his depiction of himself as "extravagant," meaning capable of bizarre actions or lacking in reason.

Although everything around him is "assourdissant," in line 6 we see that the poet is nonetheless capable of focus. Yet for the first time we also have some indication that the poet's glance (if not his fixation) is being reciprocated, that the woman is also looking either at him or in his general direction: "Je buvais . . . dans son œil." What is the nature of this reciprocated sighting (is it a glance, a gaze, a stare? does she actually look directly at him?), and is the poet capable of interpreting correctly the intent of the woman's gaze? Versluys suggests, "He is not so much drinking from the woman's eyes the meaning she possesses intrinsically as he is endowing her with his own meaning" (297). In other words, what the poet offers the reader is less an orderly and objective representation than a desperate attempt to understand her in the little time at his disposal before she fades from his memory. The preceding physical appearance (clear and orderly as it is) contrasts with the overall impact of the woman on the poet, especially the impact of her glance or gaze. Although the poet fully understands the implications of his situation, he is not spared the mental anguish that follows the woman's departure from his sight: "The woman . . . stands for two different ways in which human messages oppose disorder: as mediated, orderly communication (the beauty of her figure) and as unmediated communication (her glance). But in each of them, as we shall see, disorder inevitably lurks" (Chambers, "Storm," 159). She is both a cure for, and a cause of, the disorder in the poem and in the poet's mind.

This matter is complicated further by the depiction of her eye as a "ciel livide" (which itself is then qualified by "où germe l'ouragan"). The woman's gaze/glance appears to be dark and ominous albeit not immediately threatening. Similarly, in "Horreur sympathique" Baudelaire associates the "ciel livide" with potentially troubling thoughts:

> De ce ciel bizarre et livide,
> Tourmenté comme ton destin,
> Quels pensers dans ton âme vide
> Descendent? . . .

Even though these two individuals do not know each other, and undoubtedly never will, the potential for danger exists and succeeds in preoccupying the poet; perhaps any actual encounter with the woman would be disastrous. (For evidence, one need only examine Baudelaire's depictions of women and his relationships with these women in many of his other poems.)

What, in fact, would the "ouragan" describe: their potential relationship? the woman's volatile character? the poet's torment (the latter a likely candidate, considering the line that follows)? "Ouragan" is an appropriate choice of vocabulary, particularly in the context of our discussion of order and chaos; a hurricane might be considered a natural form of disorder, one that we might appose to the "civilized" disorder of the street scene (yet within which there is, ironically, some sense of order, in its circular motion centered on the "eye").

Line 8

After the potentially threatening tone of the previous two lines, the eighth line unites the two aspects of physical and emotional relationships that permeate Baudelaire's oeuvre: on the one hand the idealized woman—gentle, captivating, enchanting—and on the other the (here) nearly violent, physical act. Grammatically, the line is the complement of "je buvais": "La douceur" and "le plaisir" both take on physical proportions; they are the "potent potables" that the poet would consume, thus intensifying his already heightened fascination with the woman. This line is also another wonderful syntactic construction: an orderly, lucid realization on the part of the poet of the effect of the woman on him, the sequence of two-syllable nouns and verbs—"douceur," "fascine," "plaisir"—reaching a climax with the shockingly violent, monosyllabic "tue," which concludes the quatrain. While "douceur" describes the woman herself in relatively flattering tones, "plaisir" describes the potential relationship between the poet and the woman, a physical one that would lead to death.

Lines 9–12

While the woman offers the poet both gentleness and pleasure, the poet's reaction to these qualities encompasses both hope and despair. After her departure, his frustration and tension, which have been building up over the course of the description of the woman, reach a peak (a pseudosexual climax of sorts) in the ninth line, with the sudden flash followed by darkness, followed in turn by melancholic reflection. In discussing "A une passante," Walter Benjamin states, "The delight of the urban poet is love—not at first sight, but at last sight" (45). The woman's presence in the poem is reflected in two ways: through the objective description that accompanies the initial sighting and in the emotional reaction after she has disappeared; the former is based on an event that lasted but a brief moment, the latter on a mental activity unrestricted even by the underlying reality.

The "éclair" is a most suitable image for conveying (once again) the brevity of the moment depicted. Yet this same word functions on a completely different level, introducing an opposition of light and dark, followed as it is by "la nuit" and referring back to the stormy vocabulary of "livide" and "ouragan." Obviously, this opposition does not occur exclusively at a spatiotemporal level. The night is not that which follows the setting of the sun but rather that void in the poet's soul as the passerby moves away from him, the glimmer of hope apparently extinguished, their brief encounter now history (and already obscured by the crowd and by the inevitably fading memory).

The poet's sudden realization of what has occurred, and his confused reaction to this event, are dramatically reflected in the punctuation of line 9. The ellipsis could signify the temporary blindness that occurs after a bolt of lightning has struck, the void in which he feels he has been left, or the ecstasy experienced by the poet as a reaction to the woman. Time, and the woman's progression away from him, continue, while the poet would wish both to stop, in what Remacle terms "la presque simultanéité de l'espoir et de la déception" (97). The exclamation point accentuates even further the poet's startled and consequently chaotic reaction to the woman's disappearance into the crowd. The diacritic mark preceding the second hemistich creates yet another break, a pause after the poet's exclamation, before he proceeds, in apostrophic style, to address this woman. I need hardly point out the obviously disjointed nature of this line, especially by comparison with the order of the preceding line. Its physical appearance on the page suffices to demonstrate the confusion felt by the poet at this moment as events happen all too quickly around him.

The lasting impression left in the poet's mind is that of a "Fugitive beauté," an expression that logically describes the woman in the context of the poem and one that allows again for several possible interpretations. There is undoubtedly a progression from the descriptive to the interpretive in this line, from a description emphasizing the brevity of this encounter ("Un éclair . . . puis la nuit!"), to a reflection on the part of the poet about what he has just experienced. Both suggest the frustration of the poet with the elusiveness of the woman. We might particularly note the use of vocabulary in the poem to indicate the (all too rapid) passage of time: "passa," "éclair," "fugitive," "soudainement," which might be opposed to the vocabulary of the negative question in the eleventh line: "Ne te verrai-je plus que dans l'éternité?" Yet "fugitive" may also signify flight, a conscious (or perhaps unconscious) effort to distance oneself. The lightning-quick exchange of glances between the poet and the woman inspires and impassions the poet, but the woman herself is out of reach, so that he is simultaneously frustrated.

Certainly there is an element of regret about the lack of fulfillment of the potential relationship, an interesting reworking of the common Baudelairean theme of the eventual demise of love or the beloved, as seen in "L'Horloge": "Le plaisir vaporeux fuira vers l'horizon." Ultimately, the woman is that which cannot be obtained, genuinely appreciated, or understood. The poet remains, describing something that has barely existed in his own personal world. It becomes apparent that the duration of the "regard" and of this "encounter" is irrelevant in relation to its impact on the object, the poet. As for the poet's rebirth, to which this line alludes, this may well be an attempt to extricate himself from the disorder and torment caused by his surroundings. Perhaps through some form of rebirth he will inherit the calm, orderly nature of the woman. (It is imperative as well to point out the maternal element introduced into the poem at this point, although I will not elaborate on this notion here.)

The poet's distress in line 11 stands in stark contrast to the all too brief hopefulness of the "rebirth" in the previous line (a rebirth that was, admittedly, "soudain"—thus only temporary—as the maternal figure disappears). The desperation takes the form of a question— "Ne te verrai-je plus que dans l'éternité?"—for which the poet already knows the answer all too well, as will be revealed in the final tercet. In poems such as "Je te donne ces vers . . ." and (albeit cruelly) "Une Charogne," the poet states that long after her death (and decomposition), the woman will "live on," immortalized in the poet's memory and in the verses he composes. Yet in the case of "A une passante," the poet clearly finds no solace in this memory. On the contrary, he despairs at having to content himself with one fleeting moment (one can scarcely even call it an "encounter"). Although he is inspired by the passerby's beauty, the poet would rather engage in an actual relationship with her. A desperate disorder results from his inability to "capture the moment," a disorder that the poet himself provokes (as opposed to that caused by the woman's immediate impact on him). The question in line 11 is hypothetical; the woman to whom it is addressed is long gone, and the poet is left questioning not only the nature of what has just transpired but his seemingly bleak future without her. Aynesworth suggests, "She is simply a fantasy by which the man maintains consciousness in the context of chaos and dereliction" (333). But I would counter that the poet is not merely daydreaming; the fantasy is more like a nightmare. Although one might posit that this woman is merely a model on which the poet will base his "fantasy," I believe that in this case the poet would prefer reality, however disappointing it may ultimately prove to be, to imagination.

The sense of hopelessness reaches a near-hysterical apex in the twelfth line (which resembles the ninth line in its disjointed construction). Again the poet laments how he and the woman have been forever separated, a fact that is stressed by the dual references to spatial ("Ailleurs, bien loin d'ici") and temporal ("trop tard! *jamais*") separation, with the second reference in each case suggesting a more extreme condition than the first; while "ailleurs" and "trop tard" evoke a missed opportunity, "bien loin d'ici" and "jamais" reflect the impossibility of recapturing the past or finding the woman. The restricted and precise nature of the setting for this poem (one instance on a city street) is now overwhelmed by an indeterminate future in an unknown, unattainable place. (Using a similar vocabulary, the ending of "L'Horloge" is even more despairing: "Meurs, vieux lâche! il est trop tard!") The negative "jamais" reveals the ironic impossibility of the title: how can the poem be addressed to the woman—"une passante"—who is no longer there and cannot be found? As Godfrey remarks, "In a dramatic demystification of the traditional lyric preoccupation with the theme of love, Baudelaire thus transforms the love sonnet—which in its very form recalls the ideals of Petrarchan love—into a "poème sur rien'" (41). The woman—"une passante"—is qualified in the title in terms of an ephemeral action that results in her disappearance. The only mitigating factor in this line is the final "peut-être"; in spite of his lament, the poet does seem to reserve some hope for a future encounter with the woman. Yet this hope seems empty; the obstacles to any future meetings are insurmountable, as will be clearly delineated in the final two lines.

Lines 13–14

After these lines of despair, the full realization of the futility of the situation leads the poet into a moment of striking clarity at the end of the poem. The poet liberates himself from the state of confusion caused by his surroundings and by the apparition (and disappear-

ance) of the woman in order to formulate a cohesive, precisely struc-
tured summation about the encounter, an orderly structure that is
particularly remarkable when opposed to the lamentation of line 12.

In the final two lines there are a total of eight pronouns ordered
into four pairs: "j[e]"/"tu," "tu"/"je," "toi"/"je," "toi"/"le." In line
13 the two pairs form a perfect grammatical and semantic harmony
(albeit one founded on ignorance!) as the "j'ignore" of the first
hemistich matches the "tu ne sais" of the second, and as the "tu fuis"
matches the "je vais." This line again suggests a mutual bond
between the poet and the woman, an interest on the part of the poet
perhaps reciprocated by the woman (however slightly), made even
more personal by the poet's dramatic use of the familiar "tu."

Yet once again the emphasis is on the ephemeral nature of this
event, the "fugitive" of line 10 recalled by the verb "fuis" (which is
noticeably stronger than the "vais" used to convey the poet's own
movement). Although the general state of confusion of the previous
stanzas has dissipated, it has been replaced by two new states equally
unacceptable to the poet: ignorance and nothingness; the ignorance of
what has happened to the woman and what might have happened
between them, and the nothingness that results from this ignorance,
as the poet remains alone in the chaotic, anonymous bustle of this
street, what Quesnel calls "l'impitoyable réalité" (100). And this igno-
rance and hopelessness, so clearly and logically presented in the
penultimate line, lead to the final lament that closes the poem.

The last line is composed of two hemistiches with identical struc-
tures—apostrophic "ô toi," followed by relative clause—yet the impli-
cations of the two halves of this last line differ tremendously. In the
first, the poet finally admits to the possibility of a romantic interest on
his part, yet this can only be expressed in hypothetical terms through
the use of the pluperfect subjunctive. The apostrophe makes the state-
ment accusatory, blaming the woman for the power she does not
know she possesses, for being the object of an unrequited "passion."
The final hemistich, however, breaks from the pattern of the previous
three by omitting the first person pronoun. Now only the woman is
mentioned (in contradistinction to the "moi" of the very first line), the
"passante" of the title being all that lingers in the mind of the poet,
yet disembodied from the context in which she appeared. She is no
longer merely a "passante," that activity having long ceased in any
case but rather a (potentially) vindictive woman, conscious of her
devastating impact on the poet.

It is evident from these final lines of "A une passante" that it is neither the physical depiction of the woman (lines 1 through 5) nor, for that matter, the poet's immediate reaction to this woman (line 6 through the first part of 9) that will ultimately dominate the structure of the poem and provide the greatest emotional and poetic impact. The key to a true comprehension of the poem (and the vacillation between order and chaos that has been the focus of this analysis) lies in the chaos-based yet orderly summation by the poet (second part of line 9 to the end of the poem) and more specifically in the final accusatory address: "Seul l'anonymat permet le libre cours de l'imagination érotique inhérente à l'activité poétique qui, elle, est fondée sur le sentiment d'un manque, d'une absence, d'une nostalgie, de l'impossibilité de convergence de la réalité et du rêve" (Buvik 234). Only the disappearance of the woman before they can meet (and before the poet realizes that it is possible for them to meet) allows the poet to engage in the imaginative, poetic activity that subsequently results in the composition of the poem, and in the revelation of emotions that perhaps would not have existed in the case of an actual relationship. The real but chaotic event leads to an imaginary yet ordered summation.

Such an interpretation of the poem obviously emphasizes the tercets over the quatrains, a fact that the title of the poem itself would confirm as valid, since "à" implies an address rather than a mere depiction. What becomes clear after any reading of "A une passante," although this fact is not evident in the lines that precede (which are, however, remarkable in themselves), is that the progress in the poem is assuredly in the direction not only of the final tercet but also of the final two lines: the ordered yet emotional conclusion by the poet regarding this encounter. The only order that the poet can construct in these final lines is sterile—based on the hopelessness of an unrealizable relationship. Far more beneficial to the poet's creative process is the frightening chaos that allows his imagination to run free in the first place. Is it possible, therefore, to determine which prevails in the poem—order or chaos? The answer is apparently neither. The only triumph is that of the passerby over the poet, in both orderly and chaotic fashion, which frustrates his desire to capture (or to recapture) this woman and this moment experienced in the midst of a deafening street.

Chapter 13

Profaned Memory: A Proustian Reading of "Je n'ai pas oublié . . ."

BRIGITTE MAHUZIER

Je n'ai pas oublié, voisine de la ville,
Notre blanche maison, petite mais tranquille,
Sa Pomone de plâtre et sa vieille Vénus,
Dans un bosquet chétif cachant leurs membres nus,   (4)
Et le soleil, le soir, ruisselant et superbe,
Qui, derrière la vitre où se brisait sa gerbe,
Semblait, grand œil ouvert dans le ciel curieux,
Contempler nos dîners, longs et silencieux,   (8)
Répandant largement ses beaux reflets de cierge
Sur la nappe frugale et les rideaux de serge.

A fervent reader and admiring critic of Baudelaire, Marcel Proust quoted his poems extensively (and occasionally misquoted them) in his essays, articles, and correspondence. In *Contre Sainte-Beuve*, Baudelaire is one of the three writers (the others were Nerval and Balzac) whom Proust chose to defend against the critic's harsh judgment, wrongfully and unfairly based, he contended, on a study of the man's life. In "Sainte-Beuve et Baudelaire," a chapter addressed to his mother, Proust attempts to defend Baudelaire not so much against Sainte-Beuve as against his mother's low opinion of the poet. For her also, the man and his work were not separate entities, and she found in his lack of family loyalty a reason to dislike both the poet and his poetry: "Je comprends que tu n'aimes qu'à demi Baudelaire. Tu as trouvé dans ses lettres . . . des choses cruelles sur sa famille" (250). Thus Proust attempts to recreate for his mother the world according to Baudelaire: "Il me semble que je pourrais commencer, forme par forme, à t'évoquer ce monde de la pensée de Baudelaire, ce pays de son génie, dont chaque poème n'est qu'un fragment et qui, dès qu'on le lit, se rejoint aux autres fragments que nous en connaissons, comme dans un salon, dans un cadre que nous n'y avions pas encore vu, certaine montagne antique, où le soir rougeoie et où passe un poète à figure de femme" (255).

Like a child playing in front of his mother, Proust assembles fragments of Baudelaire's poetry, deploring the impossibility of the task yet awkwardly and painstakingly creating his own tableau: "pour cela, il te faudrait tous ces ports, non pas seulement *un port rempli de voiles et de mâts* et ceux *où les vaisseaux, glissant dans l'or et la moire, ouvrent leurs vastes bras . . .* mais ceux qui ne sont que des 'portiques' *que les soleils marins teignaient de mille feux.*" Among these fragments, we find the last line and a half of "Je n'ai pas oublié . . . ," a short poem that Proust found particularly touching and that he also framed with the same awkward prose: "Le soir, dès qu'il [presumably the harbor] s'allume, et où [antecedent?] le soleil met *ses beaux reflets de cierge / Sur la nappe frugale et les rideaux de serge,* jusqu'à l'heure où il est fait *de rose et de bleu mystique*" ("La Mort des amants"). A page later, faced with failure of his tableau, Proust brushes it off negligently with a pastiche of Manet's *Olympia*: "Et la négresse, et le chat, comme dans un tableau de Manet" (*Contre Sainte-Beuve*, 256).

Out of their original context, inserted as they were in a tableau that remains an odd assemblage of fragments, the quoted lines could hardly convince the reader that this is indeed one of Proust's favorite poems. We must remember, however, that Proust's first addressee is not his reader but his mother and that his reading, as dismemberment and rememberment of Baudelaire's corpus, is part of a fictional conversation between mother and son, a conversation that happens to be the kernel of the entire *A la recherche du temps perdu*. It is indeed at this point in his search for an appropriate form of representation that in 1909 Proust abandons his project to write a theoretical work "against Sainte-Beuve" and decides to incorporate his theory into a narrative addressed to his mother: "Maman viendrait près de mon lit et *je lui raconterais un article* que je veux faire sur Sainte-Beuve et *je le lui développerais*" (*Correspondance* III, 320; emphasis added). Thus Proust's reading of Baudelaire becomes at once the most private of acts and the first public profanation. It allows us not only to peer into private, familial connections (between Proust and his mother, on the one hand, and between Baudelaire and his mother, on the other) but also to displace the question of poetic influence from a paternal to a maternal connection (Baudelaire acting like Proust's "poetic mother").

I propose to focus on "Je n'ai pas oublié, voisine de la ville" and to read it as we can also read Proust's *A la recherche du temps perdu*: as an address to the poet's mother, not only recalling early childhood memories (as Proust does in "Combray"), but also gesturing toward the absent mother (Proust begins writing the *Recherche* three years after the death of this mother in 1905).

Baudelaire's poem, which recalls early childhood memories that mother and son shared, is indeed specifically addressed to the poet's mother even though the addressee is not mentioned in the poem. Jean Starobinski thoroughly explores the question of the addressee and of the poem's referentiality in his reading of the poem. For Starobinski, it is one of the greatest poems of memory and also one of the greatest poems about the power of poetry. With great subtlety, Starobinski demonstrates that this power is not so much that of the "relève" of the banal (being represented here by the metaphor of the sun/father, whose presence dominates the poem, transfiguring the mediocre, reconstituting the original family, and taking over the liminal act of memorization) as that of translating a feeling of hurt and letting the addressee hear, through figurative language (mostly metonymical: displacing contiguous elements so that the mother, as the main object of memory, is the decentered or absent center of the poem), the pain caused by a lack of love: "L'acte de langage . . . est l'aveu d'une relation blessée avec autrui, il organise ses figures et ses déplacements pour formuler la plainte devant le défaut d'amour: plainte adressée à la mère, avec le lecteur pour témoin obligé" (428). Although our reading, which offers a Proustian perspective of Baudelaire's memory at work in the poem and emphasizes the opposition between the two parts of the poem, differs in its overall approach, it recognizes the primary function of the mother as the addressee of the poem and the importance of the poem's (self-)referentiality. In the past, most editors of *Les Fleurs du Mal* have recognized the referential quality of this poem (annotated editions usually include Baudelaire's letters to his mother), and most critics quote or mention the letters as an obligatory reference to the poem.

The referentiality of the poem is indeed one of its main characteristics. Its anecdotal, autobiographical aspect, which it shares with "La servante au grand cœur," sets it apart as decentered from the theme of "Tableaux parisiens." Starobinski considers this decentering typical of the poem's metonymical nature, placing it in a metonymical posi-

Brigitte Mahuzier

163

Profaned Memory: A Proustian Reading of "Je n'ai pas oublié . . ."

tion to "Tableaux parisiens," just as Neuilly, a suburb of Paris, is in a metonymical relation to the city. This decentering indeed reflects the position of the subject in a modern city, a city that is developing a sort of bastardized extension of itself: the suburb. Thus the "modern city subject" as well as the lyric subject of "Je n'ai pas oublié . . ." is like the young Baudelaire in his relation to his mother: expelled (in suburbia) and longing (for the center).

If even more poems in *Les Fleurs du Mal* are about memory and the evocation of the past, "Je n'ai pas oublié . . ." can indeed be distinguished as concerning both memory and the poet's private life. The autobiographical component of this poem is further confirmed by Baudelaire's correspondence with his mother. As if the possessive adjective "notre" and pronoun "nous" were not explicit enough, Baudelaire, in a letter written to his mother in 1858, thirty years after the time to which the poem refers, feels the urge to make it clear to her that, along with "La servante au grand cœur," the poems contain early family memories, in which she is the first concerned:

> Vous n'avez donc pas remarqué qu'il y avait dans *Les Fleurs du Mal* deux pièces vous concernant, ou du moins allusionnelles à des détails intimes de notre ancienne vie, de cette époque de veuvage qui m'a laissé de singuliers et tristes souvenirs—l'une: *je n'ai pas oublié, voisine de la ville* (Neuilly), et l'autre qui suit: *la servante au grand cœur dont vous étiez jalouse* (Mariette)? J'ai laissé ces deux pièces sans titres et sans indications claires parce que j'ai horreur de prostituer les choses intimes de famille. (*Correspondance* I, 445)

Almost as a reproach to an oblivious mother ("vous n'avez pas remarqué [mais] *je n'ai pas oublié*"), Baudelaire insists on the specific connection between the poem (in our particular case, "Je n'ai pas oublié . . .") and its spatial referent "(Neuilly)." What was supposed to be hidden from the public (Baudelaire deliberately avoids giving the poems a title) is revealed in the privacy of a letter. With the publication of Baudelaire's private correspondence, the public stands in the shoes of the maternal addressee despite Baudelaire's desire to protect "intimate family matters," his horror of turning the private into the public. As in Proust, we find in Baudelaire an acute sense that to make public the most intimate details of one's past is a form of profanation, especially as these intimate details concern one's early past and one's first relationship with the other (in most cases, the mother).

Thus we find in both the poet and the novelist the same concern about profaning family (read maternal) matters and the same theme of the "profaned mother."

In a second letter addressed to his mother and written on May 6, 1861, Baudelaire makes more explicit his allusion to "des détails intimes de notre ancienne vie," and his tone is more pressing:

> Il y a eu dans mon enfance une époque passionnée pour toi; écoute et lis sans peur. Je ne t'en ai jamais tant dit. Je me souviens d'une promenade en fiacre; tu sortais d'une maison de santé où tu avais été reléguée, et tu me montras, pour me prouver que tu avais pensé à ton fils, des dessins à la plume que tu avais faits pour moi. Crois-tu que j'aie une mémoire terrible? Plus tard, la place Saint-André-des-Arcs et Neuilly. De longues promenades, des tendresses perpétuelles! Je me souviens des quais, qui étaient si tristes le soir. Ah! ça a été pour moi le bon temps des tendresses maternelles. (*Correspondance* II, 153)

Baudelaire's "Je n'ai pas oublié . . . ," because of its pictorial quality (short, compact, and static), is the verbal equivalent of the pen and ink drawings that his mother made for him as proof that she had not forgotten him during their separation. This privileged time, evoked by Baudelaire in his poem, is a passionate but ephemeral moment for the six-year-old boy. Framed between the death of his father (in 1827) and the intervention of his stepfather (1828), it is a time when the mother-son relationship was without paternal interference. At this time the two communicated through images and landscapes rather than with words. Thus Proust's special fondness for this poem can also be understood as a form of "correspondance" between the two writers based on similar memories of special form of intimacy existing between mother and son. The close nonverbal relationship with the other (as mother) in turn arouses in both writers an analogous anxiety when translated into words and when the details of this intimacy are published for everyone to read and thus to profane.

This period of intimacy as it is portrayed in Baudelaire's poem is not without a particular sadness. The sun that lights the poems in its middle—"et le soleil, le soir"—is an evening sun and contributes to the melancholic mood that permeates the poem. Only with time have critics become sensitive to the complexity of the poem's mood. For Robert-Benoît Chérix, writing in 1949, the "dizain" is a sort of "mirage" about an exquisite moment of intimacy, idyllically happy. For Jean Prévost, however, writing only a few years later, it is no longer a question of "bien-être" but of a pervading malaise: "Rien ne semble d'abord plus simple et plus uni que le petit poème consacré à la maison de Neuilly. . . . Pourtant la pièce laisse comme une inquié-tude . . . les tristes plâtres des bosquets, les dîners 'longs et silencieux' mettent dans ce petit morceau une mélancolie vague, un malaise qu'accentue la curiosité prêtée par le poète au soleil couchant, specta-teur de cette scène" (192–93).

But this melancholy is not to be confused with a romantic longing for an idealized and lost past. As Helen Regueiro Elam argues, "The souvenir for Baudelaire becomes an object that has no authenticity other than the transformation and the disintegration brought about by time. Indeed, it is this presumed 'loss' that constitutes its authen-ticity and gives it power. Where romantic poets tended to privilege and to seek out unmediated experience, Baudelaire has a predilection for objects that bespeak disintegration of direct experience" (151). The memories retrieved are not happy childhood memories ("Cette péri-ode de veuvage . . . m'a laissé de singuliers et tristes souvenirs"), and if the objects remembered seem to have lost their original splendor and color (reminding us of the fragility of memory), the reason, we begin to sense, may be that they never had such qualities. The house is white, and so is the plaster of the statue of Pomona. No other color is indicated, and the description of the house and its backyard, its plaster decorations, is bland and anonymous. The first four lines could describe any typical suburban house and backyard. The washed-out quality of the picture evokes an overexposed or an old faded black and white photograph and suggests the possibility of the image's multiple reproduction. If we recall that Baudelaire criticized photography as that which is eminently reproducible and lacks authenticity, we could see in these first four lines a representation of Baudelaire's memory as a photograph: memory has been robbed of its originality, its authenticity. His recollected childhood is ironically like that of anyone living in the Parisian suburb: a "cliché" that fades with time.

The systematic denigration contained in these first lines leaves nothing whole or untouched. Nature, beauty, love, and also the myths of creation, history, and memory are all depreciated in the plaster figures of Pomona and Venus. Michel Quesnel, in a chapter entitled "Pomone et Vénus," points to the double and complementary feminine presence (fecundity and love) that evokes the absent mother but in a blasphemous and violent way (there is neither fecundity nor love): "Dans l'évocation de la mère, ce texte est lourdement, violemment sacrilège, mais Baudelaire ne le sait pas" (19). Pomona, the Latin goddess of fertility in nature, and Venus, the Latin goddess of sensual love, have become the antithesis of what they originally represented in Latin mythology and its Hellenic roots. Pomona, the female figure who represents the eternal return of the seasons and the never-ending bounty of nature, is made of plaster, an artificial and cheap material that is easily eroded and can turn back into powder, in other words a material that cannot stand the test of time (unlike the enduring dream of stone in "La Beauté"). As for Venus, the goddess of sensual love, born from the ocean and often represented as very young and beautiful in her triumphant nudity, here she is old and has lost all her attributes as a "Venus." Both goddesses, each embodying one aspect of femininity (Pomona: maternity and reproduction; Venus: sensual love and carnal pleasure), have fallen from grace, hiding their naked members behind a bush. This female paradise is a paradise lost from the very beginning, a paradise demystified, defamed and simply ridiculed. Not only have the goddesses lost their stone rigidity (in a sort of Medusa reversal: from stone to flesh)—their antique splendor—but they are belittled, hiding behind a bush that has also lost its original greenery and is not even a bush but a "bosquet," the diminutive of bush. The diminutive, which in French also connotes affection and/or a personal tie to the object designated as "petit(e)," is emphasized in the first lines and is linked to the feminine in a repetition of [i] sounds, placed in a symmetrical pattern in the second hemistich of the first two lines: "voisine de la ville / petite mais tranquille."

The systematic repetition of sounds (including the consonants [v] in line 1 and [t] in line 2) turns to a kind of self-parody in the third line with "Pomone de plâtre" ([p]) and "vieille Vénus" ([v]). The fourth line finally breaks up the alliterative pattern but picks up the parodic content of the first four lines, the derisive nature of this diminutive paradise. The bush is as "chétif" (an adjective that evokes both undernourishment and captivity) and pitiful as the two plaster figures it cannot hide, as fragile as the memories themselves. Every element in lines 3 and 4 reveals the fragility of memory, its susceptibility to time, which erodes and fragments the objects remembered (places, people, and so forth). One can point out the progressive zooming-in effect of the eye, causing the fragmentation of the elements recaptured through memory in the first four lines: from "ville" to "maison" to the statues and finally their naked parts, their "mem-

bres nus." It is as if remembering were involved in a process of dis-
memberment and of disintegration of matter, from stone to dust.

But the poem does not stop on this moment of desecration/demys-
tification and disintegration/dismemberment. Formed by one long
sentence, it continues for another six lines, introduced by the conjunc-
tion of coordination "et," placed here to connect the first four lines to
the last six. This connection, however, which is awkward to the point
of being dysfunctional, serves as a clue to the entire poem: catching
the reader between the two parts of the poems, it is the clue to the
oxymoronic quality of the Baudelairean memory at work in this
dizain.

Grammatically, it is incorrect, since after a negative "ne . . . pas"
("Je n'ai pas oublié"), a second negative "ni" should follow suite. The
correct sentence should read, in its primary structure: "Je n'ai pas
oublié . . . Notre blanche maison . . . Ni le soleil . . . qui . . . semblait . . .
contempler nos dîners."

This grammatical incongruity deserves our attention. If the first
part of the poem opens with the lyrical "I," affirming the advent of
memory but through the negative "Je n'ai pas oublié," the second
part forgets (negates) the original negation and sets itself in the com-
fortable mode of full memory. Formed by one sentence, the poem can
thus be divided structurally into two parts, each one corresponding to
a different form of memory. I propose to read the two parts of the
poem according to the two modes of Proustian memory—voluntary
and involuntary—each having a different form of temporality, respec-
tively translated by the perfect and the imperfect tenses. Looking at
the verb tenses in the two parts, we notice that the first four lines are
governed by the perfect and the last six by the imperfect. The
"passé composé," a tense denoting temporal precision (marking
beginnings and endings), has the capacity to fragment time in discrete
temporal units. The memory here is that of single objects getting
smaller as the mind is trying to recapture them in a conscious effort. It
is the frustrating experience of "voluntary memory," when the more
one concentrates and wilfully attempts to recover the past, the more it
escapes. All "I" can consciously do is to retrieve memories as so many
small, disconnected clichés that may never be called one's own, since
they are identical for everyone living on the outskirts of a large city
and belonging to a sort of petit-bourgeois memory bank. "Je n'ai pas
oublié . . ." can thus be understood as a denegation of what really
happened: I have forgotten what made these memories unique, and

all I can summon from my memory is a little white house in a suburban backyard with its gaudy plaster "embellishments."

The second part, which opens with "Et," effects a radical change in the form of memory and temporality. The past tense is no longer the "passé composé" but the imperfect. It is a tense of the iterative, the continuous, setting the memory in a sort of atemporality, that of an artistic creation or re-creation. It is the mode of the "temps retrouvé," of involuntary memory, of that which is given, as a surplus when every conscious effort has failed and one has given up the hope and desire to resuscitate the past.

Grammatically, the sentence should end with the failure of memory, with the fragments of dismemberment or, in other words, with the loss of "le vert paradis des amours enfantines" ("Moesta et errabunda"). But like Proust's experience of involuntary memory, it is precisely because of this loss, precisely because time has receded so far that one feels powerless to retrieve it, that it can be recaptured:

> Oui, si le souvenir, grâce à l'oubli, n'a pu contracter aucun lien, jeter aucun chaînon entre lui et la minute présente, s'il est resté à sa place, à sa date, s'il a gardé ses distances, son isolement dans le creux d'une vallée ou à la pointe d'un sommet, il nous fait tout à coup respirer un air nouveau, précisément parce que c'est un air qu'on a respiré autrefois, cet air plus pur que les poètes ont vainement essayé de faire régner dans le paradis et qui ne pourrait donner cette sensation profonde de renouvellement que s'il avait été respiré déjà, car les vrais paradis sont les paradis qu'on a perdus. (IV, 449)

Thus, through a faulty coordination, we jump from a world of irony, lack, and fragmentation to the incommensurable world of fullness and recovery, from the destruction of myth to a mystical recovery. Indeed a certain aura of mysticality has replaced the pitiful, ironic figures of the nude goddesses. The sun, large mystical eye, the candle ("ses beaux reflets de cierge"), the white tablecloth spread out for the frugal dinner ("sur la nappe frugale et les rideaux de serge"), the silence ("nos dîners longs et silencieux")—all serve to create an atmosphere both mysterious and, with its religious connotation, strangely beautiful. On the semantic level, we are also in another register. The sun, single male element, replaces the duality of the female elements in the first quatrain ("voisine"/"ville," "petite"/"tranquille," "Pomone"/"Vénus"). As the subject of the second part of the poem, it is attached to a string of predicates: "ruisselant," "semblait," "contempler," "répandant." It is the one element that dominates the poem. Whereas the elements in the first four lines are referential, the sun is a symbolic sun, an artificial poetic creation that seems to be an eyewitness ("semblait . . . contempler") and yet casts only its candle-light reflections ("ses beaux reflets de cierge"). Like Rimbaud's "Omega" (in "Voyelles"), it encompasses all natural elements while privileging water: "le soleil, ruisselant . . . répandant" (water), "se brise" (metal/mineral), "gerbe" (vegetal), "œil" (human).

Symbolically, the sun is the phallus as it is the eye/sex of the painter/poet. What the eye (and the "I") has now recaptured is not a fragment of time, fragile and fugitive as in a photograph, but time reconstituted through a sublime representation, more akin to the art of painting than to the technique of photography. This particular quality of the poem has not escaped the critics, for whom it is a "lieu commun" to underline the multiple relationship between literature and painting in the nineteenth century, encouraged by the fact that a number of poets, such as Hugo, Gautier, Baudelaire, and Mallarmé, practiced painting and/or were interested in it as art critics. "Je n'ai pas oublié . . ." has been compared to a Corot for its "grâce saine" and more generally to a pastel or a monochromatic water color for its dis-crete aspect (Mauclair 360; Prévost 192). With the exception of Starobinski, for whom the poem calls upon the invisible presence of the absent mother through a frame displacement reminiscent of some paintings by Bonnard, the painting reference seems to have been a way for the critics to evoke the unproblematic nature of the pleasur-able memory of a peaceful family scene. My reading counters this general trend. Visual representation is not a way to settle peacefully images of the past. On the contrary, it can contain disquieting ele-ments, as is the case here.

Syntactically, the painterly quality of the poem is enhanced by its structure: whereas the first four lines are broken up with commas and appositions, and offer a cumulative effect, the last six form one sinu-ous sentence in which each part is syntactically linked to the whole: "Et le soleil . . . qui . . . semblait . . . Contempler nos dîners . . . Répandant."

As a tableau, it can be read spatially (reinvested with movement, through the eye of the reader/viewer following the eye of the sun/eye) as a move from the outside to the inside: from behind the glass window into the family dining room. The sun holds a privileged place in this poem as it penetrates through the glass window (which allows for the light and the visual to effectuate this passage from out-side to inside) and participates in the most private of scenes: that of a family dinner. In fact, in a series of "dining room scenes" in Proust's *A l'ombre des jeunes filles en fleurs,* Baudelaire is mentioned for his "soleil rayonnant sur la mer" and also as the master of poetry, an inspiration for Marcel, the young would-be writer. The sun is indeed the dominating element of the poem, the source and witness of all things, consecrating with its rays the family dinner, which becomes a religious ritual.

This dominating godlike figure, however, whose rays form a metaphorical bouquet (a "gerbe"), able to link the outside with the inside, the cosmic with the intimate space, is not an almighty fatherly "eye." The sharpness of the glass breaks its gerbe and softens its power. Two contradictory comments can be made on the word "gerbe." First, it can be seen as a poetic, glorified version of the "bosquet chétif." Whereas the bosquet is a sadly unaesthetic element of nature, still rooted into its soil, yet lacking life, the gerbe is a gath-ering of cut flowers or limbs, detached from their natural origin, an artificial man-made creation, a reminder that art is foremost artifice and that it has the lethal power to kill that which it represents. Yet, paradoxically, gerbe is also that which evokes life, the metaphor of poetic production as a vital projection (the two words "gerbe" and "fusée" are analogous, according to *Robert*: both evoke a "jet de liq-uide qui gicle").

Poetic creation can be seen as a form of physical, sexual projection or ejaculation. Liquidity is indeed the main characteristic of the Baudelairean sun in this poem. The liquid element is already present with the word "ruisselant," and after the passage through the solid "vitre," the sun diffuses its liquidity with the verb "répandant." Furthermore, the verb "répandant" is to the previous proposition what "Et le soleil" is to the first four lines: an excess and a prodigality. Again, we can divide the six lines into four and two. Whereas lines 5 to 8 form a self-sufficient proposition ("Et le soleil . . . qui . . . semblait . . . contempler nos dîners"), the last two lines can be considered an excess. What the verb "répandre" indicates figuratively is a profusion, as if the poem barely contained itself, despite its very compact struc-ture (a dizain of alexandrines in rhymed couplets, of which there is only one other example in *Les Fleurs du Mal*: "Je t'adore à l'égal de la voûte nocturne").

Stylistically, the last six lines can also be divided into two parts. From lines 5 to 8, the structural elements of the sentence (which I have outlined above) are amplified with a series of appositions: "*ruisselant et superbe,*" "derrière la vitre où se brisait sa gerbe," "grand œil ouvert dans le ciel curieux," "*longs et silencieux.*" My underlining emphasizes the repetition, enhanced by a couple of doublets: the internal containing further spatial information, the external describing the sun with its sonorous alliteration in [s], and the dinners with their insistence on silence, mimicked by the long (four syllables) "si-len-ci-eux." After this long adjective the poem reaches the end in a more even and flowing cadenza, with the last two lines: "Répandant largement ses beaux reflets de cierge / Sur la nappe frugale et les rideaux de serge."

Again we can oppose these last lines to the preceding four. The sun, with its alliteration in [s] ("Et le soleil, le soir, ruisselant et superbe") has softened into a repetition of [r] sounds: "Répandant largement ses beaux reflets de cierge / Sur la nappe frugale et les rideaux de serge." These last two lines can also be set in opposition to the first lines of the poem as the "petit," with its alliteration in [i], [p], [t], stands in opposition to the "grand," with its alliteration in [a], [r], [g].

These remarks are confirmed if we consider the changes Baudelaire made as he was correcting the 1857 proofs of *Les Fleurs du Mal* for the 1857 edition (where the poem is numbered seventy) and finally into the 1861 edition (where it is numbered ninety-nine).

The 1857 proof reads:

> —Et *les soleils,* le soir, *orangés* et superbes,
> Qui, derrière la vitre où se brisaient leurs gerbes,
> Semblaient, *au fond du ciel en témoins* curieux,
> Contempler nos dîners, longs et silencieux,
> *Et versaient doucement* leurs *grands* reflets . . .

The 1857 edition has:

> —Et le soleil, le soir, *ruisselant* et superbe,
> Qui, derrière la vitre où se brisait sa gerbe,
> Semblait, *grand œil ouvert dans le ciel* curieux,
> Contempler nos dîners, longs et silencieux,
> Et versaient *largement* ses *beaux* reflets . . .

And the 1861 edition reads:

> Et le soleil, le soir, ruisselant et superbe,
> Qui, derrière la vitre où se brisait sa gerbe,
> Semblait, grand ciel ouvert dans le ciel curieux,
> Contempler nos dîners, longs et silencieux,
> *Répandant* largement ses beaux reflets . . .

Looking at these versions, we may notice three major changes and one that may pass unnoticed but may be the most revealing. The first change is from the plural "les soleils" in the 1857 proof to the singular "le soleil" in the 1857 and 1861 editions, with the necessary grammatical changes in verbs and pronouns. Let me simply reiterate at this point what I mentioned above: the opposition between the first and second parts of the poem, between the many and the one, the fragmentation of voluntary memory and the unity of involuntary memory, between human and artistic time.

The second change—from "orangés" to "ruisselant"—also reinforces the importance of a time outside human temporality. The orange sun is specifically that of a certain time of the day, a fugitive moment. As such, the color also adds a realistic touch that the second part of the poem altogether avoids, preferring the full effect of the oxymoronic "soleil," "le soir," which evokes the "soleil noir" of the romantics. Broadly speaking, we could say that realism (and photographic memory) belongs to the first part of the poem, with its dominant elements (the house) painted white (the adjective precedes the noun, so that the color white is emphasized), while a certain form of neoromanticism (and pictorial memory) belongs to the second part, which contains no color, only the light's reflection. Moreover, as I noted above, the present participle "ruisselant," which replaces "orangés," is one of the key words of the poem. It liquefies the sun and turns it into an oxymoron: it is both fire and water. One could see in this poem the copresence of two principles: the masculine (the fire) and the feminine (the water), a fusion of masculine/paternal/sun and feminine/maternal/water elements. Phonetically, the word "ruisselant" has two functions: it reinforces the alliteration in [s] in the fifth line and creates a contrast with (at the same time as it anticipates) "répandant" in line 9. Baudelaire first replaced the softness of "orangés" with the sonorous harshness of "ruisselant" and, inversely, progressively eliminated the [s] sounds from the ninth line, replacing it with the [r] sound (from "versaient doucement" first with "versaient la*r*gement" and finally with "*r*épandant la*r*gement") while soft-ening the vowel through a nasalization in [a]. Baudelaire makes very clear the passage from [s] to [r], the liquefaction of the sun, which simply loses its original power as it breaks against the transparent glass.

The third change involves a very important rhetorical move: from comparison (and metonymy) to metaphor. In the 1857 proof Baudelaire had compared the suns (plural) to avid witnesses of the family dinners ("au fond du ciel *en* témoins curieux"). In the corrections he makes in the 1857 edition (unchanged in the 1861 edition), the sun (singular) *is* an eye ("grand œil ouvert dans le ciel curieux"). Reminiscent of Hugo, this sun has the power to enter into the life of those he watches even in their most intimate and sacred moments ("L'œil était dans la tombe et regardait Caïn" [Victor Hugo, "La Conscience"], 88). Not plural but singular, we could see it as paternal intervention or the intervention of the symbolic (as the Law) into the semiotic. A more careful observation, however, reveals that the eye is already present as an absence in the first part (the absent eye of the god from the paradise lost forces the two goddesses to hide behind a bush), whereas in the second part, the eye is high in the sky, present and visible (it is the acquiescent eye of the paradise regained, through an ideal fusion of both mother and father, liquid and sun).

Thus if we read the poem as it unfolds, from the outside to the inside, from time lost to time regained, from the absent father-as-Law to the father-as-mother (or phallic mother), there is a sense of recov-ery, the sense that we have when we read *A la recherche du temps perdu* from "temps perdu" to "temps retrouvé." It is counting on the failing memory of the reader, however, on his/her forgetting of forgetting: it assumes that the reader will be oblivious to the statement "Je n'ai pas oublié" and will perform the same act of denegation that turns "ni" into "et," a negative into a positive. We can indeed read this poem from beginning to end as a recovery. We can also (perhaps one read-ing does not exclude the other) read it as the oxymoronic experience of what Baudelaire considered as the beautiful, which he calls "bizarre": "La bizarrerie naît de l'étrange union de l'éternel et du transitoire" (Pichois, in *OC*, xx).

One final but crucial remark concerning what I proposed earlier as the "clue" to the whole poem: the conjunction "et." Baudelaire delet-ed "Et" from line 9 ("Et versaient") in the proof, which would have distracted from the fifth line ("Et le soleil") and would have split the poem into yet another part (even though it would have been a minor split: "Et le soleil . . . qui semblait . . . et versait"). At the same time he suppressed the dash before "soleil," as if he had wanted indeed to erase the difference between the first four lines and the last six and to force his reader to be caught in two irreconcilable forms of memory, in a "bizarre," and thus eminently poetic, experience of "oxymoronic memory" (see Hiddleston).

As an appendix, let us go back to our opening scene, a scene liminal to the *Recherche,* in which Proust attempts to make his own Baudelairean tableau by assembling pieces of Baudelaire's poetry. The last line and a half of Baudelaire's "Je n'ai pas oublié . . ." seem to have struck him: "Le soir, dès qu'il s'allume, et où le soleil met *ses beaux reflets de cierge / Sur la nappe frugale et les rideaux de gerbe* jusqu'à l'heure où il est fait *'de rose et de bleu mystique.'*" But as he incorporates them into his own tableau, Proust adds color to Baudelaire's own, very sober "tableau parisien": a touch of pink and a touch of blue from "La Mort des amants." The mystical element of Baudelaire's poem is thus reappropriated by Proust unbeknownst to the poet. One could see, in Proust's recreation of Baudelaire's poetry (using fragments of it, piling them up by assembling them idiosyncratically, diverting their original quality and function), a move similar to "kitsch" in popular art at the turn of the century. A striking feature of kitsch is its affinity for religious themes, its reappropriation of the sacred as it is diverted from its spiritual origin and is assigned a cheap, titillating function. For Baudelaire, undeniably, a sense of the sacred still exists that is lacking in Proust. This sense allows Baudelaire to write his *Fleurs du Mal,* to write from a Christian perspective, borrowing from Christian concepts and mythology (such as good and evil, God and Satan, and so forth). Coming after Baudelaire, after Nietzsche's proclamation of the death of God (after 1870), Proust, who was actually born in 1870 during the Commune, can only attempt to recreate this lost sense of the sacred.

If Baudelaire can write of evil, in the process profaning the most intimate part of his life by writing about it, Proust can no longer do the same. He must stage the act of profanation not only in his novel but in the liminal position in relation to his novel where his mother would watch him recreate Baudelaire's poetic world. But in this world, Baudelaire, as the figure of the poet, would be not a male poetic figure, a poetic "father" (against whom Proust would situate himself) but a feminine figure, "un poète à figure de femme," in other

words a "poetic mother." And this strange phenomenon would hap-
pen, so important to Proust's concept of poetic creation that reverses
the idea of poetic filiation: Baudelaire would become yet another
"profaned mother." Instead of seeing the influence of Baudelaire on
Proust, the reader would be able to recognize Proust (his theory of
voluntary and involuntary memory, his concept of the profaned
mother) already present in Baudelaire as so many "anticipated mem-
ories." The intimate Baudelaire would be displayed to the public
through Proust's writing in an act of profanation, just as features
belonging to a mother are displayed on the face of her son for every-
one to see: "Le visage d'un fils qui vit, ostensoir où mettait toute sa foi
une sublime mère morte, est comme une profanation de ce souvenir
sacré" (III, 1514).

Chapter 14

Recycling the Ragpicker:
"Le Vin des chiffonniers"

ROSS CHAMBERS

Souvent, à la clarté rouge d'un réverbère
Dont le vent bat la flamme et tourmente le verre,
Au cœur d'un vieux faubourg, labyrinthe fangeux,
Où l'humanité grouille en ferments orageux,   (4)

On voit un chiffonnier qui vient, hochant la tête,
Buttant, et se cognant aux murs comme un poète,
Et, sans prendre souci des mouchards, ses sujets,
Épanche tout son cœur en glorieux projets. (8)

Il prête des serments, dicte des lois sublimes,
Terrasse les méchants, relève les victimes,
Et sous le firmament comme un dais suspendu
S'enivre des splendeurs de sa propre vertu.   (12)

Oui, ces gens harcelés de chagrins de ménage,
Moulus par le travail et tourmentés par l'âge,
Le dos martyrisé sous de hideux débris,
Trouble vomissement du fastueux Paris,   (16)

Reviennent, parfumé d'une odeur de futailles,
Suivis de compagnons blanchis dans les batailles,
Dont la moustache pend comme les vieux drapeaux.
Les banniers, les fleurs et les arcs triomphaux   (20)

Se dressent devant eux, solennelle magie!
Et dans l'étourdissante et lumineuse orgie
Des clairons, du soleil, des cris et du tambour,
Ils apportent la gloire au peuple ivre d'amour!   (24)

C'est ainsi qu'à travers l'Humanité frivole
Le vin roule de l'or, éblouissant Pactole;
Par le gosier de l'homme il chante ses exploits
Et règne par ses dons ainsi que les vrais rois. (28)

Pour noyer la rancœur et bercer l'indolence
De tous ces vieux maudits qui meurent en silence,
Dieu, saisi de remords, avait fait le sommeil;
L'Homme ajouta le Vin, fils sacré du Soleil! (32)

In his early years, Baudelaire sometimes favored a quite didactic poetic form that involved *describing* a specific "case" (in such a way as to ask the implicit question: what does this mean?) and then supplying an *interpretation*, so that the whole poem had a closed, question-and-answer structure. Sailors will sometimes capture an albatross and torment the ungainly bird (what does this mean?). Answer: it means that "Le Poëte est semblable au Prince des nuées" and so forth. But later Baudelaire began to substitute for the question-and-answer poem a more open form, without a specifically supplied "answer." Now the poem merely describes an instance, asking: what does this mean? and leaving the interpretation up to the reader. Many of the prose poems of *Le Spleen de Paris* are of this type, as are the great poems of the "Tableaux Parisiens" section of *Les Fleurs du Mal*, such as "Les Sept Vieillards," "Le Cygne," and "Les Petites Vieilles."

Whether an answer is furnished or not, the question poem can be considered an apt form for a poet who is attempting to discover a poetic practice capable of responding to new and baffling historical conditions: the effects of the bourgeois political revolution with its nationalist sequel, and of the industrial revolution, with the sudden emergence of a capitalist culture and the law of the marketplace as dominant forces in the unprecedented new social formation we have learned from Baudelaire to call "modernity." The rapid urbanization of the population and the growth of large cities, especially Paris, must have seemed emblematic of this wholly new historical experience, not least because life in the city daily asks the urban dweller the question: what does this mean? One regularly sees sights—the existence of ragpickers, or of fragile, courageous, lonely old women—and one frequently encounters "cases"—a swan in a midcity gutter—that provoke the imagination and stir the *allegorizing* impulse. For if the object has no obvious meaningfulness in itself, its meaning (if it has one) has to be wondered about, pondered over, *constructed* without guarantee of validity. In this sense, the words "tout pour moi devient allégorie" in "Le Cygne" might stand for Baudelaire's whole effort as a poet of the city, with the sole proviso that early in his career he liked to supply a key to the allegory, as he does in "Le Vin des chiffonniers," whereas later he was to become the poet of the "open" allegory.

Canny readers are always suspicious, however, of "keys" and never more so than when they are supplied with didactic emphasis. Like the morals in La Fontaine's fables, such keys are sometimes so visibly inadequate as a response to the kinds and numbers of questions a case seems to pose that their function can come to be seen as one of *signaling the interpretability* of the case rather than of actually solving its riddles. When, in addition, as we know from the history of the variants of "Le Vin des chiffonniers" (brilliantly disentangled by Richard Burton), that the supplier of the interpretive key hesitated at great length over the actual interpretation to be given (is wine the gift of a charitable God to suffering humanity or the invention of a rebellious humankind seeking to improve the lot imposed on it?), readerly dissatisfaction with any "provided" solution can only be aggravated. It is in any case a law of discourse that what can be interpreted once can always be interpreted again and again (so that the original interpretation will find itself becoming subject to interpretation in turn). There are simply no apparent limits to the interpretability of an interpretable object, whether it be a verbal text like a poem, or some "chose vue" such as a ragpicker staggering drunkenly along a Parisian street or an unlikely swan stranded uncomfortably in a Parisian gutter.

Readers are not alone in knowing this, of course. Writers know it too, and—especially under circumstances of strict thought-control such as La Fontaine experienced under the Sun King and Baudelaire under the various regimes ("constitutional" monarchy, pseudorepublic, epigonic empire) under which he lived—it is for them a rather simple device to supply a relatively innocent or hypocritical interpretive key, confident in the knowledge that readers can *take the hint* and do some further interpreting of their own. When challenged, the writer can always deny responsibility for any interpretation that goes beyond the explicit key, while the text goes on generating other meanings through the history (which may be long or short) of its "reception," or what I will call (because it hints at the ragpicker's

trade and simultaneously implies an active role for the reader) its
uptake.

Richard Burton thinks, very plausibly, that Baudelaire learned
something of this kind from his experience in writing "Le Vin des
chiffonniers." The figure of the *chiffonnier* kept changing its possible
meaning as the historical circumstances of its reception (the context of
uptake) changed. That this discovery about uptake was made apropos
of a figure whose task was precisely to go about the city taking up
shreds of cloth and other materials suitable for recycling in the paper-
making industry is one of those happy historical accidents that make
one smile, or perhaps it wasn't an accident at all? In any case, the ear-
liest version of the poem, written well before the revolution of 1848,
was a piece of flaneur realism, descriptive of the drunken ragpicker as
one of the characteristic sights of the city. Shortly after the revolution,
though, Baudelaire must have realized that his ragpicker, intoxicated
on dreams of glory and justice, was the perfect emblematic figure for
(and comment on) the uprising of the working class, itself inflamed (at
least in Baudelaire's view) with misleadingly utopian socialist
rhetoric. A little later still, a few changes made it possible for the poem
to encapsulate, in sourly allegorical form, the whole sad history of the
Second Republic, Baudelaire's "verdict on the utopianism of 1848"
(Burton, "Metamorphoses," 255) being implied in "the transformation
of the *chiffonnier* from the besotted republican-socialist Utopian (with
Bonapartist leanings) of stanzas 2 and 3 into the out-and-out
Bonapartist of stanzas 4–6" ("Metamorphoses," 254). The allusion,
then, in the poem known to us from the 1857 edition of *Les Fleurs du
Mal* (and only slightly modified thereafter), is to the takeover of the
Republican revolution—an appropriation that was, so to speak, a par-
ticularly manipulative form of uptake—by the "prince-président,"
and in due course emperor, Louis Napoléon (Napoléon III).

All these interpretive metamorphoses hinge on a few semiotic
facts, notably the centrality of wine symbolism in the discourse of
pre–1848 socialism (exhaustively documented by Burton), together
with the easy reversibility whereby "ivresse" and exhilaration can be
understood interchangeably as glorious revolutionary excitement or
as pathetically illusory intoxication or even as addiction (for example,
to the ideological power of heady words). We can assume that,
equipped with these precoded meanings, alert contemporary readers
had little difficulty in 1857 in going beyond the poem's own self-inter-
preting coda (about the benefits and dangers of wine) and in reading

it as an allegorical narrative of the 1848 revolution in the sense that has been made available again to us modern readers by Burton's magisterial historical reconstruction.

But interpretability doesn't necessarily stop there. Without going beyond Baudelairean contexts of uptake, I suggest that the 1857 text not only invites the two main readings that would have been possible until then (the flaneur realism, or descriptive reading, and the "allegory of the revolution," or narrative reading) but also continues to admit further readings in the context of issues that were to emerge more specifically for Baudelaire as time went on and the Second Empire consolidated itself. Specifically, these issues include the question of the relation of poetic practice to the devices of populist demagoguery and militaristic government and the issue of the poet's affinity with the ragpicker, less in terms of their shared addiction to intoxicants (wine or rhetoric) than as one recycler or "parasite" in the cultural economy, to another in the material economy of capitalism. Baudelaire was to be increasingly concerned with the social situation and aesthetic power of the "modern" poet in an era of inauthenticity—for which the Second Empire and its methods of government are emblematic—as well as troubled about the very possibility of a genuinely "poetic" discourse in a world in which what Walter Benjamin called "loss of 'aura'" and Baudelaire "perte d'auréole" reduced the poetic function itself to gleaning what it could from the life of a city to which poets and their craft were, at best, of only passing interest and of purely incidental value. The flaneur of the 1840s was to come to think of himself, more specifically, by the late 1850s and early 1860s, as a "glaneur," a "collector" of a particularly humble kind and comparable, therefore, to the ragpicker in a way that "Le Vin des chiffonniers," focused on its drunkenness theme, seems at first glance scarcely interested in.

There is room, then, I suggest, for readings of the poem that develop the affinity of poet and ragpicker on the basis of a shared intoxication other than the political exhilaration that Baudelaire was later to call "mon ivresse en 1848" ("Mon cœur mis à nu") as well as on the basis of a common relation to history, one that distinguishes between those who *make* history as a narrative of "glory" and those who *undergo* history's effects, like the flame of a street lamp buffeted by the wind, figures like the poets and ragpickers who stagger through the city, reduced to marginal social status and a parasitic trade. Because of the excellence and availability of Burton's political exegesis of the poem through its various preliminary versions, I will refer to the 1857 version almost exclusively in what follows and will devote relatively little space to its relation to revolutionary politics. I will concentrate somewhat more carefully on the poem's implications as an enactment of a certain poetics of modernity and as an allegorization, not of French political history, but of the figure of the poet (see Gasarian), as that history had led Baudelaire to understand it.

To that end I have reproduced the 1857 version of the poem as Burton gives it ("Metamorphoses," 239–40). I will simply rehearse four different uptakes to which it lends itself, relying heavily on Burton, especially for numbers 1 and 2.

Uptake 1: Flaneur Realism

As Burton makes clear, descriptions of the ragpickers of Paris and their astounding way of life were a standard topos, a commonplace of the flaneur writing of the early midcentury. Encamped like hordes of barbarians at various places throughout the city, notably the Montagne Sainte-Geneviève on the Left Bank, the ragpickers, whose drunkenness was proverbial, emerged and roamed the streets in the exercise of their trade, spreading disquiet especially in the *beaux quartiers* (which they frequented particularly assiduously because the pickings there were good). Beyond this surface visibility and exoticism, the grimy, dingy figure of the ragpicker perhaps interested flaneur writers, however, in ways and for reasons they were less willing or able to formulate. On the one hand, he was "in business for himself" as a kind of entrepreneur, and on the other hand he made a living, like all profit takers, as a kind of parasite on the productive economy, so that he stood as a kind of caricature of the entrepreneurial spirit so prominent in early capitalism. At the same time, as a member of the Lumpenproletariat, he was one of the system's most obvious victims, reduced to the misery of a subsistence existence and readily identified, therefore, with the "dangerous" elements of the working class, perceived by the nineteenth-century bourgeoisie as a kind of enemy within the walls of their own city (especially after 1848). Finally, the ragpicker's trade made him a strikingly apt metaphor for those rather marginalized writers and journalists who themselves eked out precarious livings as parasites on the life of the city. Like the ragpicker, they collected in random fashion the sights and sounds of the streets and recycled them but into literary descriptions that were marketable in part because the new, modern way of life had made urban reality so complex and various that the literate members of the population, leading a relatively sheltered existence in bourgeois homes and workplaces, had a strong need for information about conditions of existence and social phenomena that they could not know for themselves.

What is noteworthy about Baudelaire's poem as a piece of flaneur writing, though, is that it represents an early attempt to make verse into a vehicle for a style and content that had previously been confined to prose. Partly inspired by the Sainte-Beuve of the *Vie, poésies, et pensées de Joseph Delorme* (1829), Baudelaire was interested in finding a way to make poetry modern by making it capable of treating the themes of city life, itself the most modern of phenomena. "Le Vin des chiffonniers" is remarkable therefore, not for the originality of its treatment of the ragpicker topos, but because it puts into verse a content that, as prose, was already entirely banal by the 1840s. It is as if the poet had deliberately chosen to versify a cliché of flaneur realism, precisely because of its recognizability as such. Thus none of the particular insights one might except or hope for are offered; like his predecessors and contemporaries, Baudelaire delineates the ragpicker as a figure of drunkenness and dissolution, lost in an alcoholic haze of self-aggrandizement and illusion. He was counting, perhaps, on the shock that a contemporary reader would experience upon encountering and recognizing in a startlingly unexpected genre (poetry) a figure totally familiar from the prosy flaneur journalism that had already coded the meanings that could be attached, in the ideology of the day, to the "chiffonnier" as social phenomenon, the shock of coming upon a ragpicker in a poem, like finding a swan in a gutter, qualified in this way and in this sense as the quintessential urban experience. For as Walter Benjamin perceived, shock, for Baudelaire, is at the heart of the new aesthetics of the city.

As a question-and-answer poem, a description followed by its own commentary, the text has a logical argumentative structure that segments it into three parts:

1. "Souvent . . . On voit un chiffonnier qui vient" (emphasis on the frequency of a characteristic sight), stanzas 1–3;
2. "Oui, ces gens . . . Reviennent" (reinforcement of the initial description with a reexemplification of its terms, the ragpicker as victim of alcohol-induced illusion), stanzas 4–6;

3. "C'est ainsi qu[e]," etc. (meditative commentary, responding to the question—what does this mean?—with a metaphysical interpretation of the significance of wine), stanzas 7–8.

Notice that this structure has the effect of predetermining an issue: the poem is, on the face of it, about wine and intoxication, not, for example, about the social significance of ragpickers or the history of the 1848 revolution. Only by detecting an implicit allusion to the connotations of wine in the socialist rhetoric of Baudelaire's day could Burton reinterpret the poem, discovering in it a political dimension of which, as flaneur realism, the text seems entirely devoid. My own recyclings of the ragpicker poem have their point of departure in Burton's move, but we should note before moving on that in *narrativizing* the poem as an allegorical treatment of the history of the revolution, Burton is obliged partly to negotiate carefully with, and partly to ignore, its argumentative structure as *description*. The conjunctive "Oui" at line 13 makes it awkward to read stanzas 1–3 and 4–6 as referring simply to a chronological change, and the initial "Souvent," appropriate to the description of a typical sight, is out of place if the poem is an account of a singular historical event.

Reading the poem as a structural allegory, I will have no difficulty with "Souvent" but will, like Burton, have to negotiate with the "Oui." Furthermore, my final recycling of the ragpicker poem as a meditation on history and its effects will necessarily have to evacuate wine from the "C'est ainsi qu[e]" interpretive framework of the poem, a framework entirely comfortable to Burton's reading. I *will* retain, however, for my own purposes, the question of the structure of historical agency (wine as human invention or God's gift?) that is posed by this segment and by Baudelaire's long hesitations over it. There is, in short, a certain malleability of the text, of which its various interpretive recyclings can take advantage, bringing certain textual features to the fore, soft-pedaling or even tacitly ignoring others, reinterpreting yet others whose meaning or function may have seemed obvious. Such malleability or indeterminacy as the condition of "recyclability" is a logically necessary characteristic of the interpretable text, and it is, I think, figured in this poem's key image of the flame that vacillates as it is buffeted by the wind (lines 1–2). I will suggest in due course that the staggering gait of the ragpicker, the uncertainty of his progress through the city, reproduces this image, and is itself a figure of the poem's own historical status as a recyclable product of culture, one that is subject to the ragpicker's practice of uptake and that lurches, like him, through the history of its manifold interpretations.

Uptake 2: Allegorical Narrative

This is Burton's political reading of the poem as an allegory of the history of the revolution of 1848, for details of which the reader should consult Burton's essay. Such a reading produces a chronological relation between stanzas 1–3, taken to refer to the revolution's idealistic and utopian beginnings, and stanzas 4–6, read as a comment on the demagoguery and militarism into which it had fallen by the end of the year: "If I am right in seeing the verb 'revenir' as a talismanic term in the Bonapartist lexicon, stanzas 5 and 6 . . . may be opposed after the fashion of a diptych to stanzas 2 and 3, with stanza 4—representing the *journées de juin*—marking the transition from the people's republican fervor of February–June 1848 to the upsurge of popular Bonapartism between July and December" (Burton, "Metamorphoses," 255–56). The transition itself, however, is crucial, since the anaphoric "Oui" of line 13 (looking back to the previous stanzas but introducing a sentence that enjambs from stanza 4 to stanza 5 and so links "republican fervor" with "popular Bonapartism" as if they were one phenomenon) requires emphasis on historical continuities and a less contrastive account of the diptych. Burton specifies, therefore, that "Baudelaire's point seems to be that the (cynical) authoritarianism of Bonapartism is already contained *in nuce* in the (idealistic and Utopian) authoritarianism of Republican socialist attempts to legislate for instant human happiness" ("Metamorphoses," 257), a reading that is consonant with Baudelaire's later ironic treatment of Utopianism in the prose poem "Assommons les pauvres!" The initial "Souvent," though, is more difficult to reconcile with a narrative allegory, presupposing a single series of events. It seems to favor instead another form of allegory that I shall call structural.

Uptake 3: Structural Allegory

Throughout the many versions of "Le Vin des chiffonniers," Burton notes that "one crucial theme remains constant: the assimilation of the ragpicker to the poet" ("Metamorphoses," 265), and he comments astutely on the twin issues of "l'ivrognerie littéraire" and of the poet's affinity with the ragpicker as a parasitic agent of what I have called cultural recycling. I shall return to the issue of Baudelaire's pairing of drunkenness and scavenging in relation to the work of the poet, but the ragpicker's actual trade is mentioned only once in the poem (in the reference to "hideux débris" at line 15), whereas two forms of drunkenness are opposed in stanzas 1–3 on the one hand and 4–6 on the other, and the comparison of the ragpicker's drunkenness to that of the poet ("Buttant, et se cognant aux murs") holds only for the first of these. In the second, a form of "free indirect style" identifies the vision of the ragpickers as victorious troops, returning to bring glory to "[le] peuple ivre d'amour," as that of the ragpickers themselves. In the first segment, the ragpicker is compared "externally" with a poet on the basis of gait, and his dream is that of a wise legislator. In the second, there is "internal" identification, on the part of the ragpickers, not with a poet but with returning soldiery, and the dream is militaristic and demagogic. With characteristic solipsism, the poet identifies the ragpicker as a poet while knowing that ragpickers' self-identifications can be antipoetic as well as poetic ones.

In Baudelaire's two main later treatments of the relation of poetic practice to the methods of government employed by authoritarian regimes such as that of the Second Empire, he concentrates on the difficult task of distinguishing poetry as an oppositional practice from a degenerate and/or authoritarian cultural environment in which it is embedded and of which it forms part. "Au Lecteur" (see Chambers, "Un despotisme 'oriental'") acknowledges that hypocrisy is part of the poet's own panoply in a world under the sway of Satan; "Une Mort héroïque" explores the rivalry between an artistic and tyrannical prince and the inspired clown, Fancioulle, the sublimity of whose performance is as illusionistic as it is imperious. In "Le Vin des chiffonniers," intoxication is identified as the common element against which the ragpicker as poet figure and ragpickers as would-be heroes of the admiring crowd are quite carefully but of course not absolutely distinguished. The distinction is apparent if one correspondingly segments the final two stanzas (7–8) of commentary but in reverse order (so that stanza 7 refers back to stanzas 4–6 and stanza 8 to 1–3). The paradox of wine as it is formulated here then resolves into that of a human invention (poetry) that has a power of consolation ("Pour noyer la rancœur et bercer l'indolence") comparable with God's own gift of sleep but is also an overmastering force that subjugates "l'Humanité frivole" by flatteringly celebrating its own exploits.

Instead of being a comforting gift, wine reigns in this second case by gift giving and not *as* "true kings" do but only *as if* it was truly royal (there is a crucial ambiguity in "ainsi que les vrais rois"). The "Oui" of line 13 confirms the relationship of illusion that exists between the two powers of wine, poetic and demagogic, while the poem nevertheless distinguishes poetic power as part of the divinity of humans (whose allegiance, though, is to the pagan rather than the Christian divine, to the Sun rather than to God), from the abusive power of militaristic patriotism that cannot ("Oui") be fully dissociated from poetry. Similarly the "glorieux projets" associated with poetic intoxication and the desire for justice and good government are distinguished from the illusory forms of "glory" that make the populace "ivre d'amour," while the same word ("glorieux," "gloire") ironically describes both.

Notice that in the first segment, the ragpicker as poet appears as a solitary figure ("*un* chiffonnier" versus "*ces gens*") and a solipsistic one (whose "épanchements" amount to a self-intoxication on the "splendeurs de sa propre vertu"). His habitat is the "labyrinthe fangeux" of a "vieux faubourg" (a worker's quarter) and the moral atmosphere surrounding him is, correspondingly, that of a threatening storm. A dreamer, certainly, he is on the side of the noble "projets" that dignify humanity, however much his vision of wise oaths and just laws, as stanza 3 makes clear, feeds on self-centered and self-indulgent dreams of personal glory, as he imagines himself "sous le firmament" as if the open sky were some great legislator's "dais suspendu." This picture of self-intoxication and self-aggrandizement is in turn softened, furthermore, by the recognition (in stanza 8) that it is compensatory, part of the consolation of "tous ces vieux maudits qui meurent en silence," whether poets or other wretched humans, while the same lines similarly situate all of humanity's ambitions for justice and sublimity as a merely self-indulgent consolation for misery.

But the ragpicker's dream is further contrasted, in stanzas 4–6, with the collective frenzy ("orgie") of the hordes whose escape from back-breaking toil takes the form of imagining themselves a victorious army returning from conquest and surrounded by the love of the people. Tellingly, the scene has now shifted to the glittering new quarters of Haussmann's "fastueux Paris," of which (in one possible reading) this tatterdemalion collection of down-and-outs is a "trouble vomissement." Accordingly, the "glorieux projets" of the ragpicker/poet have become—is this their actual realization?—a daz-

zling and deafening orgy of sunlit military celebration, the just laws
and oaths no more than crowd-pleasing display, an ironic "sunshine"
("soleil," 23) of victory contrasting simultaneously both with the "fer-
ments orageux" (4) to which it illusorily responds and with the
sacredness of the (upper-case) "Soleil" (32) from which wine, as the
comforter of humanity, descends. The contemporary relevance to the
bread and circuses policy of the Second Empire is clear, as is the
implication that France's leaders after 1848 were no more than a
crowd of down-and-outs masquerading as a victorious army. But
these contemporary allusions (the subject matter of Burton's allegori-
cal narrative) are generalized ("C'est ainsi qu[e]") as evidence of a
universal law, that of frivolous humankind's subjection to the dazzle
of gold and the flattering celebration of its own brutal doings
(exploits), as if they were wonderful. Against this form of objection,
the self-indulgence of the poetic would-be legislator's "glorieux pro-
jets" must count as equally ludicrous, perhaps, but relatively harm-
less and, to the extent that it brings some sort of comfort to the "vieux
maudits," even beneficial.

Uptake 4: An Allegory of History

The poem is remarkable, as I have mentioned, for its stress on the
ragpicker as drunkard (a contemporary cliché) as opposed to the (to
us, striking) particulars of the ragpicker's trade, the earning of a liv-
ing from economic system parasitically, not from production but in
scavenging and recycling. In other places ("Le soleil," perhaps, a
poem closely linked thematically with this one, or certain passages of
"Le peintre de la vie moderne," describing the activities and practices
of Constantin Guys), Baudelaire comes closer to associating a picture
of the poet or artist as a collector of chance sights or insights, or even
simply of rhymes, thrown up by city life, with the theme of exhilarat-
ing inspiration, or "ivresse." But only at lines 15–16—"Le dos mar-
tyrisé sous de hideux débris, / Trouble vomissement du fastueux
Paris" (I read "Trouble vomissement" now as referring to the
"débris" rather than to the hordes of ragpickers themselves)—does
the theme of "la glane" surface in "Le Vin des chiffonniers," whereas
the drunkenness theme pervades the poem. Conversely, much later
writing of Baudelaire's seems to invert these proportions at least by
implication; in the "Tableaux parisiens" section introduced into the
1861 edition of *Les Fleurs du Mal*, the poet figure has become very

largely a sober flaneur, and new poems like "Le Cygne" or "Les Petites Vieilles" present him as a "collector" of sights, encounters, and thoughts. Although it includes "Enivrez-vous," the volume of prose poems planned under the title of *Le Spleen de Paris* similarly deemphasizes poetic "ivresse" and highlights rather the poet's status (or lack of status) as a flaneur-collector and his general affinity with those, like prostitutes, saltimbanques, and ragpickers, who ply a parasitic trade in the street. In explicit formal contrast with the architecture of *Les Fleurs du Mal*, the overall design of *Le Spleen de Paris* is unstructured, like a random collection of items "picked up" by the poet in the course of his daily existence as a Parisian. These later texts, then, authorize a reading of "Le Vin des chiffonniers" framed by the perception of an affinity between the poet and, less drunkenness as such, perhaps, than a certain sense of dependency on *randomness*, derived from his existence in the city.

For the hesitancy in Baudelaire's treatment of wine in the poem's coda (documented by Burton), like the vacillations in his treatment of the relation between drunkenness and scavenging—now stressing the one, now highlighting the other, now weaving the two together—is interesting. This hesitancy suggests that unsteadiness, vacillation, and "trouble" (a synonym, perhaps, for indeterminacy) might be key themes of his work as well as of his life (in which he seems to have lurched almost uncontrollably from political doctrine to political doctrine, from aesthetic system to aesthetic system, from poetic practice to poetic practice; compare the opening of *Exposition Universelle-1855*). In his narrative reading of the poem, Burton is led to rely somewhat on the verbs that suggest a teleological (end-oriented) understanding of the ragpicker's movement throught the city: "un chiffonnier qui *vient*," "Oui, ces gens . . . *Reviennent*," "Ils *apportent* la gloire." But the first four stanzas, which begin with a memorable (and only apparently irrelevant) evocation of the vacillating, wind-tormented flame of a gas lamp, are as interested in the ragpicker's *gait*, his mode of movement, as in its directionality; "hochant la tête, / Buttant, et se cognant aux murs comme un poète," ragpickers are also "harcelés," "moulus," "tourmentés," and their back is "martyrisé sous de hideux débris." All these adjectives, which suggest passiveness on the part of the ragpickers as unresisting objects of various forces ("chagrins," "travail," "l'âge," "hideux débris"), also develop an implied equivalence between them, with their staggering gait, and the fitful and also pas-

sive flame of the "réverbère," "Dont le vent bat la flamme et tour-
mente le verre." It is as if the wavering light that illuminates the scene
of the ragpicker's unsteady progress—a zigzagging gait characteristic
of drunkards but also, quite independently of alcohol intake, of those
whose trade is scavenging—somehow symbolizes, in its *passive* (that
is, suffering) relation to the wind, the ragpicker's own "tourmente."
For the wind that lashes the lamp not only stands for the daily mis-
eries of "chagrins de ménage," work, and age but also suggests the
"storms," revolutionary or otherwise, of history, evoked at line 4 in
the "grouillements orageux" of the faubourg.

The latter part of the poem, though, seems more concerned with
the *making* of history as a narrative construct. In stanza 8, it tells a
story of its own about the origins of wine. The description in stanza 6
of the erstwhile battered ragpickers of stanza 4 bringing glory to the
people, after having themselves beheld the upright vision of pen-
nants, flowers, and triumphal arches, shows how staggering misery
can be reinscribed, in the exhilaration of a moment, as a *destiny* of
glory; it is done, as stanza 7 makes clear, by the trick of propaganda.
But this description also reads, not only as a contrast with, but also as
an ironic realization of, the "glorieux projets" harbored by the
unsteady ragpickers of stanza 2, as if the desire for glory on the part
of the wretched accounted for their ready acceptance of what passes
for glory when it is "brought" to them, providing in this way the
motivation for a disabused story about the fate of revolutionary fer-
vor. So does history have a narrative structure, a matter of the making
of glorious projects and of the bringing of glory? Or is it an experience
of random digressiveness, a matter of being buffeted, tormented by
the so-called "winds of change"?

In this case as in that of its other questions, the poem's "Oui" artic-
ulates a difference while forcing us to see the relatedness of its only
apparently opposed terms. The vacillations and torment of those
who, in reality, *undergo* the effects of history—they are "tourmentés
par l'âge" ("âge" in the sense, not only of old age, but also of the era,
the epoch) like a lamp tormented by the wind—are contrasted with
the illusory benefits associated with an active *making* of (narrative)
history. But these very illusions are simultaneously presented as com-
pensatory indulgences or necessary self-deceptions on the part of
those whose actual fate it is to be, not the *producers* of history, but its
ragpickers, those who stagger along, buffeted by events and picking

up the débris that history "throws up" like a "vomissement" but attempting also to recycle the bits and pieces into a form that might make sense of their experience.

If such a reading itself makes some kind of sense—if it is an acceptable recycling of the poem—then it becomes necessary to acknowledge that there is a kind of indeterminacy in the text, as between its own narrative construction of history (a practice it identifies as that of history's "winners") and the experience of history that it describes, as a buffeting that sends its "losers" lurching randomly through the city streets. Such indeterminacy, furthermore, thematized within the poem as its own ambiguous comment on the nature of history, simultaneously affects the form of the poem itself, which gives rise to *narrative* interpretations of its allegory (such as Burton's reading) as well as more *descriptive* accounts (such as my own has tended to be) that read the poem as presenting alternative options (poetic and militaristic drunkenness, wine as comfort and as humanity's deceptive master, history as narrative and history as tormented lurching) but options between which, in the end, there is not much to choose. For as that central word "Oui" keeps reminding us, the supposed alternatives are in fact aspects of the same thing (of drunkenness, of wine, of history), so that one can only vacillate digressively between them, unable to make an absolute distinction between them.

More generally, to return now to my earlier point, textual indeterminacy of this or another kind is the necessary precondition of the fact that cultural texts can be recycled and are subject to different uptakes, as I have tried to show is the case for "Le Vin des chiffonniers." In different readings, different features become prominent, or recede, or are subject to what I called "negotiation" with respect to their function or meaning, but the texts themselves, independently of a given reading, can have no particular, or positively identifiable, character that would be "their own," that is to say, proper to them as texts. Like the argumentative structure of "Le Vin des chiffonniers," textual features lend themselves in part, and in part resist—but are always malleable to—specific readings and then to further readings that "pick up" on them, as if the texts were themselves so many shapeless rags available for recycling, and send them lurching through a history of interpretations(s), like ragpickers staggering through a city. Texts, then, are so much cultural debris, the flotsam and jetsam of history, and depend on uptake for any ability they display to enter into cultural circulation and thus to participate further, both in the making of history (the illusory production of narrative) and in the random buffeting that is the real experience, Baudelaire suggests, of humanity's ragpickers, poets, and other "vieux maudits."

Does that make textual debris "hideux," as Baudelaire wrote in 1857 of the debris under which his ragpickers stagger? By 1861, he had revised the lines that contrast the ragpicker's "hideux débris" with "[le] fastueux Paris" that throws them up, and the vision in these lines had consequently become grayer and more uniform. The ragpickers, now, are "*Éreintés et pliant* sous *un tas de* débris, / Vomissement *confus* de l'*énorme* Paris." One might think that, in this final Baudelairean uptake on the poem, the alternatives in question (poet and politician, comforting versus abusive drunkenness, February and December, history as narrative and history as digressiveness) had become, like "hideux" and "faste" themselves, even less sustainable than before and the all-reconciling "Oui" that joins them that much stronger in the poet's disabused vision of a world governed by the category of the "confus." But by the same token, the status of texts as cultural debris, subject to endless historical recycling, has lost its pejorative connotation, and such texts have become, simply, the burden under which, as cultural agents, we all bend and stagger as, "éreintés et pliant," we attempt to find our uncertain way through the enormity that is history.

Chapter 15

Myth, Metaphor, and Music in "Le Voyage"

WALTER PUTNAM

(A Maxime du Camp)

I

Pour l'enfant, amoureux de cartes et d'estampes,
L'univers est égal à son vaste appétit.
Ah! que le monde est grand à la clarté des lampes!
Aux yeux du souvenir que le monde est petit! (4)

Un matin nous partons, le cerveau plein de flamme,
Le cœur gros de rancune et de désirs amers,
Et nous allons, suivant le rythme de la lame,
Berçant notre infini sur le fini des mers: (8)

Les uns, joyeux de fuir une patrie infâme;
D'autres, l'horreur de leurs berceaux, et quelques-uns,
Astrologues noyés dans les yeux d'une femme,
La Circé tyrannique aux dangereux parfums. (12)

Pour n'être pas changés en bêtes, ils s'enivrent
D'espace et de lumière et de cieux embrasés;
La glace qui les mord, les soleils qui les cuivrent,
Effacent lentement la marque des baisers. (16)

Mais les vrais voyageurs sont ceux-là seuls qui partent
Pour partir; cœurs légers, semblables aux ballons,
De leur fatalité jamais ils ne s'écartent,
Et sans savoir pourquoi, disent toujours: Allons! (20)

Ceux-là dont les désirs ont la forme des nues,
Et qui rêvent, ainsi qu'un conscrit le canon,
De vastes voluptés, changeantes, inconnues,
Et dont l'esprit humain n'a jamais su le nom! (24)

192

II

Nous imitons, horreur! la toupie et la boule
Dans leur valse et leurs bonds; même dans nos sommeils
La Curiosité nous tourmente et nous roule,
Comme un Ange cruel qui fouette des soleils. (28)

Singulière fortune où le but se déplace,
Et n'étant nulle part, peut être n'importe où!
Où l'Homme, dont jamais l'espérance n'est lasse,
Pour trouver le repos court toujours comme un fou! (32)

Notre âme est un trois-mâts cherchant son Icarie;
Une voix retentit sur le pont: "Ouvre l'œil!"
Une voix de la hune, ardente et folle, crie:
"Amour . . . gloire . . . bonheur!" Enfer! c'est un écueil! (36)

Chaque îlot signalé par l'homme de vigie
Est un Eldorado promis par le Destin;
L'Imagination qui dresse son orgie
Ne trouve qu'un récif aux clartés du matin. (40)

O le pauvre amoureux des pays chimériques!
Faut-il le mettre aux fers, le jeter à la mer,
Ce matelot ivrogne, inventeur d'Amériques
Dont le mirage rend le gouffre plus amer? (44)

Tel le vieux vagabond, piétinant dans la boue,
Rêve, le nez en l'air, de brillants paradis;
Son œil ensorcelé découvre une Capoue
Partout où la chandelle illumine un taudis. (48)

III

Etonnants voyageurs! quelles nobles histoires
Nous lisons dans vos yeux profonds comme les mers!
Montrez-nous les écrins de vos riches mémoires,
Ces bijoux merveilleux, faits d'astres et d'éthers. (52)

Nous voulons voyager sans vapeur et sans voile!
Faites, pour égayer l'ennui de nos prisons,
Passer sur nos esprits, tendus comme une toile,
Vos souvenirs avec leurs cadres d'horizons. (56)

Dites, qu'avez-vous vu?

IV

"Nous avons vu des astres
Et des flots; nous avons vu des sables aussi;
Et, malgré bien des chocs et d'imprévus désastres,
Nous nous sommes souvent ennuyés, comme ici.   (60)

La gloire du soleil sur la mer violette,
La gloire des cités dans le soleil couchant,
Allumaient dans nos cœurs une ardeur inquiète
De plonger dans un ciel au reflet alléchant.   (64)

Les plus riches cités, les plus grands paysages,
Jamais ne contenaient l'attrait mystérieux
De ceux que le hasard fait avec les nuages,
Et toujours le désir nous rendait soucieux!   (68)

—La jouissance ajoute au désir de la force.
Désir, vieil arbre à qui le plaisir sert d'engrais,
Cependant que grossit et durcit ton écorce,
Tes branches veulent voir le soleil de plus près!   (72)

Grandiras-tu toujours, grand arbre plus vivace
Que le cyprès? —Pourtant nous avons, avec soin,
Cueilli quelques croquis pour votre album vorace,
Frères qui trouvez beau tout ce qui vient de loin!   (76)

Nous avons salué des idoles à trompe;
Des trônes constellés de joyaux lumineux;
Des palais ouvragés dont la féerique pompe
Serait pour vos banquiers un rêve ruineux;   (80)

Des costumes qui sont pour les yeux une ivresse;
Des femmes dont les dents et les ongles sont teints,
Et des jongleurs savants que le serpent caresse."

V

Et puis, et puis encore?

VI

"O cerveaux enfantins!   (84)

Pour ne pas oublier la chose capitale,
Nous avons vu partout, et sans l'avoir cherché,
Du haut jusques en bas de l'échelle fatale,
Le spectacle ennuyeux de l'immortel péché: (88)

La femme, esclave vile, orgueilleuse et stupide,
Sans rire s'adorant et s'aimant sans dégoût;
L'homme, tyran goulu, paillard, dur et cupide,
Esclave de l'esclave et ruisseau dans l'égout; (92)

Le bourreau qui jouit, le martyr qui sanglote;
La fête qu'assaisonne et parfume le sang;
Le poison du pouvoir énervant le despote,
Et le peuple amoureux du fouet abrutissant, (96)

Plusieurs religions semblables à la nôtre,
Toutes escaladant le ciel; la Sainteté,
Comme en un lit de plume un délicat se vautre,
Dans les clous et le crin cherchant la volupté; (100)

L'Humanité bavarde, ivre de son génie,
Et, folle maintenant comme elle était jadis,
Criant à Dieu, dans sa furibonde agonie:
'O mon semblable, ô mon maître, je te maudis!' (104)

Et les moins sots, hardis amants de la Démence,
Fuyant le grand troupeau parqué par le Destin,
Et se réfugiant dans l'opium immense!
—Tel est du globe entier l'éternel bulletin." (108)

VII

Amer savoir, celui qu'on tire du voyage!
Le monde, monotone et petit, aujourd'hui,
Hier, demain, toujours, nous fait voir notre image:
Une oasis d'horreur dans un désert d'ennui! (112)

Faut-il partir? rester? Si tu peux rester, reste;
Pars, s'il le faut. L'un court, et l'autre se tapit
Pour tromper l'ennemi vigilant et funeste,
Le Temps! Il est, hélas! des coureurs sans répit, (116)

Comme le Juif errant et comme les apôtres,
A qui rien ne suffit, ni wagon ni vaisseau,
Pour fuir ce rétiaire infâme; il en est d'autres
Qui savent le tuer sans quitter leur berceau.   (120)

Lorsque enfin il mettra le pied sur notre échine,
Nous pourrons espérer et crier: En avant!
De même qu'autrefois nous partions pour la Chine,
Les yeux fixés au large et les cheveux au vent,   (124)

Nous nous embarquerons sur la mer des Ténèbres
Avec le cœur joyeux d'un jeune passager.
Entendez-vous ces voix, charmantes et funèbres,
Qui chantent: "Par ici! vous qui voulez manger   (128)

Le Lotus parfumé! c'est ici qu'on vendange
Les fruits miraculeux dont votre cœur a faim;
Venez vous enivrer de la douceur étrange
De cette après-midi qui n'a jamais de fin?"   (132)

A l'accent familier nous devinons le spectre;
Nos Pylades là-bas tendent leurs bras vers nous.
"Pour rafraîchir ton cœur nage vers ton Electre!"
Dit celle dont jadis nous baisions les genoux.   (136)

VIII

O Mort, vieux capitaine, il est temps! levons l'ancre!
Ce pays nous ennuie, ô Mort! Appareillons!
Si le ciel et la mer sont noirs comme de l'encre,
Nos cœurs que tu connais sont remplis de rayons!   (140)

Verse-nous ton poison pour qu'il nous réconforte!
Nous voulons, tant ce feu nous brûle le cerveau,
Plonger au fond du gouffre, Enfer ou Ciel, qu'importe?
Au fond de l'Inconnu pour trouver du *nouveau!*   (144)

This last, great poem in *Les Fleurs du Mal* was composed during the serene, productive weeks Baudelaire spent in early 1859 at the Maison-joujou in Honfleur. From this peaceful retreat at Madame Aupick's house overlooking the port, he wrote the final act in the eternal spectacle of spleen and suffering. The original title, "Les

Voyageurs," was changed to "Le Voyage" when it was included in the 1861 edition of *Les Fleurs du Mal*. On February 20, 1859, Baudelaire reported to his friend Charles Asselineau the completion of a long poem "qui est à faire frémir la nature, et surtout les amateurs de progrès" (*OC* I, 1098). Three days later, he asked Maxime du Camp to accept the dedication: besides the dutiful expression of admiration for the renowned traveler and academician, Baudelaire was also hoping to buy time in repayment of debts he had contracted. Nor should the irony of the dedication escape notice (*OC* I, 1097): du Camp, by his own voyages in Brittany and the Near East, embodied that restless lure of infinite horizons. In his own writings, du Camp had hailed "progress" as the new religion of his century. For Baudelaire, the kind of progress espoused by his contemporaries was an intellectual and artistic sham resulting from the worst form of self-delusion and denial. "Le Voyage" thus catalogs the vanity and futility of our numerous ploys designed to escape or overcome the vicissitudes of our earthly existence. Through its various movements, the poem holds up to us the despairing image of life: "Une oasis d'horreur dans un désert d'ennui!" (112). The ultimate voyage leads inevitably and unrelentingly to death or, as the concluding lines suggest, through death and the unknown to the hope and promise of renewal.

"Le Voyage" is not only the longest poem in *Les Fleurs du Mal*; it also occupies a strategic position as the final poem in the final section ("La Mort") of the 1861 and 1868 editions. The length of the poem merits consideration in view of its significance to the collection. Let us remember in passing that the very notion of a long poem was contrary to Edgar Allen Poe's aesthetic, an injunction that Baudelaire largely followed. Here as nowhere else he sets up a complex network of images and resonances that challenges the reader's acumen. Indeed, its very length creates obstacles to even the well-intentioned reader who wishes to treat the wealth of rhythmic, semantic, and metaphoric features in the poem. The rich sonority of "Le Voyage" makes it most difficult to seize in one cogent grasp: to give but one example, does the reader immediately associate the "mer"/"amer" end rhyme in lines 42 and 44 with the "amers"/"mers" of lines 6 and 8? Probably not, at least not before several readings. The significance of such repeated sound patterns is immediately obvious in a sonnet, whereas even the attentive, devoted reader cannot easily connect all of the pieces of the 144 lines of "Le Voyage." The task becomes even more daunting when we begin to consider that this final poem contains innumerable echoes of many of the preceding 126 poems of *Les Fleurs du Mal*.

As with the final scene in a Shakespearean drama, we would typically turn to the closing poem in a collection for definitive pronouncements on the themes of nature, fate, time, humanity, and, of course, death. Given the much-discussed "architecture secrète" of *Les Fleurs du Mal*, "Le Voyage" would seem to be a converging point for all that has preceded. While all of the major themes of *Les Fleurs du Mal* recur one final time, the much-awaited resolution and closure are withheld and deferred beyond the limits of the collection, beyond the limits of life. Death is, after all, the one journey from which no one returns. "Le Voyage" is related to Rimbaud's "Bateau ivre" in the sense that both are visionary poems of vision withheld; even if Baudelaire tells some of what is purportedly seen by other travelers, the reader should not expect any sort of revelation. Baudelaire's earthly search for answers has taken him through a succession of revolts only to leave him faced now with the inevitability of death. Rather than fear judgment, rather than welcome relief, the poet gives us an ambiguous approach to death: a sometimes timorous, sometimes defiant fascination with the uncharted void that might hold the promise of renewal. He is prepared to follow the paths that lead "Anywhere out of this world," according to the title of one of his prose poems. The retrospective glance, far from creating nostalgia, points to an open future and a vertiginous voyage to worlds yet unknown.

"Le Voyage" retraces an itinerary that resembles the stages of life itself: from the evocations of childhood in the opening stanza through the approach of death at the end, Baudelaire takes the reader on one final journey. It is a poem not of rupture but rather of solemn transition and transport to another world. The formal and thematic features of the poem preclude the sound and fury that so often go with death poetry. Baudelaire believed that great poems should have the steady flow of great rivers "qui s'approchent de la mer, leur mort et leur infini" (Richard, *Poésie*, 115). The regular stanzas made up of four alexandrines each contain few surprises: a couple of interesting uses of enjambment, an occasional punctuation break that interrupts the flow, a rare emphasis on a particular word versus another. The very regularity of "Le Voyage" contributes to its difficulty: an inattentive reader can be lulled into complacency or distraction by the floating rhythms that prevail.

The general organization of "Le Voyage" leads quite naturally from the opening evocation of childhood to the final section where death rules supreme. This progression is charted through a structure that is strikingly predictable and sustainably regular. Except for the two-quatrain stanzas of sections 3 and 8 as well as the pivotal one-line question in section 5, all of the others contain either six or seven quatrains. Each four-line stanza is made up of regular alexandrines, and the alexandrines generally observe a caesura (hemistich) after the central, sixth syllable. The occasional run-on line ("enjambement") tends to englobe a complex thought and never disrupts the methodical, calculated pace of the poem. I shall return to the specific use of enjambment in the one-line questions posed in sections 3 and 5. The stanzas follow a regular, alternating *a/b/a/b* rhyme pattern ("rime croisée"); in keeping with the traditional law of alternating rhymes, the "a" rhymes are feminine, while the "b" rhymes are masculine. One interesting variant on this general tendency occurs in the second and third stanzas, where the "a" rhymes continue through both stanzas and resonate with alternating consonants: "flamme"/"lame" and "infâme"/"femme." The [f] and [l] alternation provides a haunting echo to the rounded [am] group that ends each line; the final insistence on "femme" consequently receives maximum stress. Although efforts have been made to devise a theory about the properties of masculine and feminine rhyme endings, such theories do not help us much in this poem. It is widely acknowledged that Baudelaire did not indulge in many of the bold formal innovations that would soon sweep their way into French poetry. His greatness lies elsewhere and especially in the rich fabric of myth and theme, and of music and vision, that he so deftly weaves into patterns of unsurpassed subtlety.

I

The first section of "Le Voyage" contains a typology of voyagers in keeping with the original title of the poem. From lost childhood to the adventurer, from the victim of love to the refugee, all flee a negative destiny. They have all found the present world disappointing for a host of reasons; their escape involves a constant flight toward some chimeric, paradisiacal haven. As evoked in the final two stanzas, the only true voyagers are those who leave for no specific reason, those who push onward with a destination no more clearly defined than clouds and dreams. Except for a unique reference to "ballons" (18), the preferred mode of transport is by sea, perhaps out of deference to the fabled travels of Odysseus, perhaps in recollection of Baudelaire's only real journey, which took him by ship as far as Mauritius and Réunion at the age of twenty. Indeed, much of the rhythm of "Le Voyage" and a good deal of its metaphysical scope can be attributed to the rich suggestiveness of the sea. One example occurs in lines 7–8: "Et nous allons, suivant le rhythme de la lame, / Berçant notre infini sur le fini des mers," in which the first line can be considered to contain up to four stressed syllables in order to suggest the rolling waves at sea. Even the seemingly infinite sea has limits that are challenged and surpassed by the individual's limitless, internal aspirations.

The opening stanza sets the tone and direction for the rest of the poem. The imaginary travels of a child looking at maps or prints of far-off places are an expression of youthful desire for conquest; with only limited knowledge of the outside world, the child sees himself as invincible. The childhood theme so central to Baudelaire recurs here with force: it is a time of optimism and innocence, inclusion and virtuality. As put in *Le peintre de la vie moderne*: "L'enfant voit tout en *nouveauté*; il est toujours *ivre*" (*OC* II, 690). The irony of the child's *love* of maps will recur in II, 4 with the mention of the adult lookout's *love* of imaginary lands; such self-delusion can only lead to bitter disillusionment. At this stage of childhood, everything *is* as it seems, signaled as of the first stanza by the three consecutive uses of the verb "être" followed by an adjective. These lines set up a perfect sequence of comparisons that will furnish the terms for the unfolding of the poem as a whole: "égal," "grand," and "petit." Each of these terms will provide the measure of the individual against the universe that he does not yet know. The child thinks that he can devour the world, thus introducing the theme of desire that will be developed most strikingly in section 4. From the perspective of a child's pure look outward, the world seems much bigger than in the "eyes of memory," when everything seems so much smaller. It is a question of vision, which, as we know, is one of Baudelaire's central concerns. This preoccupation will be highlighted in the chiasma of lines 3–4, which constitutes a mirror image converging toward a hypothetical (but absent) center. Metaphor will provide the privileged means of suggesting the multiple contradictions in the human condition and of redefining our perceptions of reality.

Although he intimates some personal concerns, Baudelaire is careful to maintain his poem at a high level of generality. He does so by the consistent use of plurals or collective singular nouns: "l'enfant" can be any child, "les voyageurs" are nonspecific, archetypal figures without defined traits. The subject of the poem is a collective "nous": this presumably includes the poet himself and all humanity, which will inevitably succumb to death. Baudelaire is very careful to install this we/they opposition in readers' minds, reserving the familiar form of direct address—"tu"—for the final section, in which death appears in the guise of a ship's captain. The reader is thus left with the uneasy feeling of being the absent "tu" to whom the poet speaks and for whom he expounds upon the journey of life.

The generality necessary for the poem is reinforced by a subtle penchant for abstraction, quite often in the context of a more concrete passage. The aforementioned infinity rocked on the finite seas is but one example of how Baudelaire transforms images into poetry. Claude Pichois has pointed out the antithetical and paradoxical nature of qualifying the sea as finite when it is typically one of the most boundless spaces known to poets (Pichois 1098). Another example of generality in this first section can be found in the use of myths that resonate beyond the simple level of interpretation. In stanza 4, Baudelaire introduces the tale of Circe, the goddess who transformed Odysseus's men into swine. The archetype of the dangerous female is omnipresent in Baudelaire's poetry, and "Le Voyage" is no exception. For now, it is important to point out the rapid transformation in stanza 4 by which the crew members refuse the trap of eroticism and flee seduction in a space that is both metaphysical and mythological. The enjambment that links lines 13 and 14 compels the reader to accept the defense against the temptress: drunkenness brought on by space, light and flaming skies, drunkenness that approximates the infinite and hides the horrors of the void (compare "Une Mort héroïque"). Let us remember that the crew members' thirst made them vulnerable to Circe's magic potion in the first place; second, that Odysseus's willingness to share Circe's bed reversed the charm and liberated his companions. Baudelaire thus replaces the erotic solution by an injunction to contemplation of such ineffable qualities as space and light. These are extended versions of the space of maps and the light of lamps evoked in stanza 1: they become physical manifestations of the infinite and the boundless that, like the poet's imagination, defy comprehension by the common mortal. The antithetical elements of ice and sun make up this radical therapy against the perfidious kisses of the temptress.

II

Section 2 deals with hope and disillusionment, imagination and suffering, and desire and deception. Having posited the futility of any voyage that pretends to lead to a glorious destination, Baudelaire returns here to blast any illusion that man might still have about his ability to attain such common goals as love, glory, and happiness. Despite the acute focus of this section, the poem maintains a high level of generality due in large part to the use of capitalized nouns, either abstract ("Curiosité," "Ange," "Homme," "Imagination") or mythogeographic ("Icarie," "Eldorado," "Enfer," "Amériques," "Capoue"). In a universalizing mode, Baudelaire leads us to give the greatest possible extension to the "nous" that runs throughout the poem; the poet would include himself with this crew of doomed adventurers. In a resounding confirmation of the power of metaphor, Baudelaire shows that we cannot be named, but can only be compared, as occurs twice in the first stanza: we *imitate* a top or a ball as we turn in circles; then curiosity, *like* a cruel angel, pushes us to constant activity that leads nowhere except to disenchantment and bitter defeat. This exercise of our desire and will can never overcome the fundamental void, the profound absence that resides at the center of all human activity. Our goals are like mirages, always magnificent and always illusory, vanishing as soon as we seem on the verge of achieving them. The somber, nihilistic second strophe categorically subverts the idea of meaning in life: since our goals are nowhere, they are everywhere, and since hope springs eternal in the human heart, we run even harder in pursuit of a resting place "anywhere out of this world." We have exhausted all earthly possibilities, prefiguring the final conclusion in which death holds the only source of hope.

The frame of reference in this second section is a curious mixture of Christian and pagan images: in the final approach to death, Baudelaire suggests that the antagonism between such earthly distinctions is ridiculous and futile in the face of an infinitely more awe-inspiring prospect. The angel is, after all, cruel; "Enfer" is more expletory than explicatory; the "brilliant paradise" in the final stanza is not a divine place for worthy souls but rather a mirage for desperate derelicts. All of these places are illusory, providing imaginary solace for wounded souls but no real escape from the fate that lucid individuals know. The sea imagery dominates stanzas 3–5 in a rather predictable but magisterial show of Baudelairean prowess: in our metaphorical journey through life, we mistake islands and ports for safe havens from the travails and dangers that lie in our path. Baudelaire tells us that the abuse of our imagination and our capacity for self-delusion lead to cruel awakenings when we realize that we have lived for dreams and illusions. He exhorts us to open our eyes not only to the reefs and other dangerous passages that await us but also to the intrinsic futility of setting goals that do not even exist. Neither Eldorado, nor the Americas, figure on Baudelaire's map.

Classical references abound in this second section; indeed, except for the earlier mention of Circe, they are suddenly grouped here in opposition to the more specifically Christian imagery that is prevalent in other parts of the poem. This could be explained by the fact that we are still listening to the narrator-poet here, whereas the travelers' tales dominate in sections 4–6, where the Christian references become more frequent. We can already note that in sections 7–8, when the narrator-poet takes over once again, the frequency of classical references increases accordingly. Baudelaire was obviously attracted by the potential of the prestigious wanderings of Odysseus, one of the earliest founding texts of initiation and self-discovery. We should nevertheless be wary of making too much of the specifics of such a comparison, because there are as many differences as similarities. The most important divergence between the two works is their outcome: while Odysseus returns to Ithaca and lives a happy, fulfilling life of earthly satisfactions in the real world, Baudelaire catalogs the suffering and despair that make up life in hopes that the unknown realm of death will provide a possibility for renewal.

The first clearly classical reference occurs in stanza 2: "Notre âme est un trois-mâts cherchant son Icarie" (33). This allusion is generally taken to be to *Voyage en Icarie* (1840), a philosophical novel by Etienne Cabet. Cabet was a utopian pacifist close to nineteenth-century socialism; he is probably best known on this side of the Atlantic for having attempted to found utopian communities in the American Midwest (he was buried in St. Louis in 1856). Baudelaire might very well have been attracted to this image of a utopian world that contrasts so brutally with his harsh portrayal of reality. In a larger, more general sense (which is also the sense that attracted Cabet), "Icarie" refers to an earthly paradise such as one might expect to find in the Greek island that was named for the unfortunate Icarus, the son of Daedalus who flew too close to the sun and fell into the sea nearby. Islands have long been utopian places, protected by virtue of their isolation, idealized as miniature worlds, reserved for scenes that the mainland cannot host. The utopian search is above all for a small corner of perfection preserved in contrast to the surrounding ruin and devastation of the real world. It is hardly surprising that Baudelaire's poetry abounds with islands and havens of all sorts; indeed, the next stanza recounts the illusion brought on by too vivid an imagination that sees an Eldorado in each island. One other aspect of the Icarus legend might help us to argue for this interpretation: who in Greek mythology better symbolizes the vertical ascent and fall than the boy who disobeyed his father's orders and flew too close to the sun, melting his wings and bringing about his death by drowning? Much has already been made of Baudelaire's obsession with verticality (compare "Elévation," "Hymne à la beauté"): the seat of heaven with regard to abysmal hell, the evanescent air as opposed to the hard earth, the will to defy gravity itself and rise above the menacing "gouffre." Icarus epitomizes death resulting from uncontrolled curiosity and desire, both of which are central themes in "Le Voyage." He defied his father's injunction and paid the price of his disobedience. These are all constant preoccupations of Baudelaire, both the man and the poet, and seem to us to justify expanding the interpretation of this reference to "Icarie" beyond its presently accepted limits.

The other mythological places mentioned in this section are all variations on the utopian theme: "Eldorado," the fabled city of gold sought by the Conquistadors, "Amériques," the new world of promise and potential, "Capoue," the Italian city of delights where Hannibal's soldiers spent a voluptuous winter. All of these names are evoked by way of contrast with the despairing reality that Baudelaire sees everywhere. This self-deception results from our human propensity for hope and especially from our deformed vision. The sailor on watch cries out: "Ouvre l'œil" (34); another drunken sailor invents imagined Americas that are mirages (43–44); the old vagabond of the final stanza has his eyes bewitched to the point that he thinks he sees a city of pleasure instead of a slum (47–48). Is this distorted vision so common because we prefer to delude ourselves by seeing a here-and-now, that is better than it really is, out of fear that the unknown might prove to be even worse? As we know, Baudelaire will invert this duality and embrace the unknown future rather than endure further suffering in the present.

The fifth stanza of this second section also provides us with an especially striking example of Baudelaire's poetic virtuosity:

> O le pauvre amoureux des pays chimériques!
> Faut-il le mettre aux fers, le jeter à la mer,
> Ce matelot ivrogne, inventeur d'Amériques
> Dont le mirage rend le gouffre plus amer?

In one exclamation and one extended question, the poet manages to create a complex web of sound and meaning that deserves special attention. I have already pointed out that he echos the rhyme pattern "mer"/"amer" that had been used earlier in the second stanza of the poem. The other pair of end rhymes are among the richest in the poem: "chimériques"/"Amériques." Likewise, there is an internal rhyme at the caesura in line 2: "fers"/"mer." But the predominant pattern that gives the whole stanza its strong tonality is the cluster of [m] + vowel + [r]. Each of the line-ending words contains such a sequence, thus linking them beyond the usual pairs of rhymes that we expect. In addition, we find the sequence in "*am*o*ur*eux" and "*mir*age"; with an added consonant, the sequence recurs in "mettre," which contributes to the [r] string in the second line. We could also consider "*m*atelot iv*r*ogne" to contain a different version of the same pattern, although the more interesting combination of sounds there is the [v] + [r] that recurs in "inventeur." The [v] sound, as we shall see, is the predominant consonant throughout the entire poem, occurring from the title to the final word: "nouveau." This rich sonority extends to the emphasis that one must place on the key word in the poem: "gouffre." The abysmal depths are both a place of terror and of hope, a void and a space to be filled; in the felicitous words of Jean-Pierre Richard, the gouffre is the privileged place of Baudelairean spirituality (95). It is into the gouffre that the poet plunges at the end of the poem in hopes of renewal and rediscovery.

III

Section 3 consists of two stanzas and a half-line question addressed to the "étonnants voyageurs" who suddenly appear before the poet. Following the poet's monologic presentation in sections 1 and 2, Baudelaire here infuses his poem with a dynamic element: the reported tale of other voyagers. This dialogue constitutes a dramatic counterpoint to the poet's voice, one that could only exist in a long, developed poem such as "Le Voyage." Are the voyagers "étonnants" because the poet is surprised to see them at all; or is it some aspect of their appearance that he finds unusual; or is it in anticipation of their universal pronouncement about the depravity of the human race? We find ourselves here faced with a dialogue between two groups ("nous"/"vous"), neither of which we know or see well enough to personalize their discourses. This level of generality remains high because of the almost exclusive use of plurals in both stanzas, yielding an impression of density and multiplicity.

The first stanza contains an interesting convergence of two entities often connected in Baudelaire's poetry: eyes and seas. Although not bottomless, both give an impression of unfathomable depth. They are further valorized by the reference to rich memories (51), as if eyes and seas were the repositories of immense wealth. This comparison is suggested by the mention of fabulous jewels made up of stars and ether; these hidden treasures, frequent with Baudelaire, are nevertheless as inaccessible as stars or ether. The box that contains the riches of our memory, like the treasure chest, like the gouffre, are inexhaustible; we cannot, by definition, reach their depths or measure their worth. The direction of movement here becomes complex, since it seems to lead downward and inward, toward some hypothetical center represented by the jewelry box. This motion contrasts with the outward movement of the "true voyagers" of section 1. As Jean-Pierre Richard so cogently put it: "Tout effort vers le centre de l'être débouche ici sur une nostalgie" (101).

The whole presentation grows more suggestive and less descriptive, more turned to the hard, mineral sphere than to the soft, human world. In fact, beyond the two groups, the poem makes only scant, implied reference to humankind at all; it is as if we were defined by the way we travel (neither by steam nor by sail), by our current station (prison), by our ability to register and record (like a canvas). Baudelaire excels thus at writing what remains an exceptionally human poem while expelling from it recognizable human beings. The painting metaphor (55–56) invokes our thirst for new images that speak truth to our lives and that can understand the tales of other travelers. Since it is through the senses that we know the world, Baudelaire inscribes vision in the question asked: "Dites, qu'avez-vous vu?" (57). The poet first asks these astonishing travelers what they saw in the course of their travels; bringing back tales of far-off lands or peoples is fundamentally a centering act, one that displaces the original focus in favor of another.

IV

Section 4 opens the direct discourse of the travelers who have experienced the world and return to tell of what they saw in their travels. The maritime setting here reaches its richest expression. In a tale reminiscent of Poe's *Narrative of Arthur Gordon Pym*, the travelers take us through a series of landscapes that are suggested more than described, aestheticized rather than identified. Each evocation has the hardness and concentration of the jewels to which the poet referred earlier. Like an oracle, the voyager-poets of sections 4 and 5 give a past vision in trusting that it will shed light on the present and even the future; the verbs will suddenly be in the past or future rather than in an atemporal present. To relate a vision is to reveal desire; the whole fourth section leads ineluctably to an exposition of the hollowness of the wonders of the world for which we so ardently yearn.

Theirs is essentially a visual evocation, suggesting by the rapid succession of sights that they were constantly in motion. Their vision confirms the earlier remark comparing men to tops and balls (25–32), always spinning but rarely advancing to any destination worth achieving. At such a whirlwind pace, it is hardly surprising that they are never seen at rest in one place. Their boredom doubtless pushes them onward; by comparing it to the boredom of the audience, Baudelaire reinforces the relationship of size that he established in the first stanza of the poem. The exoticism deployed in the beginning of this section is rivaled only by "La Vie antérieure."

The travelers are tempted to "dive into the sky" (64), a curious reversal of a key image that requires some examination. A closely related expression will, of course, recur in the penultimate phrase of the poem: "Plonger au fond au gouffre, Enfer ou Ciel, qu'importe? / Au fond de l'Inconnu pour trouver du *nouveau*!" (143–44). One way to understand the image (at least in our three-dimensional physical world) is to imagine the sky reflected in the sea and tempting the sailor-voyagers to dive into the water, upon which they can also see the sky. "Plonger" suggests a vertical, downward movement that is the archetypal search for self-knowledge, the exploration of the inner being. The gouffre lies down there in the realm of the "Inconnu," as we have seen and will see again. Let us remember line 8: "Berçant notre infini sur le fini des mers," suggesting the boundless self as compared to the limited expanse of the sea. The sky and the sea are typically used to suggest infinite space. The mention here of "plonger dans le ciel," besides connecting sea and sky, achieves a telescoping effect of vertiginous power by turning upside down our very notion of space.

The significant transition occurs in the third stanza of section 4, a striking passage that contrasts the planned constructions of our cities and landscapes with the beautiful, random shapes of clouds in the sky. Our desire to yield to their temptation not only motivates our actions; it also creates anxiety in us (63, 68). Let us remember also that Baudelaire had earlier linked desire and clouds (21). The next two stanzas explore in more direct fashion the looming question of desire, appetite, and pleasure. The image tells us that pleasure serves as fertilizer to the tree of desire (70); given Baudelaire's distrust of the natural world, this is indeed a rare image. While its age, like hardened bark (71), restrains its ability to grow, the tree desires nevertheless to spread its branches higher and higher toward the sun. Like Icarus, the tree of desire strives to exceed its physical limits and reach the sun, leading the poet to wonder if it can continue its unchecked growth in the future. The tree is one of the richest symbols available: it connects the earth and sky, which, in Baudelairean terms, would suggest verticality. Trees have also been considered microcosms of life, death, and rebirth, since they reflect this basic life cycle throughout the seasons. From the tree of life to the tree of knowledge, which bore the forbidden fruit, this symbol has multiple biblical as well as pagan extensions.

Stanza 5 of section 4 contains several formal features that are worthy of mention. The pictorial image of "croquis" and "album" has already been prepared by the earlier mention of "nos esprits, tendus comme une toile" (55). We should remember that Baudelaire was also an outstanding art critic. There are several instances of internal repetition of consonant patterns that create rich alliteration: "*Grand*iras-tu," "*grand* arbre" or the hammering string of [k] sounds at the beginning of line three of the stanze: "*C*ueilli *qu*el*qu*es *c*roquis." The most striking phonetic feature, present throughout the poem but especially in this stanza, is the insistent use of the [v] sound in "vivace," "avons," "avec," "votre album vorace," "trouvez," and "vient." The final stanza of "Le Voyage" will also contain an unusually high frequency of [v] sounds.

The last two stanzas of section 4 contain an evocation of the exotic world of luxury and pomp that parodies so many of the tales told by travelers who return from far-off lands. Travel can take an individual out of familiar surroundings toward the strange and the marvelous sights and sounds of other lands and other peoples. Baudelaire has shown in other poems, such as "L'invitation au voyage," "La Vie antérieure," and "Parfum exotique," the attraction that can be exerted by the escape from the real world of spleen and flight toward the infinite, ideal world. Such journeys are, by definition, impossible but for the magic of the poet's art, which transports readers toward the mythical realm of "le Beau." The operation reveals a vision of condensed time that substitutes itself for the mundane, monotonous world of succeeding instants in which we live. The poet occupies a role analogous to that of the storyteller who, by his art, takes his readers or listeners away from the present to another time or place. In this evocation, we cannot but feel the subtle irony that the poet adds to his account of the many wonders that the voyagers have seen. They have already taken one ironic jab at those who prefer anything that comes from a distant land (76); now the audience will be given what it seems to want. The magnificence and splendor depicted by the travelers are the stuff of dreams and legend in the tradition of the *Thousand and One Nights*. We are rapidly told of luxurious palaces and extravagant costumes creating one of those "fêtes du cerveau" for which Baudelaire is so well known. The audience seems to want more of this fare, prodding the travelers to continue their tales by the short question that makes up section 5. Their show of interest and curiosity will be greeted by a sharp response: "O cerveaux enfantins!" (84) and a change in focus that contrasts with the pleasant and intriguing canvas of section 4.

VI

This section contains a scathing portrait of the horrors of the world; it stands as a counterpoint to the idealized vision presented in section 4. The forces of "spleen" and "ennui" take over their memories in a Dantesque vision as they paint a picture of sinners of all sorts. "Ennui" was given in the first poem of *Les Fleurs*, "Au Lecteur," as the most terrible of all sins. The line "du haut jusques en bas de l'échelle fatale" (87–88) suggests a vertical fall from the idealized, upper realm of the heavens to that of mortal sin. In a revealing turn of phrase, sin itself is characterized as immortal ("l'immortel péché," 88), outliving the sinner, omnipresent and omnipotent. Baudelaire postulates a form of original sin that is present from the origins of life and can never be pardoned or overcome. The renewed use of the singular con-

trasts with the final stanzas of section 4, in which plural nouns pre-
dominate; these singular nouns nevertheless retain their universal
dimension. When he depicts "la femme" and "l'homme," they are
uniformly base and abject creatures deserving of their fate. We should
point out the [s] sounds in line 90: "Sans rire s'adorant et s'aimant
sans dégoût," possibly replicating the hissing of a snake, an avatar of
the biblical serpent who tempted Eve and caused God to cast
humankind from Paradise. Whatever Baudelaire's religious beliefs, he
would have found in the tale of the Fall a legend full of rich applica-
tions for his purposes. In stanza 4, he alludes to the numerous reli-
gions of the world that pretend to show the path to salvation; they are
themselves prey to the very temptations against which they preach.
Voluptuousness and lust are everywhere. The sadism portrayed in
stanza 3 is a reminder of the suffering inflicted for both the pain and
pleasure of all involved: as in "Duellum," the violence of sadism has a
voluptuous aspect that makes the gouffre a hell in which the sinners
languish without regret. Humanity, here capitalized like "Sainteté"
(98), is a victim of that other deadly sin: Pride.

Besides voicing his metaphysical fear for the soul of humankind,
Baudelaire was undoubtedly lashing out one more time at the vain
belief in progress that characterized his century. There is no progress
in that most important of areas: human nature. In a Don Juanesque
gesture of defiance, humanity cries out its condemnation of God
(104). This blasphemous cry is a transposition of the appeal to his
readers in the first poem of *Les Fleurs*: "—Hypocrite lecteur, —mon
semblable, —mon frère!" From this earlier relationship based on
equality, even if equality in sin, we here move to the recognition of a
superior force. The poem, as we have seen from the opening lines,
sets up a network of hierarchies. The final stanza will evoke the
"lovers of dementia," those who refuse to accept the fate reserved for
common mortals and seek refuge in the "immense opium" (107).
Baudelaire here returns to the escapism that provides immediate
transport out of the ennui of daily life. These world-wise and world-
weary travelers close by proclaiming the universality and eternity of
their bleak depiction of the universe and its inhabitants (108).

VII

The Poet in the audience takes over speech once again in the final
two sections and advances his discourse to the only conclusion left:

death. It is indeed bitter knowledge that comes from travel, bitter like
the gouffre made even more cruel by the mirage of the drunken sailor
(44). The world seems small in retrospect (compare lines 3–4) and
sends us back an image of our own despair: "Une oasis d'horreur
dans un désert d'ennui" (112). This antithetical linking of oasis and
horror becomes plausible if one recognizes the horrible suffering that
makes up our lives; in other words, to live is to know the horror, and
every breath that gives life also reminds us of our mortality. What
nourishes life also destroys it. The real villain is named in the second
stanza of this section: Time. It is the enemy that eats life (compare
"L'Ennemi"). The accumulation of past moments that can never be
retrieved forms the basis of the tragedy of our existence. Our con-
sciousness of time makes all our actions seem futile, as will be
explored in "Le Port"; whether we stay in place or move about is of
little importance, since time will inevitably catch up with us.

In the spirit of the typologies at the beginning of the poem,
Baudelaire singles out other examples of reactions to the march of
time: on the one hand, the wandering Jew, condemned to roam the
face of the earth until the second coming; on the other, the apostles,
messengers sent out to spread Christ's message. They will be tracked
down by the "retiarii," the infamous Roman gladiators with nets and
tridents who so relentlessly killed their victims. The repeated [v] in
"ni wagon ni vaisseau" (119) echoes "sans vapeur et sans voile" (53).
The other type mentioned includes those who adopt the paradoxical
ploy of killing death in order to deny its existence. The use of this
cliché serves to underscore the futility of our most ingenious attempts
to deny or avoid the inevitable. Does the "berceau" (120) refer back to
those travelers who feel "l'horreur de leurs berceaux" (10)? Or is it a
reminiscence of Hercules killing the two serpents in his cradle and
thus proving that he is the son of Jupiter? In an interesting variant,
Juno sent two dragons who met a similar fate at the hands of the
young Hercules (Commelin 253–54). She then gave him her milk,
which bestowed upon Hercules the gift of immortality until he met
with the treachery of Nessus, who sent him the poisoned tunic that
would cost him his earthly life. While there is no specific mention of
Ulysses in this stanza, the infant-hero who slayed the monsters of
death and thereby acquired immortality would have suited
Baudelaire's purposes quite well.

Stanza 4 suddenly shifts to the future, placing the speaker in a pro-
leptic mode. He realizes that, as he approaches death, he must

recount an event that he has not experienced; that moment of step-
ping over is, by definition, an experience that cannot be related in a
narrative of firsthand experience. In that sense, "Le Voyage" is also a
poem about knowledge, especially the limits of knowledge. The fre-
quent recourse to myth and metaphor can be accounted for by the
need to express the inexpressible, to tell the untellable. They serve as
a go-between, linking the known, familiar world and the unknown,
alien one. Even as death looms, the victim of the retiarius sets his
sights on his last journey, this one on the "mer des Ténèbres." The
joyous heart of the passenger contrasts with the darkness of the sea,
although as Conrad would later show, it is quite possible to have a
heart of darkness. In a return to the Homeric intertext, Baudelaire's
voyager hears the voices tempting him to indulge in the lotus flower,
just as members of Odysseus's crew had succumbed to the temptation
of the flower that made them forget time, home, and duty. Whatever
the origin of Baudelaire's use of the Lotus-eaters (Pichois 1102), it is
interesting to note that it is the crew's hunger, their "vaste appétit,"
that makes them vulnerable to this narcotic flower. Hunger and thirst
suggest a void that can be filled up by all sorts of expedients, so that
the lotus and the apple of Eden fulfill a similar function. The lotus
flower can be taken as an erotic image, as it often is, or as a moral
commentary on society by the way in which such a beautiful, pure
flower can bud and prosper on stagnant, putrid water. The episode of
the lotus-eaters is emblematic of the "artifical paradises" so prevalent
in Baudelaire's writings. The "accent familier" (133), reminiscent of
the "regard familier" in "Correspondances," is a glimpse at the world
of Shades; in a vignette that Dante would have recognized, legendary
characters appear to the traveler-poet. They evoke the legend of
Pylades, Orestes, and Electra, symbols of loyal friendship and ever-
lasting fidelity. Orestes avenged the murder of his father by killing
his mother, Clytemnestra, and his stepfather, Aegisthus, who had
assassinated Agamemnon. Given Baudelaire's animosity for his own
stepfather, it is tempting to see some personal intent behind this
choice of mythological characters. Among other possible reasons, he
also undoubtedly wants to suggest here the fate that is reserved to
even the most deserving of souls.

VIII

Death is personified in the final section as an old captain at the
helm of a ship; as Claude Pichois thoughtfully suggests, there is a

possible nod to the legend of the flying Dutchman made popular by the Wagner opera (1102). While the specific details of the Nordic legend do not seem to have been Baudelaire's concern, the image of the captain on the deck of a ghost ship wandering the troubled seas conjures up a most suggestive scene. We should also remember that people usually gain access to Hades by crossing a body of water (the Styx) under the guidance of an emissary of the underworld. The sky and sea in this final leg of the journey are "noir comme de l'encre" (139), contrasting with the luminous rays found in the hearts of the travelers. Rather than resigning themselves to their fates, they are preparing their regeneration. The emphatic tone of this final section is underscored by the use of no fewer than seven exclamation points! In yet another ambiguous, paradoxical image, the poison will bring both death and life, deliverance and rebirth. In one final crescendo, they want to make that ultimate dive into the gouffre, into the unknown, whether it be heaven or hell, in one last, desperate search for renewal. It is only fitting that this final poem should close on the "double postulation" of Heaven or Hell, God or Satan, that lies at the heart of Baudelaire's thought. It had earlier served as the parameters in which the poet sought Beauty and hoped to unlock the doors of the Infinite that he had never known: "Que tu viennes du ciel ou de l'enfer, qu'importe, / O Beauté! monstre énorme, effrayant, ingénu!" ("Hymne à la beauté"). The only way to attain this realm is through the journey down and out, the path that leads to death and, beyond death, to a renewed sense of existence.

Chapter 16

Poet, Painter, Lover:
A Reading of "Les Bijoux"

RICHARD D. E. BURTON

La très-chère était nue et, connaissant mon cœur,
Elle n'avait gardé que ses bijoux sonores,
Dont le riche attirail lui donnait l'air vainqueur
Qu'ont dans leurs jours heureux les esclaves des Mores.   (4)

Quand elle jette en dansant son bruit vif et moqueur,
Ce monde rayonnant de métal et de pierre
Me ravit en extase, et j'aime à la fureur
Les choses où le son se mêle à la lumière.   (8)

Elle était donc couchée et se laissait aimer,
Et du haut du divan elle souriait d'aise
A mon amour profond et doux comme la mer,
Qui vers elle montait comme vers sa falaise.   (12)

Les yeux fixés sur moi, comme un tigre dompté,
D'un air vague et rêveur elle essayait des poses,
Et la candeur unie à la lubricité
Donnait un charme neuf à ses métamorphoses;   (16)

Et son bras et sa jambe, et sa cuisse et ses reins,
Polis comme de l'huile, onduleux comme un cygne,
Passaient devant mes yeux clairvoyants et sereins;
Et son ventre et ses seins, ces grappes de ma vigne,   (20)

S'avançaient, plus câlins que les Anges du mal,
Pour troubler le repos où mon âme était mise,
Et pour la déranger du rocher de cristal
Où, calme et solitaire, elle s'était assise.   (24)

214

Je croyais voir unis par un nouveau dessin
Les hanches de l'Antiope au buste d'un imberbe,
Tant sa taille faisait ressortir son bassin.
Sur ce teint fauve et brun le fard était superbe! (28)

—Et la lampe s'étant résignée à mourir,
Comme le foyer seul illuminait la chambre,
Chaque fois qu'il poussait un flamboyant soupir,
Il inondait de sang cette peau couleur d'ambre! (32)

"Les Bijoux" was first published as poem 20 of the 1857 edition of *Les Fleurs du Mal*. Located between "La Géante" and "Parfum exotique," it was clearly intended by Baudelaire to serve as the lead poem for a cycle of texts inspired by Jeanne Duval, the woman of color—usually called a "mulâtrasse" or "quarteronne" by contemporaries—whom he seems to have met shortly after returning from his voyage to the South Seas in 1842 and to whom he would remain attached, "comme le forçat à la chaîne," as he puts it in "Le Vampire," throughout his life, first as a lover and then, in later life, as a composite father-brother figure and provider. The poem is almost certainly an early one, probably written between 1842 and 1846, when the relationship between them was at its most physically and emotionally intense. The poem's evident eroticism made it an automatic target for censorship in 1857. At the trial, the fifth, sixth, and seventh stanzas were read out in court by Ernest Pirard, the prosecuting counsel, who claimed that, even for "le critique le plus indulgent," they constituted a "peinture lascive, offensant la morale publique." The judges agreed. "Les Bijoux" was banned and, excluded from the 1861 edition of *Les Fleurs du Mal,* was never reprinted in France in Baudelaire's lifetime. In modern editions it appears as poem 6 in *Les Épaves*, part of the debris, so to speak, that remained after the censors had shattered the intricately contrived architecture of the first edition of Baudelaire's poetic masterpiece.

Maître Pirard was no literary critic, but in his address to the court he did define both the style and the theme of "Les Bijoux" with some clarity (*OC* I, 1206–9). First, as we have seen, he described the three stanzas that he read out in court as constituting a "peinture," pointing to the intensely visual, pictorial character of the poem as a whole, which all subsequent commentators have dwelled upon and which will receive close attention here. Second, in giving "Les Bijoux" the unofficial subtitle "La femme nue, essayant des poses devant l'amant fasciné," he gave the best possible summary of the poem's situation and subject: a woman, wholly naked but for her jewels, *poses*, like an artist's model, before her fascinated lover, whose rapture is at once aesthetic and erotic, without being sexual, because, as we shall see, nothing is further from his mind, at least initially, than any sexual (in the sense of genital) transaction with the woman who so alluringly flaunts herself before him. "Les Bijoux" is, in the first instance, a poem of erotic-aesthetic fantasy, but it also describes the breakup of that fantasy brought about by the later irruption of sexual desire, first within the woman (whom the man would prefer to remain an entrancing aesthetic-erotic object) and then within the man himself, who, for his part, would prefer to remain a spectator of his beloved rather than her active sexual partner. Like "La Chevelure," a later poem also inspired by Jeanne Duval, "Les Bijoux" first constructs a fantasy and then shows its disintegration, the transition between the two "phases" of the poem occurring, as we shall see, in the course of its sixth stanza.

So vivid is the pictorial quality of "Les Bijoux" that critics have often sought to locate its "source" in one or more paintings known to Baudelaire and thus to make of the poem a verbal icon transcribing paintings such as Delacroix's *Odalisque couché, dite la Femme au perroquet* of 1827, or the same artist's *Odalisque sur un lit de repos* of 1827–1828, both of which have as their subject a suggestively posed woman of "exotic" origin, naked but for her jewels. In "Les Bijoux," says Prévost, Baudelaire *"revoit son propre souvenir avec les images et selon le style de Delacroix"* (115–16). Baudelaire's passion for Delacroix's work was such that the influence of these well-known paintings on "Les Bijoux" cannot be discounted; more generally, the poem, or at least its final stanza, inhabits the same "limbes insondés de la tristesse" that, in his *Salon* of 1846, Baudelaire detected in a still more famous Delacroix canvas, his *Femmes d'Alger dans leur appartement* of 1834. Other likely visual correlates of "Les Bijoux" are the two "Odalisque" paintings by Ingres, the so-called *Grande Odalisque* of 1814 and the later *Petite Odalisque*, also known as *Odalisque à l'esclave*, which exists in two versions, dating from 1839 to 1842. Baudelaire knew both the *Grande Odalisque* and the *Petite Odalisque* well and wrote appreciatively of them in 1846, around the time that "Les Bijoux" was probably written. Both paintings, he says, are "des œuvres d'une volupté profonde" and testify to their creator's "amour de la femme": "les muscles, les plis de la chair, les ombres des fossettes, les ondulations montueuses de la peau, rien n'y manque." "Nous ne serions pas étonnés," Baudelaire adds in a footnote, "qu'il [Ingres] se fût servi d'une négresse pour accuser plus vigoureusement dans *L'Odalisque* certains développements et certaines sveltesses" (*OC* II, 413, 460). It is not clear to which of the *Odalisques* Baudelaire is referring here, but the opulent forms of either could have suggested the equally resplendent "développements," not to mention the entrancing "sveltesses" of the woman of color, Jeanne Duval, with whom he was associated at the time.

Of the two paintings, it is perhaps the later *Petite Odalisque*, "cette délicieuse et bizarre fantaisie qui n'a point de précédents dans l'art ancien," which is closer in spirit to "Les Bijoux," not least because it depicts not one female figure but two: a recumbent woman, fair-skinned and brown-haired, apparently asleep or just waking, naked apart from a necklace, a bracelet, and a drape that conceals only her thighs and lower legs, and, crouched at her feet, a fully clothed female slave, darker in complexion, playing on a lute and singing, apparently entranced by the beauty displayed before her. Two figures, then, as in "Les Bijoux," one observing and serenading the other; the fact that both are female and both are slaves ("odalisque" is the general term used for a female slave confined for sexual purposes in a harem or seraglio), and that the roles of "light" and "dark" are, so to speak, transposed by Baudelaire, point forward to some of the sexual and other ambiguities that will emerge as our reading of the poem unfolds.

In line 4 of "Les Bijoux," Baudelaire likens Jeanne's posture to that of "les esclaves des Mores," a comparison that, of itself, situates the poem within a fairly precise literary, artistic, and historical context. Although the French obsession with "the Orient" long predated the beginnings of actual colonization in North Africa, the landing of a French expeditionary force in Algeria in 1830, followed by a brutal military campaign of annexation that lasted until the late 1840s, prompted a whole generation of French artists and writers— Delacroix, Gautier, Flaubert, Nerval, and Fromentin, to name but the best known—to visit North Africa and/or the Middle East and to incorporate "oriental" themes into their work. No French writer or painter of the 1840s or 1850s, even if, like Baudelaire, he or she never visited North Africa or the Levant, could remain immune to the

Orientalist obsession, whose unstated purpose and effect were, as Edward Said has shown, to immobilize, exoticize and, so to speak, to "feminize" (in the sense of rendering passive and malleable) a whole area, culture, and people in order the more easily to dominate and appropriate them: the "oriental" woman, langorously reclining in harem, zenana, or souk, becomes a figure of the passivity and possessibility of the "Orient" as a whole. That "Les Bijoux" participates in, and draws on, the discourse of Orientalism is hardly to be doubted, but it does so in a highly ambiguous and ultimately subversive fashion. Just as the poem constructs an erotic-aesthetic fantasy only to explode it, so it draws on Orientalist themes, figures, and images only to turn them against themselves and against their source in the "occidental" male before whom the "exotic" woman essays her various provocative poses. She may, at the outset of the poem, be a (willing) slave to her master's erotic-exotic fantasy, but she is a slave possessed of an "air vainqueur" (3) who will in due course assert her power over the man to whom, initially, she is, or seems to be, in thrall. The aesthetic-erotic-exotic *object* gradually becomes a fully human sexual *subject,* and as she does so, she turns her master's Orientalism on its head and, in forcing him to confront *his* humanity, *his* sexuality, consigns him once more to the realm of the body that, as we shall see, he seeks above all to negate and transcend.

The first stanza of "Les Bijoux," then, situates the relationship between man and woman, "colonial" white subject and "colonized" object of color, in a context of power, domination, and servitude that, in his later writings, Baudelaire would liken to the sadomasochistic bond between "bourreau" (executioner) and victim: "Je crois que j'ai déjà écrit dans mes notes que l'amour ressemblait fort à une torture ou à une opération chirurgicale. . . . Quand même les deux amants seraient très épris et très pleins de désirs réciproques, l'un des deux sera toujours plus calme ou moins possédé que l'autre. Celui-là, ou celle-là, c'est l'opérateur, ou le bourreau; l'autre, c'est le sujet, la victime" (*Fusées, OC* I, 651).

But this power relationship is, by its very nature, subject to abrupt reversal, as the development of "Les Bijoux" will graphically demonstrate. At the beginning of the poem, "la très chère" is a willing accomplice in her partner's exotic-erotic fantasy ("connaissant mon cœur") and allows herself to be molded and manipulated by his idiosyncratic desire ("se laissait aimer"). She is his slave but a slave who, in keeping with Hegel's classic analysis of the master-slave dialectic, is in fact more powerful than her master, who needs her far more, ulti-

mately, than she needs him. Or, varying the image, she is a wild ani-
mal who is only temporarily and imperfectly "tamed" ("comme un
tigre dompté") and who will, in due course, "revert" to her "natural"
sexual self and so turn the subject-object, "bourreau-victime" dyad on
its head. At the outset, the "master" *seems* "plus calme ou moins pos-
sédé" than his female slave, but if the latter "[sourit] d'aise" as she
abstractedly ("d'un air vague et rêveur") tries this pose and that, it is
because, ultimately, she is controlling their relationship through her
very passivity. The woman may be a slave, even an "esclave vile,"
but, in the later formulation of "Le Voyage," the "master" is a yet
more abject figure, an "esclave de l'esclave," a slave to the very desire
that causes him to wish to enslave and dominate the Other:

> La femme, esclave vile, orgueilleuse et stupide,
> Sans rire s'adorant et s'aimant sans dégoût;
> L'homme, tyran goulu, paillard, dur et cupide,
> Esclave de l'esclave et ruisseau dans l'égout. . .

For the moment, though, the man is able to keep the woman at the
desired distance from him and contemplate her body and its "riche
attirail" (3) or jewels as he would a work of art, with no threat of
being lured into a sexual engagement with his partner. It is not so
much her body that entrances him as the jewels that adorn it, or
rather, it is precisely the point of contact between body and jewels,
the time-bound and the timeless, the relative and the absolute, "exis-
tence" and "essence," "nature" and "art," that is the focus of his long-
ing. By identifying with the jewels, he seeks to appropriate the
absolute realm of being that they represent and so to rise above the
relative, contingent realm both of his lover's body and, more impor-
tant, of his own. As so often in Baudelaire, the eroticism of "Les
Bijoux" conceals an inveterate repugnance toward mere genital sexu-
ality. Whereas most of the love poems in *Les Fleurs du Mal* are suf-
fused with the all-pervasive perfume of the beloved, which envelops
the lover and draws him into her embrace, here the visual and the
aural ("bijoux sonores," "les choses où le son se mêle à la lumière")
reign supreme until, in line 28 of the poem, the olfactory reimposes
itself and instantly transforms a secure aesthetic-erotic relationship
into a potentially dangerous sexual one. Not only is the woman's
body detached from the spectator, but its component parts are, as it
were, detached from each other and confront the viewer as a series of
discrete, self-contained, anatomical entities. "Yeux" lead to "bras,"
"jambe," "cuisse," and "reins," to "ventre" and "seins," and so on to

"hanches," "taille," and "bassin," as the lover's eyes are drawn inexorably down from his partner's timeless "bijoux" to the all too human "bijou rose et noir" ("Lola de Valence") that opens between her thighs (the word "bijou" was widely used in eighteenth- and nineteenth-century erotic parlance to designate the female genitalia), reminding us of how, according to Baudelaire, Ingres himself dissects the female body "avec une âpreté de chirurgien" that often produces "des épaules simplement élégantes associées à des bras trop robustes": "Ici nous trouverons un nombril qui s'égare vers les côtes, là un sein qui pointe trop vers l'aisselle" (*OC* II, 460, 587).

Aesthetically entranced by his lover's jewels and by the successive "métamorphoses" in her position, the poet is able, for the moment, to remain immune to any properly sexual desire for her person. His love is "profond et doux comme la mer," offering no threat to his individual autonomy as he is drawn toward her *in imagination*, his thoughts ebbing and flowing about her like waves round a cliff ("qui vers elle montait comme vers sa falaise"). She is his cliff, but by the same token, he is her sea: although he remains, for the moment, in control of his fantasy, he is nonetheless curiously passive, lapping around the woman like the sea, the "female" element par excellence, while her location on her cliff-top "divan" places her in a position of "male" power and dominance. This confusion or interchangeability of "male" and "female" sexual roles indicates the close links between "Les Bijoux" and contemporaneous poems such as "Lesbos" and the two "Femmes damnées" poems. "Les Bijoux" highlights less the desire of man for woman and of woman for man than that of man-woman for woman-man. It is situated, so to speak, on a sexual continuum of male and female in which all kinds of "slippages" from one to the other are possible and which cannot but threaten the man's quest for a position of autonomy that will permit him to control both his partner's sexuality and, more important, his own.

The woman displays both "candeur" and "lubricité," and her sexuality, her desire for the man, from line 17 onward, will increasingly dominate the poem, triggering a sexual response in the poet that will comprehensively destroy his erotic-aesthetic fantasy. She moves provocatively toward him, a tiger no longer tamed, and "son bras et sa jambe, et sa cuisse et ses reins" pass alluringly before his eyes, which, for the last time, are "clairvoyants et sereins." This shift from erotic-aesthetic to the unambiguously sexual is bitterly resented by the poet. His partner's belly and breasts are "plus câlins que les Anges du mal," expressions of a properly diabolic force that instantly destroys "le repos où mon âme était mise" and lures it, despite itself, "du rocher de cristal / Où, calme et solitaire, elle s'était assise." In focusing on his lover's jewels as much as, if not more than, on her physical body, the poet had sought to rise above his own physicality and enthrone himself in a hard, mineralized universe (compare "Rêve parisien") in which, as on a crystal rock, he could deny the desires of the body and its subjection to change, decay, and, finally, death. He had been in a kind of paradise, "calme et solitaire," a voyeur in charge of his fantasy and its object: the eruption of sexuality, first that of the woman and then of his own, destroys that Eden of asexual self-containment and draws him, just as surely as "les Anges du mal" draw Adam and Eve, into an undesired but irresistible sexual exchange with his partner.

As the woman moves toward her lover, she appears to him as an androgynous figure, at once woman and boy, uniting "les hanches de l'Antiope au buste d'un imberbe." This "nouveau dessin" is itself inspired by a celebrated painting in the Louvre that Baudelaire undoubtedly knew, Correggio's *Jupiter et Antiope*, painted in 1524–1525 and depicting the naked figure of Antiope asleep in a wooded grove with, to her right, a satyr lasciviously eyeing her voluptuous body prior to possessing it; the satyr is, of course, Jupiter in disguise. There are two Antiopes in Greek mythology. The Antiope referred to here is the daughter of Nycteus and widow of Polydorus, King of Thebes, who, after being raped by Jupiter in the form of a satyr, gave birth to twin sons, Amphion and Zethus. (Ingres also painted a version of *Jupiter et Antiope*, and Baudelaire speaks disparagingly of it in his *Exposition universelle* of 1855. The Ingres painting dates from 1851 and is less likely to have provided Baudelaire with his comparison). Baudelaire could hardly have chosen a more suggestive and appropriate comparison for what is about to take place between him and Jeanne than this exquisite "amalgamation of erotic emanation and idealized shape." In the words of a modern critic, "by foreshortening, the figures shape out a concavity of explicitly erotic implication: sinuous oblique arabesques quicken the sleeping figure of Antiope, and a rotating impulse spurs the action into continuity and makes us know how the satyr's movement must conclude"; in a few seconds, the satyr "will replace the spectator (who is put in a voyeur's situation towards the Antiope) in the concavity her body makes" (Freedberg 282, 691). So, too, is the erstwhile voyeur of "Les Bijoux" drawn irresistibly toward and into the concavity of the woman's body. Her "bassin" thrusts forward to meet him, and he is overwhelmed by the wild animallike darkness of her skin ("ce teint fauve et brun") made still more alluring by the "fard" that adorns it. The "fard" is "superbe," not so much in the banal sense of "magnificent" as in the Latinate sense of "haughty, vainglorious, arrogant." It compels submission: the woman is now the "bourreau," and the man her "victime."

Stanza 7 ends with an exclamation mark, a graphic marker of the sexual arousal that has now replaced the erotic-aesthetic contemplativeness of the opening scene. The final stanza begins with a dash, which, I suggest, Baudelaire intends to represent the sexual act in which he and Jeanne then engage. What follows is an expression of postcoital melancholy and exhaustion similar to that evoked in near-contemporaneous poems such as "Sed non satiata" and "Une nuit que j'étais près d'une affreuse Juive." The lamplight ebbs and gutters ("la lampe s'étant résignée à mourir") like the man's physical powers after making love with his partner. All that remains are the glowing embers in the hearth ("le foyer seul illuminait la chambre"), but the light they dispense is now decidedly sinister. The hearth pants and sighs like the exhausted lover, flooding the woman's burnished skin with a lurid, bloody glow: "Il inondait de sang cette peau couleur d'ambre." The jewels have disappeared, and what remains is the body and above all the blood that issues monthly from the woman, locating her firmly in the time-bound and death-bound world from which her jewels seemed to deliver her, which is also the surest evidence of the poet's own mortality:

> Il me semble parfois que mon song coule à flots,
> Ainsi qu'une fontaine aux rythmiques sanglots.
> Je l'entends bien qui coule avec un long murmure,
> Mais je me tâte en vain pour trouver la blessure.
> ("La Fontaine de sang")

"Les Bijoux" begins with the poet enthralled in a self-contained ecstasy of contemplation before a bejeweled exotic object of fantasy; it ends with him beside an all too human, all too sexual woman, exhausted and dejected, "comme au long d'un cadavre, un cadavre étendu" ("Une nuit que j'étais près d'une affreuse Juive . . ."). The Baudelairean ideal of "concentration" has been supplanted by the dreaded condition of "vaporisation" or "dissipation" brought about by the intrusion, and expression, of sexual desire (as in *Mon cœur mis à nu*: "De la vaporisation et de la centralisation du *Moi*. Tout est là"

[*OC* I, 676]). The paradox of "Les Bijoux" is that, like so many of Baudelaire's poems, it betrays, beneath its manifest eroticism, the poet's abiding horror of genital sexuality. Or as Gustave Flaubert memorably wrote Baudelaire in a letter of 1857: "Vous chantez la chair sans l'aimer" (*Lettres à Charles Baudelaire*, 150).

Having indicated a number of visual images that may have inspired or contributed to the writing of "Les Bijoux," I shall conclude by mentioning an image that the poem in its turn inspired. This is a drawing by Auguste Rodin entitled "Les Bijoux" that forms part of a sequence of twenty-seven drawings inspired by *Les Fleurs du Mal*, which the collector Paul Gallimard commissioned from him in 1887. The bejeweled woman is barely visible: what dominates the drawing is the figure of the poet, depicted seated on a rock in a cavern in the classical pose, chin resting on clenched fist, arm buttressed by knee, that Rodin used for the successive sculptures that are now known as *The Thinker* but that, interestingly, were first called *The Poet*. How better to indicate the true theme of "Les Bijoux"? It is not about the woman, or even about her jewels, but *about the poet himself*, about the endless, obsessive thoughts that he weaves around the object of his fantasy. Even when he seems most in contact with her, he is, in reality, wholly self-absorbed, a part, almost, of that "rocher de cristal" on which he squats and from which he hopes never to be budged. Yet neither the woman's sexuality nor his own can ultimately be denied. Aesthetic distance is destroyed as he engages, despite himself, in sexual exchange with her, after which he is flung back once more into himself, no longer self-sufficient and serene but scattered and exhausted by the physical exertion to which he has succumbed. The fantasy has gone, and we leave the poet in a room suffused in a bloody hue, stranded in those "limbes insondées de la tristesse" that Baudelaire detected in the work of Delacroix. Whether lost in rapt contemplation of his beloved, engaged with her in the grotesque "opération chirurgicale" of sex, or plunged into postcoital melancholy, the Baudelairean lover is always alone, so true is it, as Jean Prévost wrote of Baudelaire, that "il chante, dans l'amour, une nouvelle forme de la solitude" (191). Ironically, Baudelaire's poems of ecstasy—"La Chevelure" or "Les Bijoux"—often express most fully the "sentiment de destinée éternellement solitaire" (*Mon cœur mis à nu*, OC I, 680), that haunted him all his life.

REFERENCES

Adatte, Emmanuel. *"Les fleurs du mal" et "Le Spleen de Paris": Essai sur le dépassement du réel.* Paris: José Corti, 1986.

Aguettant, Louis. *Baudelaire.* Paris: Editions du CERF, 1978.

Ariès, Philippe. *The Hour of Our Death.* Translated by Helen Weaver. New York: Knopf, 1981.

Arnold, Paul. *Esotérisme de Baudelaire.* Paris: J. Vrin, 1972.

Auerbach, Eric. "The Aesthetic Dignity of the 'Fleurs du mal.'" *Scenes from the Drama of European Literature.* New York: Meridian, 1959.

Austin, Lloyd J. "Baudelaire: Poet or prophet?" *Studies in Modern French Literature Presented to P. Mansell Jones.* Manchester: Manchester University Press, 1961.

Avni, Abraham. "A Revaluation of Baudelaire's 'Le Vin'; Its Originality and Significance for *Les fleurs du mal.*" *French Review* 44:2 (December 1970): 310–21.

———. "'Les Sept Vieillards': Judas and the Wandering Jew." *Romance Notes* 16:3 (Spring 1975): 590–91.

Aynesworth, Donald. "A Face in the Crowd: A Baudelairian Vision of the Eternal Feminine." *Stanford French Review* 5:3 (Winter 1981): 327–39.

Bachelard, Gaston. *L'Eau et les rêves.* Paris: José Corti, 1964.

———. *La Poétique de la rêverie.* Paris: Presses Universitaires de France, 1960.

———. *La Poétique de l'espace.* Paris: Presses Universitaires de France, 1989.

———. *La Terre et les rêveries du repos.* Paris: José Corti, 1974.

Badesco, Luc. "Baudelaire et la revue *Jean Raisin*: La première publication du *Vin des chiffonniers.*" *Revue des sciences humaines* 85 (January–March 1957): 55–88.

Bandy, W. T. "Le chiffonnier de Baudelaire." *Revue d'histoire littéraire de la France* 57:4 (October–December 1957): 580–84.

Bandy, W. T., and Pichois, Claude, eds. *Baudelaire devant ses contemporains.* Paris: Union Générale d'Editions (10/18), 1957.

Barberis, Marie-Anne. *"Les fleurs du mal" de Baudelaire.* Paris: Editions Pédagogie Moderne, 1980.

Barko, Ivan P. "'Le balcon' de Baudelaire: Une nouvelle lecture." *Essays in French Literature* 18 (November 1981): 1–9.

———. "La méditation chez Baudelaire; ou, L''accord de contraires.'" *Australian Journal of French Studies* 16:2 (January–April 1979): 182–86.

Barrère, Jean-Bertrand. "Chemins, échos, et images dans 'L'Invitation au voyage' de Baudelaire." *Revue de littérature comparée* 31:4 (October–December 1957): 481–90.

Bassim, Tamara. *La femme dans l'œuvre de Baudelaire.* Neuchâtel: La Baconnière, 1974.

Baudelaire, Charles. *Correspondance.* 2 vols. Bibliothèque de la Pléiade. Paris: Gallimard, 1973.

———. *Les fleurs du mal.* Edited by Antoine Adam. Classiques Garnier. Paris: Garnier, 1962.

———. *Œuvres complètes.* 2 vols. Edited by Claude Pichois. Bibliothèque de la Pléiade. Paris: Gallimard, 1975–76.

Bauer, Roger. "De 'Mignon' à 'L'Invitation au voyage.'" *Revue de littérature comparée* 60:1 (January–March 1986): 51–57.

Bays, Gwendolyn. *The Orphic Vision.* Lincoln: University of Nebraska Press, 1964.

Beauverd, Jacques. "Avez-vous compris 'L'Invitation au voyage'?" In *Hommages à Jacques Petit,* edited by Michel Malicet. Annales littéraires de l'Université de Besançon. Paris: Belles Lettres, 1985.

Beebee, Tom. "Orientalism, Absence, and the Poème en Prose." *Rackham Journal of the Arts and Humanities* 2:1 (Fall 1981): 48–71.

Benjamin, Walter. *Charles Baudelaire: Ein Dichter im Zeitalter des Hochkapitalismus.* Frankfurt: Suhrkamp, 1969.

———. *Charles Baudelaire: A Lyric Poet in the Era of High Capitalism.* Translated by Harry Zohn. London: New Left Books, 1973.

———. *Essais.* 2 vols. Translated by Maurice de Gandillac. Paris: Denoël/Gonthier, 1971–83.

———. *Illuminations: Essays and Reflections.* Edited by Hannah Arendt. Translated by Harry Zohn. New York: Schocken Books, 1969.

———. "Das Kunstwerk im Zeitalter seiner technischen Reproduzierbarkeit." *Illuminationen.* Frankfurt: Suhrkamp, 1977.

———. "The Work of Art in the Age of Mechanical Reproduction." Translated by Harry Zohn. In *Illuminations,* edited by Hannah Arendt. New York: Schocken, 1969.

Benveniste, Emile. *Problèmes de linguistique générale.* Vol. 1. Paris: Gallimard, 1966.

Bersani, Leo. *Baudelaire and Freud.* Berkeley: University of California Press, 1977.

Blin, Georges. *Le sadisme de Baudelaire.* Paris: José Corti, 1948.

Bloom, Harold, ed. *Charles Baudelaire.* Modern Critical Views. New York: Chelsea, 1987.

Brombert, Victor. *The Hidden Reader.* Cambridge, Mass.: Harvard University Press, 1988.

Burke, Kenneth. *The Philosophy of Literary Form.* 3d ed. Berkeley: University of California Press, 1973.

Burton, Richard D. E. *Baudelaire and the Second Republic: Writing and Revolution.* Oxford: Oxford University Press, 1991.

———. "Baudelaire and Shakespeare: Literary Reference and Meaning in 'Les

Sept Vieillards' and 'La Béatrice.'" *Comparative Literature Studies* 26:1 (1989): 1–27.

———. *Baudelaire in 1859: A Study in the Sources of Poetic Creativity.* Cambridge: Cambridge University Press, 1988.

———. *The Context of Baudelaire's "Le Cygne."* Durham: University of Durham Press, 1980.

———. "Metamorphoses of the Ragpicker: Interpreting 'Le Vin des chiffon- niers." In *Baudelaire and the Second Republic: Writing and Revolution.* Oxford: Clarendon Press, 1991.

Butor, Michel. *Histoire extraordinaire.* Paris: Gallimard, 1961.

Buvik, Per. "Paris, lieu poétique, lieu érotique. Quelques remarques à propos de Walter Benjamin et de Baudelaire." *Revue Romane* 20.2 (1985): 231–242.

Bynum, Caroline Walker. *Fragmentation and Redemption: Essays on Gender and the Human Body in Medieval Religion.* New York: Zone Books, 1992.

Cabanis, Jean. "Méthodes nouvelles: Charles Baudelaire: 'L'Albatros.'" *Ecole des lettres* 70:7 (January 1, 1979):33–39; 70:9 (February 1, 1979): 29–32.

Campbell, W. "Two Readings of Baudelaire: A Consideration of the Criticism of Consciousness." *Criticism* 13:4 (Fall 1971): 386–401.

Cargo, Robert T. *A Concordance to Baudelaire's "Les fleurs du mal."* Chapel Hill: University of North Carolina Press, 1965.

———. "A Further Look at Baudelaire's *Le Cygne* and Victor Hugo." *Romance Notes* 10:2 (Spring 1969): 277–85.

Carlier, Marie. *Baudelaire: "Les fleurs du mal": Dix poèmes expliqués.* Profil lit- téraire. Paris: Hatier, 1985.

Cassagne, Albert. *Versification et métrique de Charles Baudelaire.* Paris: Hachette, 1906; Geneva: Slatkine Reprints, 1972.

Cellier, Léon. *Baudelaire et Hugo.* Paris: José Corti, 1970.

Chambers, Ross. "Are Baudelaire's 'Tableaux parisiens' about Paris?" In *On Referring in Literature,* edited by Anna Whiteside and Michael Issacharoff. Bloomington: Indiana University Press, 1987.

———. "Baudelaire's Street Poetry." *Nineteenth-Century French Studies* 13:4 (Summer 1985): 244–59.

———. "Un despotisme 'oriental.'" In *Mélancolie et opposition: Les débuts du modernisme en France.* Paris: José Corti, 1987.

———. "The Flaneur as Hero (on Baudelaire)." *Australian Journal of French Studies* 28:2 (May 1991): 142–53.

———. "'Je' dans 'Les Tableaux parisiens' de Baudelaire." *Nineteenth-Century French Studies* 9:1–2 (Fall–Winter 1980–81): 59–68.

———. *Meaning and Meaningfulness: Studies in the Analysis and Interpretation of Texts.* Lexington, Ky.: French Forum, 1979.

———. *Mélancolie et opposition.* Paris: José Corti, 1987.

———. "Poetry in the Asiatic Mode." Translated by Mary Trouille. In *The Writing of Melancholy: Modes of Opposition in Early French Modernism.* Chicago: University of Chicago Press, 1993.

————. "The Storm in the Eye of the Poem." In *Textual Analysis: Some Readers Reading*, edited by Mary Ann Caws. New York: Modern Language Association, 1986.

————. "Trois paysages urbains: Les poèmes luminaires des 'Tableaux parisiens.'" *Modern Philology* 80:4 (May 1983): 372–89.

Charles, Michel. "Lecture d'un poème des *Fleurs du mal* intitulé 'Le Balcon.'" *Scolies* 1 (1971): 49–64.

Chérix, Robert-Benoît. *Commentaires des 'Fleurs du mal.'* Geneva: Pierre Cailler, 1949.

————. *Essai d'une critique intégrale: Commentaire des "Fleurs du mal."* Geneva: Pierre Cailler, 1949.

Chevalier, Jean, and Gheerbrant, Alain. *Dictionnaire des symboles.* Paris: Seghers et Jupiter, 1982.

Cixous, Hélène. *La jeune née.* Paris: Union Générale d'Editions, 1975.

Commelin, P. *Mythologie grecque et romaine.* Classiques Garnier. Paris: Garnier, 1960.

Le Corps. 2 vols. Ellipses. Paris: Edition Marketing, 1992.

Dagens, Jean, and Pichois, Claude. "Baudelaire, Alexandre Dumas, et le haschisch." *Mercure de France* 331:1130 (October 1957): 357–64.

Dard, Michel. "Commentaire sur un poème de Baudelaire." *Nouvelle revue française* 262 (October 1974): 69–76.

Derche, Roland. *Etudes de textes français.* Paris: SEDES, 1959.

Desonay, Fernand. *Le rêve héllenique chez les poètes parnassiens.* Paris: Champion, 1928.

Dufour, Pierre. "*Les fleurs du mal*: Dictionnaire de mélancolie." *Littérature* 72 (December 1988): 30–54.

Durand, Gilbert. *Les structures anthropologiques de l'imaginaire.* Paris: Bordas, 1969.

Durling, Robert, ed. *Petrarch's Lyric Poems: The Rime Sparse and Other Lyrics.* Cambridge, Mass.: Harvard University Press, 1976.

Eigeldinger, Marc. *Lumières du mythe.* Paris: Presses Universitaires de France, 1983.

————. *Le Platonisme de Baudelaire.* Paris: Editions de la Baconnière, 1951.

————. "La symbolique solaire dans la poésie de Baudelaire." *Revue d'histoire littéraire de la France* 67:2 (April–June 1967): 357–74.

Eliot, T. S. *Old Possum's Book of Practical Cats.* New York: Harcourt, Brace, 1939.

————. *Selected Essays.* New York: Harcourt, Brace, 1964.

Fairlie, Alison. *Baudelaire: "Les fleurs du mal."* London: Arnold, 1960.

François, Carlo. "'La Vie antérieure' de Baudelaire." *Modern Language Notes* 73:3 (March 1958): 194–200.

Freedberg, S. J. *Painting in Italy, 1500–1600.* Harmondsworth: Pelican, 1971.

Freud, Sigmund. *The Standard Edition of the Complete Psychological Works.* Edited and translated by James Strachey. 24 vols. London: Hogarth Press, 1961.

Friedrich, Hugo. *The Structures of Modern Poetry: From the Mid-Nineteenth to the Mid-Twentieth Century*. Evanston: Northwestern University Press, 1974.

Fuller, John. *The Sonnet*. London: Methuen, 1972.

Galand, René. *Baudelaire: Poétiques et poésie*. Paris: Nizet, 1969.

Gallagher, Catherine, and Laqueur, Thomas, eds. *The Making of the Modern Body: Sexuality and Society in the Nineteenth Century*. Berkeley: University of California Press, 1987.

Gasarian, Gérard. "La figure du poète hystérique ou l'allégorie chez Baudelaire." *Poétique* 86 (April 1991): 182–90.

Gautier, Théophile. Preface to *Œuvres complètes* by Charles Baudelaire. Paris: Michel Lévy Frères, 1869.

Geninasca, Jacques. "Les figures de la perception et du voyage dans 'Parfum exotique' et leurs représentations sémantiques." *Etudes baudelairiennes* 8 (1976): 119–46.

Gilman, Margaret. "'L'Albatros' Again." *Romanic Review* 41:2 (April 1950): 96–107.

Gnosis 26 (Winter 1993).

Godfrey, Sima. "Foules Rush In: Lamartine, Baudelaire, and the Crowd." *Romance Notes* 24:1 (Fall 1983): 33–42.

Goldbaek, Henning. "A l'ombre du voyage: Une interprétation du 'Voyage' de Baudelaire." *Revue romane* 25:1 (1990): 73–91.

Grimaud, Michel. "Psychologie et littérature." In *Théorie de la littérature*, edited by Aron Kibédi Varga. Paris: Picard, 1981.

Häufle, Heinrich. "Nervals und Baudelaires 'Schöne Unbekannte': 'Une allée du Luxembourg' und 'A une passante' im Vergleich." *Die neueren Sprachen* 88:6 (December 1989): 590–606.

Heck, Francis S. "Baudelaire and Proust: Chance Encounters of the Same Kind." *Nottingham French Studies* 23:2 (October 1984): 17–26.

Hiddleston, J. A. "Baudelaire et l'art du souvenir." *Baudelaire, "Les fleurs du mal": Intériorité de la forme*. Paris: Max Milner, 1989.

Hosek, Chaviva, and Parker, Patricia, eds. *Lyric Poetry Beyond New Criticism*. Ithaca: Cornell University Press, 1985.

Hubert, Judd David. *L'Esthétique des "Fleurs du mal": Essai sur l'ambiguïté poétique*. Geneva: Droz, 1953.

———. "Symbolism, Correspondence, and Memory." *Yale French Studies* 9 (1952): 46–55.

Hugo, Victor. "La Conscience." *La Légende des siècles*. Paris: Garnier-Flammarion, 1967.

———. *Cromwell*. Edited by Annie Ubersfeld. Paris: Garnier-Flammarion, 1968.

———. *Œuvres poétiques de Victor Hugo*. 2 vols. Edited by Pierre Albouy. Bibliothèque de la Pléiade. Paris: Gallimard, 1964.

Humphries, John Jefferson. "Poetical History or Historical Poetry: Baudelaire's Epouvantable Jeu of Love and Art." *Romance Quarterly* 30:3 (1983): 231–37.

Huxley, Aldous. *The Doors of Perception*. New York: Harper and Row, 1970.

Jakobson, Roman. "Closing Statement: Linguistics and Poetics." In *Style in Language*, edited by T. A. Sebeok. Cambridge, Mass.: MIT Press, 1960.

———. "Linguistics and Poetics." In *Style and Language*, edited by T. A. Sebeok. Cambridge, Mass.: MIT Press, 1960.

———. *Questions de poétique*. Paris: Seuil, 1973.

Jakobson, Roman, and Lévi-Strauss, Claude. "'Les Chats' de Baudelaire." In *"Les Chats" de Baudelaire: Une confrontation de méthodes*, edited by Maurice Delcroix and Walter Geerts. Namur: Presses Universitaires de Namur, 1980.

———. "'Les Chats' de Charles Baudelaire". *L'Homme: Revue française d'anthropologie* 2 (January 1962): 5–21.

Jennings, Michael W. *Dialectical Images: Walter Benjamin's Theory of Literary Criticism*. Ithaca: Cornell University Press, 1987.

Jenny, Laurent. "Le poétique et le narratif." *Poétique* 28 (1976): 440–49.

Johnson, Barbara. *The Critical Difference*. Baltimore: John Hopkins University Press, 1980.

———. *Défigurations du langage poétique: La seconde révolution baudelairienne*. Paris: Flammarion, 1979.

———. "Dream of Stone." In *A New History of French Literature*, edited by Denis Hollier. Cambridge, Mass.: Harvard University Press, 1989.

———. *A World of Difference*. Baltimore: John Hopkins University Press, 1987.

Johnson, Robert A. *Owning Your Own Shadow: Understanding the Dark Side of the Psyche*. San Francisco: Harper Collins, 1993.

Johnston, John H. *The Poet and the City: A Study in Urban Perspectives*. Athens: University of Georgia Press, 1984.

Jones, Percy Mansell. *"Le Cygne*: An Essay on Commentary." In *The Assault on French Literature and Other Essays*. Manchester: Manchester University Press, 1963.

Jouve, Nicole. *Baudelaire: A Fire to Conquer Darkness*. New York: St. Martin's, 1980.

———. *Tombeau de Baudelaire*. Paris: Seuil, 1958.

Jung, C. G. *Collected Works*. Princeton: Princeton University Press, 1971.

Kadish, Doris, and Price, L. Brian. "A View from the Balconies of Baudelaire and Genet." *French Review* 48:2 (December 1974): 331–42.

Kristeva, Julia. *Révolutions du langage poétique*. Paris: Seuil, 1974.

Lapaire, Pierre J. "L'esthétique binaire de Baudelaire: 'A une passante' et la beauté fugitive." *Romance Notes* 35:3 (Spring 1995): 281–91.

Leakey, F. W. *Baudelaire and Nature*. Manchester: Manchester University Press, 1969.

———. "Two Poems of Baudelaire: A Problem of Ambiguity." *Littérature moderne* 6:4 (1956): 482–89.

Leakey, F. W., and Pichois, Claude. "Les sept versions des 'Sept Vieillards.'" *Etudes baudelairiennes* 3 (1973): 262–89.

LeBoulay, Jean-Claude. "Commentaire composé: Charles Baudelaire." *L'information littéraire* 41:3 (May–June 1989): 24–28.

Le Hir, Yves. *Analyses stylistiques.* Paris: Armand Colin, 1965.

Levin, Samuel. *Linguistic Structures in Poetry.* Le Hague: Mouton, 1959.

Maclean, Marie. *Narrative as Performance: The Baudelairian Experiment.* London: Routledge, 1988.

McLees, Ainslie Armstrong. *Baudelaire's "Argot Plastique": Poetic Caricature and Modernism.* Athens: University of Georiga Press, 1989.

Mauclair, Camille. *Charles Baudelaire.* Paris: Maison du Livre, 1917.

Miller, Christopher L. *Blank Darkness: Africanist Discourse in French.* Chicago: University of Chicago Press, 1985.

Modiano, René. "Explication d'un poème de Baudelaire: 'L'Albatros.'" *Moderna Språk* 57:3 (1963): 320–24.

Morice, Louis. "'La Vie antérieure.'" *Etudes littéraires* 1 (April 1968): 29–49.

Morier, Henri. *Dictionnaire de poétique et de rhétorique.* Paris: Presses Universitaires de France, 1961.

Mossop, D. J. "Baudelaire and 'L'Art Mnémonique.'" *Symposium* 33:4 (Winter 1979): 345–57.

Musset, Alfred de. *Poésies nouvelles, 1836–1852, suivies des poésies complémentaires et des poésies posthumes.* Edited by Maurice Allem. Paris: Garnier Frères, 1962.

Nelson, Lowry, Jr. "Baudelaire and Virgil: A Reading of *Le Cygne.*" *Comparative Literature* 13:4 (1961): 332–45.

Nochlin, Linda. *Realism.* New York: Penguin Books, 1971.

Nuiten, Henk. *Les variantes des "Fleurs du mal" et des "Epaves" de Charles Baudelaire.* Amsterdam: APA-Holland University Press, 1979.

Oxenhandler, Neal. "The Balcony of Charles Baudelaire." *Yale French Studies* 9 (1952): 56–62.

Patillon, Michel. *Précis d'analyse littéraire.* Vol. 2. *Décrire la poésie.* Paris: Nathan, 1977.

Patty, James S. "Light of Holland: Some possible sources of 'L'Invitation au voyage.'" *Etudes baudelairiennes* 3 (1973): 147–57.

Le Petit Robert. Paris: Société du Nouveau Littré, 1967.

Peyre, Henri. *Qu'est-ce que le romantisme?* Paris: Presses Universitaires de France, 1971.

Pichois, Claude. *Album Baudelaire.* Paris: Gallimard, 1974.

———. *Baudelaire: Etudes et témoignages.* Neuchâtel: Editions de la Baconnière, 1967.

———, ed. *Lettres à Charles Baudelaire. Études baudelairiennes* 4–5 (1973).

Pichois, Claude, and Pichois, Vincenette, eds. *Lettres à Charles Baudelaire.* Neuchâtel: La Baconnière, 1973.

Pichois, Claude, and Ziegler, Jean. *Baudelaire.* Paris: Julliard, 1987.

———. *Baudelaire.* Translated by Graham Robb. London: Hamish Hamilton, 1989.

Pizzorusso, Arnaldo. "Analisi de 'La Vie antérieure.'" *Belfagor* 26 (November 30, 1971): 619–26.

Pommier, Jean. "A propos de 'L'Albatros.'" *Dans les chemins de Baudelaire,* 348–54. Paris: José Corti, 1945.

———. *Dans les chemins de Baudelaire.* Paris: José Corti, 1945.

Porter, Laurence. *The Crisis of French Symbolism.* Ithaca: Cornell University Press, 1990.

Poulet, Georges. *La poésie éclatée: Baudelaire-Rimbaud.* Paris: Presses Universitaires de France, 1980.

Poulet, Georges, and Kopp, Robert. *Qui était Baudelaire?* Geneva: Albert Skira, 1969.

Prendergast, Christopher, ed. *Nineteenth-Century French Poetry: Introductions to Close Reading.* Cambridge: Cambridge University Press, 1990.

Prévost, Jean. *Baudelaire: Essai sur l'inspiration et la création poétiques.* Paris: Mercure de France, 1953.

Proust, Marcel. *Contre Sainte-Beuve.* Bibliothèque de la Pléiade. Paris: Gallimard, 1971.

———. *Correspondance.* Edited by Philip Kolb. 20 vols. Paris: Plon, 1970–92.

Putnam, Walter C. "Baudelaire's 'Le Voyage' and Conrad's *Heart of Darkness.*" *Revue de littérature comparée* 65:3 [251] (July–September 1989): 325–39.

Quesnel, Michel. *Baudelaire solaire et clandestin.* Paris: Presses Universitaires de France, 1987.

Raser, Timothy. "Language and the Erotic in Two Poems by Baudelaire." *Romanic Review* 79:3 (May 1988): 443–51.

Regueiro Elam, Helen. "Temporality in Baudelaire." In *Charles Baudelaire,* edited by Harold Bloom. Modern Critical Views. New York: Chelsea House, 1987.

Remacle, Madeleine. *Analyses de poèmes français.* Paris: Les Belles Lettres, 1975.

Rémy, Paul. "'L'Albatros' de Baudelaire est-il un poème de jeunesse?" *Revue des langues vivantes* 17:5 (1951): 365–77.

Richard, Jean-Pierre. "Mettons-nous au Balcon!" *Baudelaire, Mallarmé, Valéry: New Essays in Honour of Lloyd Austin,* edited by Malcolm Bowie, Alison Fairlie, and Alison Finch. Cambridge: Cambridge University Press, 1982.

———. *Poésie et profondeur.* Paris: Seuil, 1955.

Robb, Graham M. "Baudelaire and the Ghosts of Stone." *Romance Notes* 25:2 (Winter 1984): 137–44.

———. *La Poésie de Baudelaire et la poésie française, 1838–1852.* Paris: Aubier, 1993.

Rollins, Yvonne B. "Le motif des tentations dans 'Les Sept Vieillards.'" *Selecta: Journal of the PNCFL* 4 (1983): 28–33.

Ruff, Marcel. "Notules baudelairiennes." *Revue d'histoire littéraire de la France* 51:4 (October-December 1951): 483–88.

Ruwet, Nicolas. "Limites de l'analyse linguistique en poétique." In *Langage, musique, poésie*. Paris: Seuil, 1972.

Sartre, Jean-Paul. *Baudelaire*. Paris: Gallimard, 1963.

Schaettel, Marcel. "Schèmes sensoriels et dynamiques dans 'Parfum exotique' de Baudelaire." *Etudes baudelairiennes* 8 (1976): 97–118.

Schenk, Eunice Morgan, and Gilman, Margaret. "'Le Voyage' and 'L'Albatros': The First Text." *Romanic Review* 29:3 (October 1938): 262–77.

Smadja, Robert. *Poétique du corps: L'image du corps chez Baudelaire et Henri Michaux*. Publications Universitaires Européennes. New York: Peter Lang, 1988.

Souffrin, E.-M., ed. *Les stalactites de Théodore de Banville*. Paris: Didier, 1942.

Spånberg, Sven-Johan. "*A Moon for the Misbegotten* as Elegy: An Intertextual Reading." *Studia Neophilologica* 61:1 (1989): 23–36.

Stamelman, Richard. *Lost Beyond Telling*. Ithaca: Cornell University Press, 1990.

Starobinski, Jean. "Je n'ai pas oublié . . ." In *Au bonheur des mots: Mélanges en l'honneur de Gérald Antoine*. Nancy: Presse Universitaire de Nancy, 1984.

———. *La mélancolie au miroir*. Paris: Julliard, 1989.

Todorov, Tzvetan. *Les genres du discours*. Paris: Seuil, 1978.

Tucci, Nina S. "Baudelaire's 'Les Sept Vieillards': The Archetype Seven, Symbol of Destructive Time." *Orbis litterarum* 44:1 (1989): 69–79.

Tucker, Cynthia Grant. "'Pétrarchisant sur l'horrible': A Renaissance Tradition and Baudelaire's Grotesque." *French Review* 48:5 (April 1975): 887–96.

Ulanov, Barry. *Jung and the Outside World*. Willmette, Ill.: Chiron Publications, 1992.

Unwin, T. A. "The 'Pseudo-narrative' of *Les fleurs du mal*." *Orbis litterarum* 46:6 (1991): 321–33.

Versluys, K. "Three City Poets: Rilke, Baudelaire, and Verhaeren." *Revue de littérature comparée* 54:3 (July–September 1980): 283–307.

Vier, Jacques. "Histoire, substance, et poésie des *Fleurs du mal*." *Archives des lettres modernes* 23 (May 1959): 1–71.

Weinberg, Bernard. *The Limits of Symbolism*. Chicago: University of Chicago Press, 1966.

Whitlow, James. "Baudelaire's 'Sept vieillards': A Case of Literary Identity." *South Central Bulletin* 17:4 (Winter 1967): 4–8.

Wing, Nathaniel. *The Limits of Narrative*. Cambridge: Cambridge University Press, 1986.

Yoshimura, Kazuaki. "Baudelaire et le souvenir." *Etudes de langue et littérature françaises* 44 (1984): 71–86.

CONTRIBUTORS

SUSAN BLOOD is Associate Professor of French at Yale University. She is the author of *Baudelaire and the Aesthetics of Bad Faith* (Stanford University Press, 1997).

RICHARD D. E. BURTON is Professor of French and Francophone Studies in the School of African and Asian Studies at the University of Sussex (England). His numerous publications include *Baudelaire in 1859: A Study in the Sources of Poetic Creativity* (Cambridge University Press, 1988) and *Baudelaire and the Second Republic: Writing and Revolution* (Oxford University Press, 1991).

ROSS CHAMBERS teaches French and Comparative Literature at the University of Michigan. His work on Baudelaire includes chapters in *Mélancolie et Opposition* (Corti, 1987), translated as *The Writing of Melancholy* (University of Chicago Press, 1993), and in a forthcoming volume entitled *Loiterature.*

ÉLIANE DALMOLIN is Associate Professor of French and Head of French Studies at the University of Connecticut, Storrs. She is also the editor of *Sites: The Journal of Contemporary/20th Century French Studies*. Her articles have appeared in *The Comparatist*, in *Nineteenth-Century French Studies*, and in *The French Review*, among other prominent journals.

GÉRARD GASARIAN is Associate Professor of French at Tufts University. He is the author of *Yves Bonnefoy: La poésie, la présence* (Champ Vallon, 1986) and *De loin tendrement: Etude sur Baudelaire* (Champion, 1996). He has also published many articles on modern French poetry.

CLAUDINE GIACCHETTI is Associate Professor of French at the University of Houston. Her publications include articles on Maupassant, George Sand, and la Comtesse de Ségur, as well as a book, *Maupassant: espaces du roman* (Droz, 1993).

KAREN HARRINGTON is Associate Professor of French at East Tennessee State University. Her publications include work on Baudelaire, as well as a French reader, *Faisons le point* (Prentice-Hall, 1996).

The late MARIE MACLEAN taught in the Romance Languages Department and the Center for Comparative Literature and Cultural Studies at Monash University in Melbourne. She is the author of *Le jeu suprême* (Corti, 1973) and *Narrative as Performance: The Baudelairean Experiment* (Routledge, 1988).

BRIGITTE MAHUZIER is Assistant Professor of French at Princeton University. She has published articles on Stendhal, Zola, Rodin and Proust. She co-edited an issue of *Yale French Studies* on gay and lesbian authors in nineteenth- and twentieth-century French and Francophone literature, and has written a book on the ethical function of Proust's aesthetics of homoeroticism.

MARGARET MINER teaches French at the University of Illinois at Chicago. She has published articles on the poetry of Baudelaire, Rimbaud, and Mallarmé, as well as a book, *Resonant Gaps: Between Baudelaire and Wagner* (University of Georgia Press, 1995).

WILLIAM OLMSTED is Professor of Humanities in Christ College, the honors college of Valparaiso University. He has translated essays by George Dumézil and Paul Ricoeur and has written articles on Baudelaire, Manet, Joseph Cornell, the architecture of museums and malls, as well as a manuscript entitled "Censoring Baudelaire: The Trial(s) of "Les Fleurs du Mal."

WALTER PUTNAM is Professor of French and chair of the Department of Foreign Languages and Literatures at the University of New Mexico. He has published two books, *L'Aventure littéraire de Joseph Conrad et d'André Gide* (Anma Libri, 1990) and *Paul Valéry Revisited* (Twayne, 1995), as well as more than a dozen articles on such authors as Gide, Verne, and Le Clézio.

GRETCHEN SCHULTZ is Assistant Professor of French Studies at Brown University. She has published articles on Desbordes-Valmore, Verlaine, Nina de Villard, and Valéry. She is currently completing a book manuscript entitled "The Gendered Lyric: Subjectivity and Difference in 19th-Century French Poetry."

WILLIAM THOMPSON is Associate Professor of French at the University of Memphis. Among his publications is his editorial work for and introduction to a collection of essays entitled *The Contemporary Novel in France* (University Press of Florida, 1995). He is also the editor of the annual *French XX Bibliography*.

NINA TUCCI teaches French at the University of Houston. She has published articles on Claudel, Baudelaire, and Malraux. Her areas of interest include the usefulness of Jungian thought applied to literature, as well as the applications of mythology and oriental philosophy to twentieth-century French literature.

JEANNE THEIS WHITAKER graduated from Bryn Mawr College with a dissertation on poetic movement in *Les Fleurs du Mal*. She is Professor of French at Wheaton College in Norton, Massachusetts.

INDEX